Leipziger Schriften zum Völkerrecht, Europarecht und ausländischen öffentlichen Recht

Edited by

Prof. Dr. Markus Kotzur

Prof. Dr. Stephanie Schiedermair

Prof. Dr. Dominik Steiger

Prof. Dr. Mattias Wendel, Maître en droit

Institut für Völkerrecht, Europarecht und ausländisches öffentliches Recht der Universität Leipzig

Volume 26

Félicité Akonkwa Mugombozi

The Responsibility to Protect (R2P)

R2P and International Humanitarian Law Violations in the Democratic Republic of Congo

Nomos

The Deutsche Nationalbibliothek lists this publication in the Deutsche Nationalbibliografie; detailed bibliographic data are available on the Internet at http://dnb.d-nb.de

a.t.: Leipzig, Univ., Diss., 2025

ISBN 978-3-7560-3534-2 (Print)
978-3-7489-6597-8 (ePDF)

Online Version
Nomos eLibrary

1st Edition 2025

To Nzinga, Corneille, Gabriella and Adan: your sacrifice made it true!

Abstract

This thesis analyzes the relationship between Responsibility to Protect(R2P) and International Humanitarian Law (IHL) in the context of the Democratic Republic of Congo. It examines how international humanitarian law is applied in the implementation of the R2P mandate in the UN Security Council Resolution 2098. The aim of this thesis is to show that the implementation of R2P raises questions about the applicability of International Humanitarian Law and the shared international responsibility of the United Nations, troop-contributing countries, the DRCongo and individual peacekeepers for violations of international law through the implementation of 2098 UNSC resolution.

The present thesis argues that resolution 2098 contains an R2P mandate in all three pillars, although this is not literally stated. This is proven by the mandate included in the preamble and paragraphs 10-12 of the resolution. However, the fact that the Brigade implementing this mandate was established within a peacekeeping force and under the same command raises questions about the neutrality of IHL and the protection of UN members and facilities enshrined in IHL. Moreover, the nature of the Brigade's mandate does not affect the qualification of the conflict, still less the international responsibility of those involved in violations of IHL.

This thesis specifies the criterion for sharing international responsibility between the UN, the countries contributing to the Brigade and the DRC, which will be established on a case-by-case basis according to the test of effective control and organization as set out in the Behrami and Saramati cases. Individual responsibility will be established notwithstanding the immunities of peacekeepers or the limits of the DRC's jurisdiction to try UN forces. Victims of violations of IHL committed during the implementation of R2P in the DRC may therefore have recourse to international, regional and national remedies to obtain reparation.

Table of Contents

Acknowledgements 13

Abbreviations 15

Table of Legal Instruments 17

Table of Cases 19

Table of United Nations Resolutions and Documents 21

Introduction 23

1. Background to the Problem 23
2. Legal Implications 29
3. Research Methodology 32
4. Organisational Lay Out 34

Title I: The Responsibility to Protect (R2P) and International Humanitarian Law in the Context of the DRCongo 35

Chapter I: Legal Understanding of R2P in Conjuction with IHL 37

1. Background and Definition of the Responsibility to Protect 38
   A. Background of the R2P 38
   B. Definition of R2P 40
2. Legal status of R2P 45
3. Implementation of R2P 51
   A. The "duty" to prevent 52
   B. The "duty" to react 57
   C. The "duty" to rebuild 63
4. Relation between Responsibility to Protect (R2P) and International Humanitarian Law (IHL) 68
   A. Analysis by origin and legal nature of IHL and R2P 68

B. States' obligations under IHL and R2P 70
C. Applicability of IHL and R2P 75

Chapter II: Responsibility to Protect in the Specific Context of DRCongo. 81

1. Crimes in the context of the Responsibility to Protect in the DRC 81
A. War crimes 82
B. Crimes against humanity 86
C. Ethnic cleansing 89
D. Genocide 91

2. The "Duty" of DR Congo under Responsibility to Protect 94

3. The "Duty" of the International Community 97
A. Regional intervention 98
B. The Intervention of the European Union (EU) 102
C. United Nations' intervention 106

4. The UNSC resolution 2098 (2013) 110
A. Background to the Resolution 2098 110
B. Scope of Resolution 2098 114
C. Resolution 2098: "R2P measure" or "robust peacekeeping mandate"? 118
D. Implementation of the Resolution 2098 124

Title II: Legal Implications of Applicability of IHL in the Implementation of R2P in the DRCongo. 129

Chapter I: Applicability of IHL in the Implementation of R2P Under Resolution 2098 131

1. Qualification of the conflict in the Democratic Republic of the Congo 131

2. Legal consequences of applicability of IHL to the implementation of resolution 2098 139

3. International Humanitarian Law violations during the implementation of R2P in DR Congo 153

Chapter II: Responsibility for Violations of IHL in the Implementation of R2P under the Resolution 2098 165

1. Legal framework of the responsibility of the Brigade for IHL violations during R2P implementation in DRC 166
   A. Basis of International Responsibility for violations of IHL 166
   B. Attribution of an IHL violation committed by the Brigade to the United Nations. 169
2. Shared responsibility between the UN, the Troops Contributing Countries and the host Country 173
   A. Basis of concurrent responsibility between the United Nations, Troops Contributing Countries and the host country for violations of IHL 174
   B. Mechanisms for sharing responsibility between entities for IHL violations committed during the implementation of resolution 2098 179
   C. The specific responsibility of entities involved in the implementation of resolution 2098. 182
3. Individual international criminal responsibility for IHL violations during the R2P implementation 188

Chapter III: Victims Reparation Remedies for Violations of IHL in the Implementation of R2P 195

1. Judicial remedies for violations of International Humanitarian Law 197
   A. Mechanisms provided for at International and Regional level 198
      i. Mechanisms provided for under Public International Law 198
      ii. Mechanisms under International Criminal Law 210
   B. Domestic remedies 213
      i. Jurisdiction of the Troops Contributing States and the DRC 214
      ii. The jurisdiction of other Courts: Universal Jurisdiction 217
2. Non-judicial Mechanisms for violations of International Humanitarian Law 221

Conclusion 227

Bibliography 235

Books 235

Articles and Book Chapters 237

Reports 249

Thesis 256

Acknowledgements

Having grown up in conflict-affected region, I have witnessed firsthand the immense challenges faced by communities and the crucial role played by peace actors. These early experiences have shaped my academic journey and inspired me to pursue this research. This journey has now culminated in the writing of this Thesis, which I had the honor to defend at Leipzig University on 2nd June 2025. I am also grateful that this thesis was awarded the Wolfgang-Scheuffler Research Prize.

I would like to express my deepest gratitude to my supervisor Prof. Dr. Stephanie Schiedermair for her invaluable guidance, patience, and encouragement throughout this project. Her mentorship has not only shaped the development of this dissertation but has also been a source of constant academic and personal growth.

I am sincerely grateful to the member of the jury, Prof. Dr. Mattias Wendel, Maîtr. en droit (paris 1) for his insightful comments, constructive feedback, and for dedicating his time to evaluate my work. His Contributions have greatly enriched the quality of this thesis.

My heartfelt thanks go to Brot für die Welt, whose generous financial support made this research and doctoral studies possible.

I am deeply grateful to my family for their unconditional love and support. My mother, Leontine Ngangura, and my brothers and sisters, Liliane Mugombozi, Francine Mugombozi, Dr. Francis Mugombozi, Roger Mugombozi, Ir. Victor Mugombozi, Fidelie Mugombozi, and Stéphane Mugombozi, have been a constant source of inspiration and strength throughout my life. I also wish to thank my in-laws for their generosity and understanding, as well as Godwin Weide, Dr. Ingrid Weide, and Angela Lindner, together with all my friends, who were always there to encourage me and remind me of the bigger picture. To all of you, I owe more than words can express.

Leipzig, August 2025
Félicité Mugombozi Akonkwa

Abbreviations

ACT	Accountability, Coherence and Transparency
ADF	Allied Democratic Forces
APCLS	Alliance of Patriots for a Free and Sovereign Congo (French: Alliance des patriotes pour un Congo libre et souverain)
API	Additional Protocol I
APII	Additional Protocol II
ARS	Articles on States Responsibility
AU	African Union
DARIO	Draft Articles on the Responsibility of International Organization
DRC	Democratic Republic of the Congo
EAC	East African Community
EUSR	European Union Special Representative
FARDC	Forces Armées de la République Démocratique du Congo
FDLR	Forces démocratiques de libération du Rwanda
FIB	Force Intervention Brigade
FNL	Force Nationale de Libération (National Force of Liberation)
GC	Geneva Convention
IAC	International Armed Conflict
ICGLR	International Conference on the Great Lakes Region
ICISS	International Commission on Intervention and State Sovereignty
IHL	International Humanitarian Law
IO	International Organization

LRA	Lords' Resistance Army
M23	Mouvement du 23 Mars
MONUC	United Nations Organization Mission in the Congo
MONUSCO	United Nations Organization Stabilization Mission in the Democratic Republic of Congo
NIAC	Non-International Armed Conflict
OAGs	Organized Armed Groups
POC	Protection of Civilian
PSC	Peace Security and Cooperation
R2P	Responsibility to Protect
RMM	Regional Monitoring Mechanism
ROE	Rules of Engagement
SADC	Southern African Development Community
SOFA	State of Agreement
SG	Secretariat General
TCC	Troops Contributing Country
TSC	Technical Support Committee
UN	United Nations
UNAMID	United Nations African Union Hybrid Operation in Darfur
UNSC	United Nations Security Council
UNSG	United Nation Secretary-General

Table of Legal Instruments

African Charter on Human and People's Rights, adopted on June 27, 1981, and entered into force Oct. 21, 1986.

Agreement between the Government of the Federal Democratic Republic of Ethiopia and the Government of the State of Eritrea, Vol. 40, No. 2, March 2001, International Legal Materials (2001).

Agreement between the Parties to the North Atlantic Treaty regarding the Status of their Forces, 19 June 1951.

Agreement between the United Nations and the Lebanese Republic on the establishment of a Special Tribunal for Lebanon,30 May 2007, UNSC Res 1757(2007).

Agreement for the prosecution and punishment of the mayor war criminals of the European Axis. London, 8 August 1945.

American Convention of Human Rights, signed at Inter-America specialized Conference on Human Rights, Costa Rica 22/11/1969.

Cairo Declaration and Cairo plan of action, adopted at the Africa-Europe Summit under the auspices of the Organization of African Unity and the European Union, 3-4 April 2000.

Charter of Fundamental Rights of the European Union, 1st December 2009.

Charter of the United Nations, 26 June 1945.

Constitution de La République Démocratique du Congo, 18 Février 2006.

Convention (I) for the Amelioration of the Condition of the Wounded and Sick in Armed Forces in the Field. Geneva,12 August 1949.

Convention (II) for the Amelioration of the Condition of Wounded, Sick and Shipwercked Members of Armed Forces at Sea. Geneva, 12 August 1949.

Convention (III) relative to the Treatment of Prisoners of War. Geneva, 12 August 1949.

Convention (IV) Relative to the Protection of Civilian Persons in Time of War. Geneva12 August 1949.

Convention against Torture or Other Cruel, Inhuman or Degrading Treatment or Punishment,1984.

Convention on the Elimination of All Form of Discrimination against Women, adopted and opened for signature, ratification and accession by General Assembly resolution 34/180 of 18 December 1979.

Convention on the Prevention and Punishment of the Crime of Genocide (1948) Entry into force: 12 January 1951.

Convention on the Safety of United Nations and Associated Personnel, 1994.

Covenant of the League of Nations, 28 June 1919.

Criminal Tribunal for the former Yugoslavia, Rules of Procedure and Evidence, IT/32/ Rev. 37 (2006), online: Criminal Tribunal for the former Yugoslavia <http://www.un.org/icty/legaldoc-ffindex-f.htm> (page visited on 1 August 2007) [TPLY Rules].

International Criminal Court (ICC), *Elements of Crimes*, 2011, ISBN No. 92-9227-232-2.

Loi n° 06/019 et 06/018 du 20 juillet 2006 modifiant et complétant le Décret du 06 août 1959 portant Code de Procédure Pénale Congolais *in J.O*, du 20/07/2006.

Loi n° 13/005 du 15 janvier 2013 portant statut du militaire des forces armées de la république démocratique du Congo, *in JO*, 54e année, du 25 janvier 2013.

Loi nº 15/023 du 31 décembre 2015 modifiant la Loi nº 024-2002 du 18 novembre 2002 portant Code pénal militaire in J.O, 31/12/2015.

Loi nº 15/023 du 31 décembre 2015 modifiant la Loi nº 024-2002 du 18 novembre 2002 portant Code pénal militaire.

Protocol Additional to the Geneva Conventions of 12 August 1949 and Relating to the Protection of Victims of International Armed Conflicts (Protocol I), 8 June 1977.

Protocol Additional to the Geneva Conventions of 12 August 1949 and Relating to the Protection of Victims of Non-International Armed Conflicts (Protocol II), 8 June 1977.

Protocol on Prohibitions or Restrictions on the Use of Mines, Booby-Traps and Other Devices as amended on 3 May 1996 (Protocol II to the 1980 Convention as amended on 3 May 1996.

Protocol to the African Charter on Human and Peoples' Rights on the Establishment of an African Court, adopted on June 10, 1998, entered into force January 25, 2004, OAU Doc. OAU/LEG/EXP/AFCHPR/PROT(III).

Regulations of the Court, ICC-BD/O 1-0 1-04/Rev.0 1-05, adopted on 26 May 2004 and amended on 9 March 2005, regulations 86 et seq. [ICC Regulations].

Rome Statute of the International Criminal Court, 1st July 2002.

Statute of the Special Court for Sierra Leone, UNSC Res. 1315 (2000) of 14 August 2000.

United Nations Convention on the law of Treaties 1969. Vienna, 23 May 1969.

Table of Cases

Affaire MONUSCO Kasindi, RI no 129/IOP/AMG/Bni/022 registered le 04/08/2022.

CETHR. *Agim Behrami and Bekir Behrami v. France* (App. No. 71412/01), CETHR (2007).

ICJ. *Application of the Convention on the Prevention and the Punishment of the Crime of Genocide* (Bosnia and Herzegovina v. Serbia and Montenegro), 91, 1427,438, 26 Feb. 2007, para. 166, 413, 430.

ICJ. *Armed Activities on the Territory of the Congo (DRC v. Uganda)*, 19 December 2005, para.179 and 180.

ICTR. *Decision on the Prosecutor's Motion to Withdraw the Indictment, Ntuyahaga* (ICTR-98-40-T), Trial Chamber I, 28 September 1998.

Preliminaries Exceptions (*Case Las Palmers),* Judgement of 04 de February 2000, Serie C, No. 66 Paras. 205-210.

SADC. *Mike Campbell (Pvt) Ltd and others v Republic of Zimbabwe*, SADC (T) (case no. 2/2007, 28- 11-2008).

ICJ. Certain Expenses of the United Nations (*Chorzów Factory Case)* (Advisory Opinion) ICJ Rep.151, at 165. *(Jurisdiction)* (1927) Series A no 22 [102] ,1962.

IT. Decision on Appeal from Denial of Judgment of Acquittal for Hostage Taking, *Karadzkic* (IT-95-5/ 18-AR73.9), Appeals Chamber, 11 December 2012.

ICJ. *Democratic Republic of Congo v. Burundi, Rwanda and Uganda*, African Commission on Human and Peoples' Rights, Communication No. 227/99 (2006).

ICJ. *Democratic Republic of the Congo v. Rwanda*, request for the indication of provisional measures, Order of 10 July 2002.

ICJ. *Diference Relating to Immunity from Legal Process of a Special Rapporteur of the Commission on Human Rights*, Advisory Opinion, ICJ Reports 1999.

E.D.H. Court, *A. v. United Kingdom*, Judgment, 22 September 1998, para. 22.

ICJ. *Corfu Channel case*, Judgment, 9 April 1949, para. 23.

ICJ. *United States Diplomatic and Consular Staff in Tehran*, Judgment, 24 May 1980).

ICJ. *Legality of the Threat or Use of Nuclear Weapons*, Advisory Opinion, 1996, paras 78–79.

ICTY. *Brdjanin*, Trial chamber, 1 September 2004, para. 703; Krstić, ICTY, Trial chamber, 2 August 2001, para. 590.

ICTY. *Krstić decision*, Appeals chamber, no. IT-98-33-A, 19 April 2004, p. 134.

ICTY. *Limaj Case*, Judgment of 30 November 2005, para. 170.

ICTY. *Procutor v. Strugar*, case No IT-01-42-A, judgement 17 jully 2008, par. 178.

ICTY. *Prosecutor v. Dario Kordić and Mario Cerkez*, Decision on the Joint Defence Motion (ibid., para. 136).

ICTY. Prosecutor v. Zoran Kupreskic et al, judgment, 14 Jan. 2000, § 49 and 132.

ICTY. Tadić (Appeals Chamber), Judgment of 15 July 1999, at paras. 131,137.

ICTY. *The Prosecutor v. Dusko Tadić*, Judgment on the appeal by the defence challengingjurisdiction, no. IT-94-1-A, 2 October 1995, para. 70.

James Katabazi and 21 Others v. Secretary General of the East African Community and the Attorney General of the Republic of Uganda, Reference n° 1 of 2007, 1st November 2007, para 16.

ICTY. Kordić and Cerkezs, Appeals Chamber, no. IT-95-14/2-A, 17 December 2004, para. 94.

ICTR. *Ndindiliyimana et al.*, judgement (ICTR-00-56), Appeals Chamber, 11 February 2014 (Military II Appeals Judgment), para 323.

ICJ. *LaGrand (Germany v United States of America)*, Provisional Measures, Order of 3 March 1999 (1999) Rep 466.

ICJ. *Military and paramilitary activities in and against Nicaragua* (Nicaragua v. United States if America), Merits Judgement, Reports 1986, pp64-65 paras 109-;

Court of First Instance of Brussels. *Mukeshimana- Ngulinzira and Others v. Belgium and Others*, RG Nos. 04/4807/A and 07/15547/A, Judgment of 8 December 2010..

ILDC. *Nuhanović v. State of the Netherlands (Ministry of Defense of Foreign Affairs)*, First Instance Judgement, Decision no. LJN: BFO181, case No. 265615, 1092(NL 2008) 10 September 2008, Netherlands; The Hague; District Court, para. 4.12.3, 4.8.

ICJ. *Paraguay v United States of America*, Provisional Measures, Order of Posted: 1998-04-09

ICJ. *Prosecutor v. Naletilic and Martinovic*, Case No. IT-98-34-T, judgment of 31 March 2003 (Trial Chamber I).

ICJ. *Prosecutor v. Zoran Kupreškić et al.*, Judgment, IT-95-16-T, 14 January 2000, 202-203, para. 518.

ICJ. *Reparation for injuries suffered in the service of the Nations*, Advisory Opinion, [1949] Rep 174, ICGJ 232 (ICJ 1949), 11th April 1949.

ICJ. *Ruzhdi Saramati v. France, Germany and Norway* (App.no. 78166/01) ECtHR (2007); *Al-Jedda v. the United Kingdom* (App. No. 27021/08) ECtHR (2011).

ICJ. *Ruzhdi Saramati v. France, Germany and Norway* (App.no. 78166/01) ECtHR (2007)

RUF. Sesay, Kallon and Gbao ('RUF') (SCSL-04-15-T), Trial Chamber I, 2 March 2009 (RUF Trial Judgment), Para 215.

ICC. *The prosecutor v. Ali Muhammad Ali Abdalrahman* Ali kushayb, para 30, p 54, No. ICC-02/05-01/20, 9 July 2021.

ICTR. *The Prosecutor v. Augustin Ndindiliyimana, François-Xavier Nzuwonemeye and Innocent Sagahutu*, ICTR-00556-A, 27.02.2014.

ICC. *The Prosecutor v. Thomas Lubanga Dyilo*. Decision on the confirmation of charges, 29 January 2007, ICC-01/04-01/06.

ICC. *The State of Netherlands v. Hasan Nuhanovic*, 12/03324, Supreme Court, 06Septeebre 2013.

Table of United Nations Resolutions and Documents

GA Res. 2676 (XXV) (1970).

GA Res. 60/1 (2005).

GA Res. 63 (2008).

SC Res. 1279 (1999).

SC Res. 2076 (2012).

SC Res 2098 (2013).

SC Res. 1234 (1999).

SC Res. 1291 (2000).

SC Res. 1291 (2000).

SC Res. 1304 (2000).

SC Res. 1316 (2000).

SC Res. 1332 (2000).

SC Res. 1355 (2001).

SC Res. 1376 (2001).

SC Res. 1399 (2002).

SC Res. 1417 (2002).

SC Res. 1484 (2003).

SC Res. 1592 (2005).

SC Res. 1653 (2006).

SC Res. 1925 (2010).

SC Res. 1973 (2011).

SC Res. 1975(2011).

SC Res. 2147(2014).

SC Res. 341 (2001).

SC Res. 827 (1993).

SC Res. 837 (1993).

SC Res. 955 (1994).

SC Res. 143 (1960).

SC Res. 169 (1961).

SC Res. 687 (1991).

SC Res. 819 (1993).

Secretary-General's bulletin on compliance with international humanitarian law by United Nations forces, UN Doc off CES, 1999, UN Doc ST/SGB/1999/13.

UN SCOR, 61st Sess., 5359th mtg. at 18, U.N. Doc. S/PV.5359 (Jan. 27, 2006).

UN Doc S/PV.5781, declaration of Belgium on behalf of the European Union, SC Verbatim Record of the 5781st Meeting, (Resumption 1) 11 November 2009.

UN Doc S/PV.6151, declaration of the United States, SC, Verbatim Record of the 6151st Meeting, 26 June 2009.

UN Doc S/PV.6216, (declaration of France), SC, Verbatim Record of the 6216th Meeting,11 November 2009.

UN Doc S/PV.6427 declaration of Ghana, SC, Verbatim Record of the 6427th Meeting, (Resumption 1), 22 November 2009.

UN Doc S/PV.6790, declaration of Germany SC, Verbatim Record of the 6790th Meeting, 25 June 2012.

UN Doc S/PV.6943, Security Council provisional records of the 6943rd meeting, 28 March 2013.

UN General Assembly, A/55/305-S 2000/809

UN Doc S/PV.6024, 26 November 2008.

United Nations General Assembly, 2005 World Summit Outcome (A/RES/60/1) (24th October 2005)

Introduction

1. Background to the Problem

War is as old as humanity and its proven harmful effects can be short or long term. It has been shown that in many armed conflicts, civilians are the main victims.[1] To counter this phenomenon, International Humanitarian Law (IHL) from the Second World War, and later, the Responsibility to Protect(R2P), are among the responses to protect the civilians.

Indeed, the Second World War was characterized by mass exterminations, deportations and hostage-taking that took a heavy toll on civilians. For this reason, the Geneva Conventions and their additional protocols were adopted to ensure the protection of civilians and their property, the wounded, the sick, shipwrecked and captured combatants.[2] These conventions paved the way for international humanitarian law. International humanitarian law (IHL) is a set of rules that aims to limit the effects of armed conflict and applies to all parties to the conflict. Also known as the law of war or the law of armed conflict, it applies to international armed conflicts, non-international armed conflicts and in cases of occupation.[3]

However, in a situation where millions of human beings are at the mercy of civil wars, insurgencies, state repression and state collapse and where the state does not have the power, the capacity or the will to meet its responsibility to protect, the need for international action arises.[4]

After the failure to protect people in Rwanda, in the former Yugoslavia, the Responsibility to Protect (R2P) norm was created to address this problem. The Responsibility to Protect (R2P) is an international norm that seeks to ensure the protection of civilians against mass atrocity crimes

1 Camilla Waszink, "Protection of civilians under international humanitarian law: trends and challenges", *NOREF report*, 2011, p. 27.

2 Niteesh Kumar Upadhyay, "Law of Armed Conflict: Applications and Practice", *ISIL Y.B. Int'l Human. & Refugee L.* 394, 2020-2021, p. 42.

3 Roberta Arnold and Noëlle Quénivet, "International Humanitarian Law and Human Rights Law: Towards a new merger in International Law", *Leiden: Martinus Nijhoff Publishers*, 2008, p.13.

4 Anne Orford, *International authority and the responsibility to protect*, Cambridge Cambridge University Press, 2011, p.11.

which are genocide, war crimes, ethnic cleansing and crimes against humanity.

The R2P principle has three pillars of protection. The responsibility to perform the functions of protecting citizens and promoting their welfare resides first and foremost on the state whose people are directly affected. Secondly, other states have the responsibility to assist states to achieve their responsibility to protect. Thirdly, the international community has the responsibility to protect through collective action under Chapters VI, VIII and VII (as the case may be) of the UN Charter.[5]

According to paragraph 139 of the World Summit Outcome Document, the Security Council is the preeminent U.N. organ responsible for implementing R2P in the U.N. system when all other actions have failed.[6] Collective action by the international community flows through the actions of the Security Council. This is consistent with the role of the Security Council under Article 24 in Chapter V of the Charter, in which members of the U.N. "confer on the Security Council primary responsibility for the maintenance of international peace and security".[7] R2P intervenes to prevent or stop the four crimes that can be considered as violations of IHL in armed conflict. It should be noted that these crimes can also be committed outside a conflict, in which case R2P would still apply.

In order to protect the population in the Democratic Republic of Congo, especially in its eastern part, which remains a theatre of interminable conflicts and which currently leaves behind more victims than in the past, the international community, in this case the UN, has intervened by virtue of the R2P.[8]

The current crisis in the Democratic Republic of Congo (DRC) dates back to the Rwandan genocide of 1994. Former genocidaires had crossed the border and founded an armed group called the Forces Démocratiques de Libération du Rwanda (FDLR). This armed group and others operating on Congolese territory literally placed the republic in a crisis that led the

---

5 United Nations, *General Assembly, 2005 World Summit Outcome (A/RES/60/1)*, 24th October 2005, Paragraphs 138-139.

6 Jared Genser, "The United Nations Security Council's Implementation of the Responsibility to Protect: A Review of Past Interventions and Recommendations for Improvement", *Chi. J. Int'l L. 18*, 2017; p. 420.

7 UN, "Panel on UN Peace Operations", *Report to the Secretary General*, p. ix.

8 Danielle N. Allyn, "The Promise of Peace: UNSC Resolutions 2098 and 2147 and the Protection of Congolese Civilians", *Carolina Digital Repository*, 2015, *available at* https://cdr.lib.unc.edu/, accessed on 7th July 2022.

UN to react in order to protect the civilian population.[9] Thus, by resolution 1279, the UN launched a peace operation called the United Nations Organization Mission in the Congo (MONUC) in 1999 with a mandate to observe the ceasefire and disengagement of forces in the first instance; and later, the protection of human rights.[10]

Unfortunately, all attempts at peace, various peace agreements and ceasefires have failed to bring political stability. The 2000s were characterized by violence. Apart from the FDLR, the Congolese armed forces FARDC were confronted with other internal and foreign rebel groups supported by Rwanda and Uganda.[11] These rebel groups committed rape, burnt villages, etc.[12] A report by the Office of the UN High Commissioner for Human Rights stated that the systematic and widespread attacks by these rebel groups could constitute crimes of genocide, crimes against humanity or/and war crimes.[13]

Even after all attempts to stabilize the region and end the continuing violence, the UNSC adopted Resolution 1653 in 2006, invoking R2P in its first pillar, specifically the DRC's responsibility to protect the population on its soil. This came after an attack by the Ugandan rebel group, the Lord's Resistance Army (LRA), in which eight MONUC peacekeepers were killed. Indeed, in paragraphs 8-10, resolution 1653 stresses that "governments in

9 Félicité Akonkwa Mugombozi, *Examination of the impact of the United Nations Security Council Resolution 2098 on the protection of civilians in North-Kivu, Democratic Republic of the Congo,* Master diss., Kampala International University, 2018, p. 20.

10 *UNSC Res. 1279 (1999) and the UNSC Res. 1291 (2000).* See also Reynaert J. "NONUC/MONUSCO and civilian protection in the Kivus", *Interns and Volunteers series,* IPIS, 2010.

11 The U.N., High Commissioner for Human Rights (OHCHR), Democratic Republic of the Congo, *Report of the Mapping Exercise Documenting the Most Serious Violations of Human Rights and International Humanitarian Law Committed within the Territory of the Democratic Republic of the Congo between March 1993 and June 2003,* October 15, 2017, pp. 463–642.

12 Jared Genser, *The United Nations Security Council's Implementation of the Responsibility to Protect: A Review of Past Interventions and Recommendations for Improvement,* p.426.

13 The U.N., High Commissioner for Human Rights (OHCHR), Democratic Republic of the Congo, *Report of the Mapping Exercise Documenting the Most Serious Violations of Human Rights and International Humanitarian Law Committed within the Territory of the Democratic Republic of the Congo between March 1993 and June 2003,* para 520. See also Charbonneau, Louis and Nichols, Michelle. "Exclusive: Rwanda, Uganda Arming Congo Rebels, Providing Troops", *U.N. Panel* (Reuters 2012).

the region have the primary responsibility to protect their populations, including from attacks by militias and armed groups".[14]

According to several reports, the conflicts in the DRC have done more harm to the community, especially in its eastern part. The Human Rights Watch report from February 2009 shows that the LRA rebel group has raped a thousand women and girls, including children, killed 1500 civilians, burned a thousand homes and entire villages.[15] Another report mentions the massacre of 150 civilians in less than 24 hours and 15,000 cases of rape and sexual violence from 2008 to 2009.[16]

In a bid to put an end to this situation, the UNSC took a step forward by adopting resolution 1925 in 2010, transforming MONUC into the United Nations Organization Stabilization Mission in the Democratic Republic of Congo (MONUSCO). By resolution 1925, the Security Council recalled the responsibility of the Congolese State to protect its population and gave MONUSCO a mandate to protect civilians and humanitarian personnel against the imminent threat of physical violence. This resolution clearly stated that the SC will support the DRC government in its efforts to stabilize and consolidate state authority and finally authorized the mission to use all means necessary to fulfill its mandate.[17] Accordingly, it is clear that the resolution invoked the DRC's responsibility to protect its civilian population (first pillar) and fully committed to the third pillar obligations under the responsibility to protect.

Despite military offensives conducted by the government armed forces (FARDC) with assistance from the UN peacekeeping mission in the DRC (MONUSCO), violence continues to escalate. More than 120 militias and armed groups are currently active in the eastern part of DRC.[18]

---

14 *UNSC Res. 1653,* Jan. 27, 2006, p : 8–10. Moreover, at the time of the adoption of Resolution 1653, some states were even ready to support the third pillar of R2P. These were France and the United Kingdom.

15 Perma, "The Christmas Massacres: LRA attacks on Civilians in Northern Congo", *Human Rights Watch,* Feb. 16, 2009, available at https://perma.cc/W3ZM-24DT, accessed on 7th July 2022.

16 Perma, "Tackling Sexual Violence Must Include Prevention, Ending Impunity", *U.N. Official, U.N. News Centre,* (Apr. 27, 2010), available at https://perma.cc/2G4V-CARW, accessed on 7th July 2022.

17 *UNSC Res. 1925,* p:11-12 (May 28, 2010).

18 *Global Centre for the Responsability to Protect, Democratic Republic of the Congo,* 31 May 2021 available at https://www.globalr2p.org/countries/democratic-republic-of-the-congo/, accessed on 7th July 2022.

MONUSCO's ineffectiveness in protecting civilians was starkly demonstrated when the M23 rebels, a Rwandan-supported group[19], seized the town. M23 fighters also perpetrated serious violations of international humanitarian law, as well as gross human rights violations. M23 rebel fighters were responsible for at least 59 cases of sexual violence. The UN investigation also documented at least 11 arbitrary executions, cases of child recruitment and forced labor, cruel, inhuman and degrading treatment and looting committed by M23 fighters.[20]

Through the good offices of the Secretary-General of the UN, on February 24, 2013, the Peace, Security and Cooperation Framework for the DRC and the region (PSC Framework), called the Addis Ababa Agreement, was signed by 11 countries of the region, the International Conference on the Great Lakes Region (ICGLR). This conference and SADC proposed another step to end the crisis in the DRC. They proposed that a specialized intervention brigade be created within MONUSCO to support the objectives of the PSC framework agreement.[21]

The Secretary-General proposed in his 2013 Special Report on the Democratic Republic of the Congo and the Great Lakes Region to create a specialized Intervention Brigade within MONUSCO to disable these rebel groups and protect civilians.[22] The UN adopted resolution 2098 on 28 March 2013 and established the Intervention Brigade within the framework of MONUSCO with the mandate to undertake military operations to defeat armed groups and to protect civilians. Composed of military components from Troop Contributing Countries (TCCs),[23] the Brigade was mandated to use all necessary means to neutralize armed groups, which goes beyond

19 MONUSCO, *"The M23 is a militia of the Rwandan army" says the DRC representative during the discussions at the United Nations Security Council,* 9081e SÉANCE, MATIN CS/14952 29 JUIN 2022, available at https://press.un.org/fr/2022/cs14952.doc.htm, accessed on 1st July 2022.

20 OHCHR, *Rapport du BCNUDH sur les violations des droits de l'homme à Goma, Sake et Minova,* 15 Nov - 2 Dec 2012, 8.05.2013.

21 On 24 February 2013 the Peace, Security and Cooperation Framework for DRC and the region (PSC Framework), called the Addis Ababa Accord, was signed by 11 countries in the region, the International Conference on the Great Lakes Region and by the Chairs of the African Union and the Southern African Development Community to end the conflict in DRC. See KOK N., "From the International Conference on the Great Lakes Region-led negotiation to the Intervention Brigade", *African Security Review,* vol. 22, issue 3, 2013, pp. 175-176.

22 UN, *Special Report of the Secretary-General on the Democratic Republic of the Congo and the Great Lakes Region, UN Doc S/2013/119,* para 60-64.

23 *TCCs in the brigade are South Africa, Malawi and Tanzania.*

the existing MONUSCO military mandate.[24]The UN Security Council reaffirmed MONUSCO's expanded mandate and authority in the DRC by adopting Resolution 2147(2014).[25]

Pursuant to resolution 2098, which provides that the Brigade be involved, together with the DRC armed forces in offensive operations against the named armed groups, the Brigade became *ipso facto* party to an armed conflict. Consequently, the International Humanitarian Law rules on conduct of hostilities apply to such an operation. The reports on the Brigade's military operations against M23,[26]ADF (Allied Democratic Forces)[27] and APCLS(French: Alliance des patriotes pour un Congo libre et souverain) are sufficient evidence to conclude that the Brigade has become party to an armed conflict and IHL rules are therefore binding for its members.

This thesis examines the implementation of the R2P, on its third pillar, which is the use of force by the Brigade under resolutions 2098 and 2147. In implementing the resolution 2098 mandate, the Intervention Brigade Forces fight under pressure against these rebel groups,[28] and it is conceivable that mistakes, such as civilian deaths, would be made in the "fog of war".[29]

Moreover, UN Special Rapporteurs have themselves raised questions about the UN's complicity in violations of International Humanitarian Law or International Human Rights Law because of its support for FARDC forces during operations where such violations are committed.[30] Some of the Brigade's unilateral operations and those carried out jointly with the FARDC are said to have violated the principles of distinction and precau-

---

24 *UNSC Res. 2098* para 12-13.

25 *UNSC Res. 2147*(2014).

26 Jay Benson, "The UN Intervention Brigade: Extinguishing Conflict or Adding Fuel to the Flames", *A One Earth Future Discussion Paper* 2, 2016, p.10.

27 Jamestown Foundation. *Congolese Forces Take the Offensive Against Uganda's ADF-NALU Militants, 20 March 2014,* available at https://www.refworld.org/docid/5333fc864.html, accessed 6 August 2019.

28 Indeed, the Task Force was under pressure from the presence of the M23 rebel group. Inasmuch as it had the mandate to disable M23 and many other armed groups, the Brigade force was intended to protect the city of Goma and its surroundings from possible attack. Indeed, the M23, which had already taken the town of Goma, had withdrawn to the outskirts of the town in the territory of Rustshuru.

29 Scott Sheeran and Stephanie, "Case, The Intervention Brigade: Legal issues for the UN in the Democratic Republic of the Congo", *New York, International Peace Institute,* 2014.

30 Patrick Cammaert and Fiona Blyth, "The UN intervention brigade in the Democratic Republic of the Congo", *New York, International Peace Institute,* 2013, p.32.

tion in IHL. To name but a few, the dropping of bombs on the inhabitants of Rugari and Kisimba in North Kivu caused deaths and injuries among civilians.[31]

In addition, the Brigade's operations or those carried out jointly with the FARDC to neutralize the APCLS, ADF and Mai-Mai groups have raised questions about responsibility for the loss of civilian lives and the destruction of non-military targets.

In the context of joint operations by the Brigade and the FARDC (Ruwenzori II), for example, the Brigade Commander is aware of the likelihood of civilian casualties when an air strike was launched on 12 May 2021 to destroy two ADF camps. In his press release, he points out that the FARDC, which will assess the impact of operations on the ground, will be able to report on violations of IHL or not during these operations.[32]

Moreover, in the afternoon of Sunday, 31 July 2022, members of the Intervention Brigade shot at people at the border at Kasindi in the DRC, the border area with Uganda. Three people were killed and 15 wounded.[33] This incident has been classified as dramatic because "the mission that was there to protect the civilians is still the one that is shooting at them".[34] Thus, in the view of what is highlighted above, this thesis will examine the legal consequences of IHL violations during the implementation of the R2P under the resolution 2098 mandate, and who could be held responsible for such violations.

2. Legal Implications

The fact that UN peacekeepers, in particular Brigade forces, may be engaged in conflict against rebel groups during the implementation of UN Security Council Resolution 2098 in the eastern DRC in the name of the

31 Thomas Ntamwira Cheshe, *The responsibility of the International Organization for damages caused to the civilians: Case of UN during peacekeeping operations in North-Kivu*, Mater Thesis, Kigali Independent University, ULK, December 2018.

32 ONU, *Transcription de la conférence de presse ONE UN en RDC*, le 19 mai 2021 à Kinshasa.

33 UN, *DR Congo: Guterres outraged over peacekeepers aggression*, calls for accountability on 31 July 2022 available at https://news.un.org/en/story/2022/07/1123692, accessed on 1st August 2022.

34 I*nterview with Joseph Kitausa, president of the Beni civil society*, available at https://www.rfi.fr/fr/afrique/20220731-rdc-des-soldats-de-la-monusco-tuent-au-moins-personnes-dans-le-territoire-de-beni, accessed on 1 August 2022.

principle of the "responsibility to protect" civilians from mass atrocities, has several legal implications.

Firstly, Resolution 2098 links the protection of civilians (POC) to the responsibility to protect. This association between the mission to protect civilians and the responsibility to protect emphasized the need for coercive intervention by the UN to put an end to violations of the rules of international humanitarian law relating to the protection of civilians. This association is not without consequence, however, as questions of the impartiality and neutrality of the UN force arise on the one hand and the protection under IHL of UN personnel and installations on the other.

It is therefore important to distinguish between impartiality with regard to the Security Council mandate and impartiality in the implementation of the mandate[35], which is at the level of UN peacekeeping operations.

In the specific context of the Brigade's intervention, some would question not the neutrality of the Security Council's mandate but rather that of MONUSCO's operational mandate. On the one hand, there is MONUSCO in general, which must respect the principle of impartiality and neutrality. On the other hand, there is the Brigade, which has a different status and is not concerned by the principle of neutrality because it is considered to be a "combatant". However, the fact that the Brigade was created within a peacekeeping force and placed under the same command led to some confusion in the operationalization of the mandate.[36]

While recognizing that peacekeeping forces have been engaged in hostilities of such a nature to trigger the application of IHL (either through acts of *self-defense* or in the execution of a mandate authorized by the UN Security Council under Chapter VII of the UN Charter), this is not without enormous consequences in the context of the Brigade.

Thus, the members of the Brigade will be considered as combatants and will lose the protection provided by IHL for UN personnel and installations. When the Brigade is "legally" susceptible to be attacked, other MONUSCO forces will still benefit from this protection. A major remaining challenge would be to identify when MONUSCO forces would

35 UN, *UN General Assembly, A/55/305,* 2000, p.9. See also Boulden Jane, Mandates Matter, "An exploration of Impartiality in United Nations Operations", *Global Governance*, 2005, pp. 147-160 available at http://www.atypon-link.com, accessed on 13th February 2019.

36 UN, *UN Doc. S/PV.6943, Security Council provisional records of the 6943rd meeting,* 28 March 2013. P.3-4. See Devon Whittle, "Peacekeeping in conflict: The Intervention Brigade, MONUSCO and the application of international humanitarian law to United Nations forces", *Geo. J. Int'l L. 46,* 2014, p. 837.

lose their protection. Don't MONUSCO installations become military objectives because they are inhabited by combatants? When, for operational reasons, MONUSCO's regular forces and those of the Brigade must act in a joint operation, don't they all become combatants?

This question, which concerns the scope of application of IHL, its duration, and the time at which it is applied, is particularly important because the application of IHL may result in a corresponding loss of the legal protection afforded to peacekeepers under the Security Convention and the Rome Statute of the International Criminal Court (hereinafter "the Rome Statute").

Another question is that of the applicable law. However, the classification of the conflict is very important in deciding which IHL rules apply when the conflict is between the regular armed forces of the DRC (FARDC), UN forces (the Brigade) and national rebel groups, or foreign rebel groups, or national rebel groups acting on behalf of a foreign country. Depending on the circumstances, the International or Non-International armed conflict rules will apply. In all cases, the nature of the brigade force plays no part in the classification of the conflict.

In addition to the above, there is the question of the scope of R2P and the application of IHL during the implementation of R2P. Indeed, it is well known that the responsibility to protect included in the mandate of Resolution 2098 is not limited to the conflict. Thus, for other violations, such as genocide or ethnic cleansing committed outside the conflict, protection will be provided by the legal arsenal that supports R2P, such as the law of genocide and international human rights law in general. However, this thesis will limit itself to R2P in the context of the responsibility to intervene, i.e. during conflicts and the application of IHL in this context.

Inasmuch as the R2P aims to protect the world's most vulnerable people from the most heinous international crimes and IHL sets rules that seek to limit the effects of armed conflict on people and objects, both rules have the same objective, namely the protection of civilians. The issue arises when those who are supposed to protect civilians oppress them when implementing the R2P principle under Resolution 2098. For instance, as a result of attacks by the Brigade on rebel groups, civilians have been injured. IHL contains basic rules designed to protect human dignity in war and when those rules are violated, there are legal consequences which can be broadly divided into state responsibility and individual responsibility on the part of those who abet, order or supervise the perpetration of such violations.

Accountability for IHL violations by Brigade members or Congolese armed forces is a way for victims of those violations to obtain reparation.

Accordingly, to assess accountability for these violations, it is relevant to determine to what extent the United Nations or the Troop Contributing Countries, or even the DRC incur responsibility. Consequently, the present thesis provides an assessment criterion for the distribution of responsibility between UN and TCCs for IHL violations.

3. Research Methodology

This thesis examines the doctrine of the Responsibility to Protect (R2P) and its links with international humanitarian law (IHL), with a particular focus on its implementation in the Democratic Republic of Congo (DRC). Given the plurality of methodological approaches in the field of international legal studies[37], it is necessary to clarify the methodological orientation of this study. The following section presents the methods used, the reasons for their adoption, and how they are applied to the research questions.

The central method used is legal dogmatics, understood as the systematic analysis of existing international legal norms in order to clarify their scope, consistency, and internal logic. Legal dogmatics is particularly suited to situating R2P within the normative framework of international law and examining its intersection with IHL. This approach allows the study to address fundamental questions such as: How does R2P relate to the obligations established by IHL? To what extent can R2P be understood as an autonomous legal norm or rather as a political principle with normative implications? And how could responsibility be shared in cases where R2P operations coincide with violations of IHL?

While doctrinal analysis is essential, it alone cannot fully capture the practical realities in which R2P is invoked and applied. That is why the study incorporates a sociology of international law as a complementary approach. The aim is to examine how international norms function in practice, particularly in fragile contexts such as eastern DRC, where legal rules interact with political, military, and social dynamics.

The socio-legal analysis draws on two sources. First, documents that provide information on how R2P and IHL standards have been implemented

37 Olivier Corten, *Méthodologie du Droit International Public*, Bruxelles, Edition de l'Université de Bruxelles, 2009, p.19.

in the DRC. These include UN resolutions, mission reports, human rights reports, and academic analyses. Second, interviews were designed to gather the views of practitioners and observers on how R2P was understood, implemented, and linked to issues of accountability for violations of IHL. Semi-structured interviews were conducted with UN mission staff, NGO representatives, members of the FARDC, and legal experts familiar with the DRC context. The interviews were not intended to produce statistically representative data, but rather to generate qualitative information to supplement the archival documents. They enabled the research to compare the normative framework of R2P with the experiences and perceptions of those involved in its implementation. Ethical safeguards, including informed consent, anonymization, and secure storage of documents, were respected throughout the process.

By incorporating documentary analysis and testimonies gathered during interviews, the socio-legal dimension of the thesis provides a more comprehensive account of how R2P works in practice and how it is perceived by those responsible for its implementation.

In addition to doctrinal and socio-legal analysis, the thesis incorporates a philosophical-normative dimension. This is necessary because the implementation of R2P, by its very nature, raises questions of justice, legitimacy, and accountability that cannot be answered by referring solely to positive law. Drawing selectively on theories of justice and accountability, this dimension allows for the evaluation of questions such as: Who can be held accountable for violations of international humanitarian law committed in the context of R2P operations? And what remedies, if any, are available to victims? Furthermore, this dimension will help to uncover ideas and perspectives that allow for a better understanding of a situation. Thus, it is necessary to establish “what” happened on the ground when the Brigade implemented R2P in the context of the conflict and "how " it happened in order to determine the distribution of responsibility between the UN and troop-contributing countries (TCCs) for violations of international humanitarian law, as this has not yet been examined by many researchers and therefore constitutes a limited area of scientific study.

This normative research is not presented as an independent method, but as a critical complement that enriches doctrinal and socio-legal conclusions with evaluative ideas. By exploring these issues in depth, legal dogmatics provides the fundamental structure of the thesis and ensures doctrinal clarity.

4. Organisational Lay Out

Apart from the introduction and conclusion, this thesis is divided into two main titles: R2P and IHL in the context of the DRCongo (Title I) and the legal implications of the applicability of IHL during the implementation of R2P (Title II).

The first title is divided into two chapters. The first chapter covers the legal understanding of R2P in conjunction with IHL. In this Chapter, four sections are developed: The background and definition of R2P, the Legal Status of R2P, principles of the implementation of R2P and the relation between R2P and IHL. The second chapter deals with the implementation of R2P in the specific context of the DRC. The analysis discusses the crimes in the context of R2P in the DRC, the duties of DRC under R2P, and the duties of the international community (African Union, European Union and UN interventions). A specific section analyzes UNSC resolution 2098 as a tool of R2P in DRC.

The Second Title is divided into three chapters. Before determining the legal implication of the applicability of IHL in the implementation of R2P, the analysis focuses on how IHL has been applied during the implementation of the R2P (first chapter). In this chapter, issues related to qualification of the conflict, the consequences of the application of IHL to the conflict and the IHL violations in the implementation of R2P are examined. The second chapter tackles the responsibility for IHL violations during the implementation of the R2P in the DRC. In this chapter the legal framework of the responsibility of the Force Intervention Brigade (FIB), shared responsibility between United Nations, Troops contributing countries (TCCs) and the DRC and individual responsibility are analyzed. The third chapter covers the victim's reparation remedies for IHL violations in the context of the R2P in the DRC. It describes the jurisdictional and non-jurisdictional mechanisms.

Title I: The Responsibility to Protect (R2P) and International Humanitarian Law in the Context of the DRCongo

Chapter I: Legal Understanding of R2P in Conjuction with IHL

The 19th century was a defining period in the protection of civilians. This century was marked by levels of cruelty and human violence comparable to "those of the Second World War".[38] The failure to protect people against the killing of 800,000 in 100 days in Rwanda,[39] qualified as 'a faster rate of killing than the Holocaust';[40] together with the massacre in the former Yugoslavia,[41] led the international community to feel a 'deep sense of shame'[42]and to recognize that it was time to be better equipped to deal with the massive human rights violations that people suffer.

This was the reason for the military intervention to protect the Albanian population of Kosovo. This intervention was criticized for not having been authorized by the United Nations Security Council (UNSC).[43]This led many[44] to question the legality of the intervention and to fear that state sovereignty would be violated because of these so-called humanitarian actions.[45] Moreover, the question is related to the analysis of art 2(4) of the UN Charter on the use of force.

Kofi Annan, the then UN Secretary General, played a role by asking governments in his Millennium Report of 2000: "If humanitarian intervention is indeed an unacceptable infringement of sovereignty, how should we

38 Jay Crush, "The Responsibility to Protect in International La" *E-international relations,* (May 31st 2013) available at https://www.e-ir.info/2013/05/31/the-responsibility-to-protect-in-international-law/, on 13th February 2019.

39 Feil and Scott R. "Could 5,000 Peacekeepers Have Saved 500,000 Rwandans?", *Early Intervention Reconsidered, Institute for the Study of Diplomacy III,* 1997, pp 1-5.

40 Alex J. Bellamy, *Responsibility to protect,* Cambridge, Polity Press, 2009.

41 U.N., *The Case of Srebrenica. U.N. Doc. A/54/549,* November 15, 1999 ; UN, "In Larger Freedom: Towards Development, Security and Human Rights for All", *Report of the Secretary-General, U.N. Doc A/59/2005* (2005), available at http://www.un.org/largerfreedom/contents.htm, accessed on may 12, 2022; *Report of the Secretary General. Implementing the Responsibility to Protect. U.N. Doc. A/63/677,* 12 may 2021.

42 Jack Donnelly, *International Human Rights,* Boulder, Colorado: Westview Press, 2007, p. 180.

43 Christopher Greenwood, "International Law and the NATO Intervention in Kosovo", *The International and Comparative Law Quarterly,* vol. 49, no. 4, (2000):34. JSTOR, available at http://www.jstor.org/stable/761769., accessed 1 Jun. 2022.

44 *Ibid,* p. 178.

45 Erin Creegan, "Justified uses of force and the crime of aggression", *Journal of International Criminal Justice 10,* no. 1 (2012) p.62.

respond to a Rwanda, to a Srebrenica -to gross violations of human rights that affect every precept of our common humanity?"[46]

Leaders and practitioners unanimously realized that they had to find a way to reconcile two seemingly contradictory international standards. The Responsibility to Protect seems to answer this question. This chapter will focus first on the definition and the background of the R2P (1). This will be helpful to determine the legal status of the R2P (2) according to the duties of states and the UN under the principle. On this basis, the analysis of the link between R2P and IHL will be the subject of a section (4).

1. Background and Definition of the Responsibility to Protect

A. Background of the R2P

R2P is underpinned by the challenges of protecting populations in relation to pre-established principles of international law. The horrors of war and their consequences for all humankind have convinced many of the need to address these challenges by establishing or further developing a principle of international law that can, in one way or another, consider the rights and obligations of States and the international community.

In response to this challenge, the Canadian government created the International Commission on Intervention and State Sovereignty (ICISS). This Commission first raised the concept of Responsibility to Protect (R2P) in one of its reports published in 2001.[47] Two elements stand out in this report. Firstly, the report sets out and develops the idea of sovereignty as responsibility. When a state considers itself to be sovereign, it must take into account its responsibilities towards its people. The report suggests that the principle of non-intervention in the internal affairs of the state should be conditional on the ability and willingness of the state to protect the rights of the population; the human rights.

Furthermore, the report stated that if a state is unwilling or unable to meet its responsibilities to its people, the international community has a responsibility to intervene to prevent or respond to atrocities in order

46 United Nations Secretary-General, "We the Peoples: The Role of the United Nations in the Twenty-First Century", *Report of the Secretary General, (A/54/2000)*, 27th March 2000, paragraph 217.

47 International Commission on Intervention and State Sovereignty, *The Responsibility to Protect*, 2001

to assist populations at risk. In practice, the report believes that military intervention would be a solution in such cases.

The R2P was discussed in the UN and endorsed by member states on the basis of the report from the High-Level Panel on Threats, Challenges and Change. This independent panel was set up by the UN Secretary General, Kofi Annan. He formed this independent group of international experts to look at how to improve the UN and ensure that it would be able to cope with the increasing internal conflicts and other challenges of the 21st century. The report produced by this panel in 2004 recommended that the UN should adhere to the idea that "States have a responsibility to protect their populations from serious threats to human rights".[48] This led leaders to agree to the meaning of R2P at the 2005 World Summit.[49]

The UN celebrated 60 years of its existence in 2005. Member States renewed their commitment to the organization while recognizing that actions must be taken in line with the challenges of the day. The conclusions of the Summit were unanimously summarized in the Responsibility to Protect. Paragraphs 138 and 139 of the Summit Outcome documents reflect the views of Member States.

In the wording of paragraph 138, States agree that each State has a responsibility to protect its population from the following four crimes: ethnic cleansing, genocide, crimes against humanity and war crimes. Furthermore, it is the responsibility of the international community to encourage and assist States in this task.

Paragraph 139, on the other hand, deals with the situation where States fail to protect their populations. In this situation, the responsibility lies with all States as members of the international community. Indeed, States undertake to protect their populations through several measures, such as the peaceful resolution of conflicts[50] and/or the use of force.[51]

However, the use of force must be conditioned by the authorization of the UNSC. During this summit, states agreed to discuss the implication of R2P in the General Assembly.

---

48 High Level Panel on Threats, "Report of the High-Level Panel on Threats Challenges and Change: A More Secure World: Our Shared Responsibility", *Challenges and Change, (A/59/565),* 2nd December 2004.

49 United Nations General Assembly, *2005 World Summit Outcome (A/RES/60/1),* 24th October 2005.

50 *Chapter 6 and 8 of the UN Charter.*

51 *Chapter 7 of the UN Charter.*

A clearer formulation of R2P comes from Secretary-General Ban Ki-moon's 2009 report. R2P is understood as having three pillars. The first is the responsibility of the state to protect its population, which is a corollary of the principle of sovereignty. The second is the responsibility of the international community to assist states in this task and the third is that when a state fails to meet this obligation, the international community has an obligation to respond. This response can be by peaceful means, but also possibly by more coercive measures as deemed appropriate.[52]

B. Definition of R2P

R2P is among the few ideas that have advanced more rapidly in international law.[53]Based on the R2P's three pillars of protection, the state concerned, other states and the international community have the responsibility to protect the populations against mass atrocities.

R2P has its roots not only in international humanitarian law, human rights law and refugee law, but also in the principle of sovereignty.[54]This reaffirms Thomas Hobbes' idea[55] that the sovereign power has the obligation to protect the people under its rule. It is thus appropriate that the primary responsibility for protecting the people lies with the power that rules over them. Sovereignty implies the power to dominate but also implies responsibilities towards that population. These responsibilities include the responsibility to protect that population against any form of violation. As a principle, R2P reconciles two aspects by stating that the principle of state sovereignty includes not only rights but also obligations. It contains

52 United Nations Secretary-General, *Report of the Secretary-General, Implementing the Responsibility to Protect, (A/64/677),* 12th January 2009.

53 Lemkin's efforts to organise the repression of the crime of genocide, recognised in the 1990s and the 1948 Genocide Convention were the most dictated ideas to spread in the international sphere. R2P is a new addition to the that list. See *Anson Rabinbach,* "Raphael Lemkin et le concept de génocide", *Revue d'Histoire de la Shoah,* 2 N° 189, 2008, p. 514.

54 Francis M. Deng, Kimaro Sadikiel, Terrence Lyons, Donald Rothchild and William Zartman. I, "Sovereignty as responsibility: conflict management in Africa", *Rowman & Littlefield,* 2010.

55 Peter Berkowitz, "Leviathan Then and Now", *Policy Review 151,* 2008, p.18.

a right to the territory (right to govern) and a 'responsibility towards the population living in that territory'.[56]

R2P strengthens the essential elements of state sovereignty by its definition as a principle of protection of the population against "organized" violence.[57]

Thus, as reaffirmed by the Secretary General, the basis of R2P lies in the responsibility of the state. This remains legally and politically valid in the face of the very essence of sovereignty. This justifies the first pillar of R2P in the paragraph 138 on the Responsibility to Protect of the 2005 World Summit Outcome Document:

> "Each individual State has the responsibility to protect its populations from genocide, war crimes, ethnic cleansing and crimes against humanity. This responsibility entails the prevention of such crimes, including their incitement, through appropriate and necessary means. We accept that responsibility and will act in accordance with it (...)."[58]

Wording this paragraph 138, States have the responsibility to prevent mass crimes and their incitement as well. This responsibility is based on a set of international obligations of States contained in international treaties and agreements, international jurisprudence and are developed through State practice.[59] These obligations require States to refrain from and take measures to prevent and punish crimes such as genocide, war crimes, ethnic cleansing and crimes against humanity.

The obligation of States to prevent mass crimes has been taken up in other international conventions. For instance, article 1 of the Genocide Convention states that the Contracting States expressly undertake to "prevent and punish genocide".[60] The ICJ has given an interpretation of Article 1 in relation to the obligation to prevent genocide. For the Court, States have

---

56 Buskie Alexander, *Understanding the Responsibility to Protect: an introduction,* December 2014, available at https://una.org.uk/news/understanding-responsibility-protect-introduction, accessed 1st June 2022.

57 Edward Luck, "Sovereignty, choice and the responsibility to protect." *Global Responsibility to Protect 1,* no. 1, 2009, p. 13.

58 United Nations General Assembly, *2005 World Summit Outcome (A/RES/60/1),* 24th October 2005.

59 Louise Arbour, "The responsibility to protect as a duty of care in international law and practice", *Review of International Studies 34,* no. 3, 2008, p. 448.

60 *Convention on the Prevention and Punishment of the Crime of Genocide Approved and proposed for signature and ratification or accession by General Assembly resolution 260 A (III) of 9 December 1948 Entry into force: 12 January 1951.*

to prevent the commission of genocide by individuals and by themselves. According to the Court: "*It would be paradoxical if States were ... under an obligation to prevent, so far as within their power, commission of genocide by persons over whom they have a certain influence, but were not forbidden to commit such acts through their own organs, or persons over whom they have such firm control that their conduct is attributable to the State concerned under international law.*"[61]

Moreover, the Court considered that Article 1 has an "operative and non-preambular"[62] character, i.e., that it creates an obligation other than those contained in the Convention and should not be considered as an introduction to the Convention. While recognizing that this obligation for States to refrain from committing genocide is not expressly provided for in Article 1, its implication is "to prohibit States from committing genocide themselves".[63] Therefore, States have a combined responsibility to prevent, stop, suppress and halt genocide.[64]

The protection of population is the primary responsibility of the State concerned. It is only when this State is not able or unwilling to protect its population that other states can intervene.

According to the ICISS, States have the primary responsibility to protect and the residual responsibility rests with the international community. Wording the World Summit's Outcome Document 2005, States agreed to take all necessary measures to help States protect their population. The paragraph 138 states that: "(...) *We also intend to commit ourselves, as necessary and appropriate, to helping States build capacity to protect their populations from genocide, war crimes, ethnic cleansing and crimes against humanity before crises and conflicts break out.*" This is pillar II of R2P.

The UN Secretary-General (UNSG) report on 'Implementing the Responsibility to Protect' 2009 clarifies that Pillar II means "international assistance and capacity building".[65]

---

61 Bosn. & Herz. v. Serb. & Mont, *Application of the Convention on the Prevention and the Punishment of the Crime of Genocide,* 2007 I.C.J. 91, 1427,438 (Feb. 26.), at para. 166.

62 Paola Gaeta, "On what conditions can a state be held responsible for genocide ?", *European Journal of International Law 18,* no. 4, 2007, p. 646.

63 Bosn. & Herz. v. Serb. & Mont, *Application of the Convention on the Prevention and the Punishment of the Crime of Genocide,* para. *162.*

64 Eyal Mayroz, "The legal duty to prevent : After the onset of genocide", *Journal of Genocide Research 14,* no. 1, 2012, p. 89.

65 UN, "Implementing the responsibility to protect", *Report of the UN Secretary-General (A/63/677),* 12 Jan. 2009.

The tenets of pillar II are the international assistance to States by helping them build the capacity to protect their populations from the four crimes.[66] This is considered by the UNSG as an 'active partnership between the international community and the State'.[67]

In light of paragraphs 138 and 139, Pillar Two refers to the responsibility of the international community to assist States to strengthen their capacity to prevent crime and to address the root causes of mass atrocities. Several aspects flow from this second pillar: encouraging states to fulfil their responsibility to prevent and eventually punish those who commit these crimes; supporting states in their security efforts by enabling them to intervene rapidly in the event of a threat; and strengthening the economic capacity of states through development aid in order to reduce inequalities.[68]

In fact, Pillar II applies when any state requests assistance from the international community to protect its population from these crimes. This assistance can come from regional or sub-regional actors[69]. Thus, Pillar II is the responsibility of other actors than the UN but should be coherent and coordinated. Wording the paragraph 139[70] the international community has the responsibility to take timely and decisive action to protect populations from the four crimes through diplomatic, humanitarian and other peaceful means and when needed to use force to stop atrocities. This is the R2P's third pillar.

Pillar III involves two steps. The first step is the use of peaceful means. This is in line with what states committed to in 2005.[71] Indeed, all these peaceful measures are also enshrined in Chapters VI and VIII of the United Nations Charter, with the aim of protecting populations from the four crimes.

---

66 Adrian Gallagher, "The promise of pillar II: analysing international assistance under the Responsibility to Protect", *International Affairs 91,* no. 6 (2015): 1265.

67 Thierry Tardy, "The dangerous liaisons of the Responsibility to Protect and the protection of civilians in peacekeeping operations", *Global Responsibility to Protect 4,* no. 4, 2012, p. 427.

68 Samia Aggar, *La responsabilité de protéger : un nouveau concept?,* PhD diss., Bordeaux, 2016, p. 37.

69 UN, "The role of regional and sub-regional arrangements in implementing the responsibility to protect", *Report of the Secretary-General (A/65/877–S/2011/393),* June 2011.

70 United Nations General Assembly, *2005 World Summit Outcome (A/RES/60/1),* 24th October 2005.

71 Alex J. Bellamy, "The responsibility to protect and the problem of military intervention", *international Affairs 84,* no. 4, 2008, p. 620.

The second step sets out the possibility of the use of force. This step is the most controversial aspect of R2P to prevent or stop the four crimes.[72] The point here would be the justification of state aggression through the use of force to protect people from crimes. However, the use of force would be included in the exception provided under the Charter of Nations, which is the authorization to use force through the UNSC under Chapter VII. Therefore, the use of force in the framework of R2P is limited to the four crimes and can only be invoked through a UNSC resolution.

Accordingly, the use of force is subject to two conditions: it must be proven that peaceful means are inadequate and that the States concerned are failing to protect their population. As military intervention is not the only measure of the responsibility to protect, the effective use of non-coercive measures would be more important in the fight against the four crimes. The rapid deployment of military personnel and the strengthening of cooperation between the United Nations and other regional and sub-regional actors will determine the effectiveness of the third pillar of the responsibility to protect.[73]

It is important to recognize that the principle of R2P as developed in the ICISS report is not identical to the one adopted by states at the 2005 World Summit. For the ICISS report, R2P sets out the responsibility of states to protect people 'at risk', which includes protecting people from all forms of violations at all times. In 2005, by contrast, at the World Summit, states decided that the R2P principle was limited to the four crimes and their prevention: genocide, war crimes, ethnic cleansing and crimes against humanity. This scope of application of R2P is therefore considered narrow and universal.[74]

This thesis is in line with the same idea by specifying that R2P can be invoked only in the specific framework provided by States and not all human rights violations in general. It does not pertain to all violations arising from all armed conflicts in general or other human rights violations and abuses, or other serious threats to human security such as pandemics, natural disasters, etc.

72 Daniel Fiott, "The use of force and the third pillar", *The Responsibility to Protect and the Third Pillar: Legitimacy and Operationalization*, London: Palgrave Macmillan UK, 2015, p. 135.

73 UN, "Responsibility to protect: timely and decisive response", *Report of the UN Secretary-General,* 25 July 2012 (A/66/874-S/2012/578).

74 Alex J. Bellamy, "The three pillars of the responsibility to protect", *Pensamiento propio* 41, 2015.

Moreover, the protection under R2P does not only include the citizens of the state concerned. The thesis makes it clear that the protection is generalized and applies to the entire population. The term Population refers to all categories of people within the territory of a State, regardless of their origin or status.

Furthermore, as a third element, the obligations of the State under R2P are well specified in international law. Through different instruments, they already have the legal obligation to prevent and punish, for example, genocide, war crimes and crimes against humanity. This thesis is based on the tenet that R2P must be implemented exclusively in the contexts provided for by the UN Charter. R2P cannot be talked about outside the principles and procedures provided for by the UN Charter. This work will therefore examine the limits and challenges of this principle in its application on the ground, in the present case in the DRC.

Indeed, prevention is the guiding principle of the R2P. Other measures can only be considered when prevention has failed. Thus, any recourse to Chapter VII of the Charter can only be envisaged if other measures fail. For the effectiveness of all these measures, the States have declared their support for the Special Council for the Prevention of Genocide.[75]

From the above, several questions arise. Is R2P binding on states? Thus, in the following section, this paper discusses the legal status of R2P.

2. Legal status of R2P

The legal status of R2P is still a matter of serious debate. Some authors believe that R2P should be recognized as an international law principle because it has its foundations in international law such as the rules governing sovereignty, human rights and international humanitarian law.[76] Other scholars, however, contest the legality of R2P on the grounds that it is not specifically and clearly invoked in international instruments.[77]

This section will discuss the legal nature of R2P in relation to the understanding of the concept as a source of law or as an international custom or, finally, as a norm creating a new obligation for states.

---

75 Bellamy, *"The three pillars of the responsibility to protect"*, p. 51.

76 Mehrdad Payandeh, "With Great Powers Comes Great Responsibility? The Concept of the Responsibility to Protect Within the Process of International Lawmaking" *Yale Journal of International Law 35* no. 2, Fall 200, p. 471.

77 Alex J. Bellamy and Ruben Reike, "The Responsibility to Protect and International Law", *Global Responsibility to Protect 2*, 2010, p.268.

Wording the ICISS report,[78] section 2(24) R2P is an emerging norm of customary law section 2.24 provides that: "(...) *While there is not yet a sufficiently strong basis to claim the emergence of a new principle of customary international law, growing state and regional organization practice as well as Security Council precedent suggest an emerging guiding principle – which in the Commission's view could properly be termed 'the responsibility to protect'.*"

This is repeated in section 6(17) and in the High-Level Panel Report. This being the case, some people could directly take the concept of "standard" in its broad definition as being what must be or what is pre-established. This narrow definition of the concept "norm" refers to its legal conception.

This understanding, although widely accepted, does not prove that R2P is a legal standard. For the concept 'norm' can be used in a political sense as well as in a legal sense.

Indeed, States did not take up the content word for word in the draft wording of the section on collective responsibility (the new paragraph 139)[79]. Therefore, it is right to consider R2P as a norm even if the concept 'norm' should not necessarily refer to the legal status of R2P.[80]

In accordance with Article 38(1) of the ICJ Statute, R2P would be considered a source of law. The general principles of international law are contained in international treaties, declarations of states and decisions of courts and tribunals.[81] Indeed, several treaties, customs and general principles of law related to human rights and IHL have established the legal basis for R2P.[82]The fact that R2P is included in these instruments clarifies the perception of States towards this principle.[83] This was evident in the 2005

78 ICISS, "The Responsibility to Protect: Report of the International Commission on Intervention and State Sovereignty", *hereinafter ICISS REPORT,* 2001, 2.24, 6.17.

79 Spencer Zifcak, *United Nations reform: Heading north or south ?,* Routledge, 2009, p.116.

80 Ramesh Thakur and Thomas G. Weiss. "R2P: from idea to norm—and action?" *Global Responsibility to Protect 1,* no. 1, 2009, pp.32-33.

81 Grigory Tunkin, "Is General International Law Customary Law Only", Eur. J. Int'l L. 4, 1993, p. 53.

82 Tunkin, "Is General International Law Customary Law Only", p. 67.

83 Hui-Chol Pak, Son Hye-Ryon and Jong Son-Kyong, "Analysis on the Legal Nature of 'Responsibility to Protect", *International* Studies 57, no. 3, 2020, pp. 282-285 ; Quoted in Jay Crush, "A Critical Analysis of the Status and Implementation of the Responsibility to Protect in International Law", *e-international relations,* May 31 2013, available at https://www.e-ir.info/2013/05/31/the-responsibility-to-protect-in-international-law/ accessed on 6 June 2022.

World Summit document and the UNSC 1973 resolution in Libya. Nevertheless, the R2P in the context of Libya looks like a justification of strategic military intervention with the aim of plundering natural resources.[84]

A closer look at the Resolution 1973/2001 concerning the so-called application of R2P in Libya shows that, the first condition before the use of force under R2P according to paragraph 139 was not respected.[85] Some days before the resolution, the International Crisis Group[86]suggested means such as cooperation between Libya's neighboring countries and other African countries to solve the conflict, without use of force. Unfortunately, that was rejected. Some will therefore argue that the lack of methods and scope of application of R2P in international law leads to arbitrariness in its application.[87]As a result, it is claimed that R2P violates the principle of non-interference in the national affairs of states, which, according to Oxford Anna, is based on filling the "political vacuum" left by decolonization.

Furthermore, the fact that R2P is endorsed in the 2005 World Summit Outcome and several other UN resolutions is not sufficient to justify its legal status.[88]The use of force in the context of R2P may be considered as legal in the sense that it is authorized by the UNSC. However, the problem about the qualification of the four crimes arises. Therefore, the determination of the preconditions for R2P is unclear and, as a result, military intervention in the response to human rights violations is used in an arbitrary manner. On the question of whether R2P is a customary norm, both tendencies recognize that it is a principle in the process of what can be called practice under customary law. It seems to be clear that R2P is in the process of evolving, that is, in the process of forming what can be called practice and would already be considered as *opinio juris* by a good number of States.[89]

---

84 Elizabeth O'shea, "Responsibility to Protect (R2P) in Libya: ghosts of the past haunting the future", *International Human Rights Law Review 1,* no. 1, 2012, p. 173.

85 Hugh Roberts, "Who said Gaddafi had to go?", *London Review of Books 33,* no. 22, 2011, p. 10.

86 International Crisis Group, *A ceasefire and negotiations the right way to resolve the Libyan crisis,* 2011, *Retrieved from https://www.crisisgroup.org/middle-east-north-africa/north-africa/libya/ceasefire-and-negotiations-right-way-resolve-libya-crisis.,* on 13th February 2019.

87 Orford, *International authority and the responsibility to protect,* p.22.

88 Elizabeth O'shea, *Responsibility to Protect (R2P) in Libya,* p.175.

89 Robert A. Pape, "When duty calls: A pragmatic standard of humanitarian intervention", in *International Security 37,* no. 1, 2012, pp. 41-80.

However, R2P cannot be considered as a customary norm or a general principle of law. The determination of a customary rule is not a function of the intention or assessments made by a group of people. Two elements of custom are very important to qualify a principle as a customary norm. The two constitutive elements of international custom are practice and *opinio juris*, which means that these practices must be habitually and regularly undertaken by the State and considered as custom or tradition.[90]

The existence of a humanitarian crisis and the need for military intervention remains a matter for the permanent members of the UNSC. Only state practice (which is objective) and *opinio juris* (which is subjective) determine its nature. Unfortunately, many states have opposed or are silent on R2P.[91] This thesis cannot consider R2P as customary rule because the two elements of customary law are cumulative. When one of them is not fulfilled, one cannot speak of international custom. In addition to this, The World Summit Outcome Document does not clarify the legal status of R2P. Another area of debate concerned the responsibility to protect as a new obligation.

Several arguments have been developed to support this thesis. For the most part, R2P has created a new obligation for the international community to combat the spread of atrocities around the world.[92] As a new concept, R2P has helped to clarify the UN Security Council's "legal obligation" to promote human rights.[93] In fact, R2P legitimizes the humanitarian actions or interventions of the UN Security Council.

Indeed, the emergence of R2P on the international scene has brought about a change in international law and more particularly in the notion of sovereignty. Since the dawn of time, sovereignty has been considered an inviolable and absolute right of States. With R2P, sovereignty implies not only rights but also obligations.[94] Through R2P, states, the international

---

90 Jean d'Aspremont, Samantha Besson and Sévrine Knuchel, (Eds.) *The Oxford handbook of the sources of international law,* Oxford University Press, 2017.

91 Anne-Marie Judson, *Where is R2P grounded in International law?* Master diss., University of Otago, 2012, p.17.

92 Anne Peters, "Humanity as the A and Ω of Sovereignty", *European Journal of International Law 20,* no. 3, 2009, p. 517.

93 Mehrdad Payandeh, "With Great Power Comes Great Responsibility-The Concept of the Responsibility to Protect within the Process of International Lawmaking", *Yale J. Int'l L.* 35, 2010, p.499.

94 Lee Feinstein, *Darfur and beyond: what is needed to prevent mass atrocities,* 2007 available at http://www.cfr.org/sudan/darfur-beyond/p12444, Accessed 9th June 2022.

community and the United Nations clearly recognize the "duty" to protect not only their citizens, but also foreign populations within the framework of the principle of sovereignty.[95]

However, this thesis asserts that the notion of "sovereignty-responsibility" was not created by R2P.[96] It has long been provided for in the United Nations Charter. This is clear from Articles 1(3) and 55 of the UN Charter, which stipulate that the protection of populations is one of the duties of sovereignty.

Moreover, the basis for the fight against the four crimes would not only be R2P, as the R2P crimes of genocide, ethnic cleansing, war crimes and crimes against humanity are *ius cogens* norms to which no derogation or limitation is permitted. By their very nature, states have, even before the advent of R2P, an obligation to respect and protect the rights of the population against these crimes. Therefore, R2P is not a legal concept; it creates no legal change as it is embedded within the existing international law order. This thesis is in line with the fact that R2P is not a legal norm. Its recognition and endorsement by states has an influence on existing norms and thus leads to a change in international law. Such a change would only occur if the declarations of international actors reach a sufficient level of uniformity. Although this thesis is consistent with the fact that R2P is not a legal norm, R2P is not devoid of legal character. R2P can therefore be considered "soft law". Generally opposed to hard law, soft law is often seen as a precursor to the development of binding legal norms, whose legal effects are not, however, non-existent. R2P has thus contributed to the interpretation of States' obligations to protect populations against mass crimes at all times. It is also influenced by existing principles of international law such as IHL, IHRL, etc.

While the interpretation of paragraphs 138 and 139 has given rise to controversy, the "open and malleable language" used in these paragraphs clarifies the very nature of R2P as a soft law.[97]

95 Alicia L. Bannon, "The responsibility to protect: The UN world summit and the question of unilateralism", *Yale LJ 115*, 2005, p. 1157.

96 Jay Crush, "A Critical Analysis of the Status and Implementation of the Responsibility to Protect in International Law." *e-international relations,* May 31, 2013, available at https://www.e-ir.info/2013/05/31/the-responsibility-to-protect-in-international-law/ accessed on 6 June 2022.

97 Jennifer M. Welsh and Maria Banda, "International Law and the Responsibility to Protect: Clarifying or Expanding States' Responsibilities?" *Global Responsibility to Protect 2,* 2010, p.230.

The recognition and endorsement of R2P by States has an influence on existing norms and thus leads to an evolution of international law.[98] For example, it was with the R2P controversy that the principle of non-intervention set out in Articles 2(4) and 2(7) and the powers conferred on the Security Council regarding the authorization of force under Chapter VII were once again called into question, leading to the conclusion that the legality of applying the R2P principle would only be admitted within the framework of the UN Charter.[99]

This thesis concedes, with Aidan Hehir, that since 2005, R2P has undergone a transformation and the subsequent reports can be read as a complete reformulation of how the existing legal commitments of states and the international community should be interpreted and applied in the future.[100] In considering all the above, it would be appropriate to ask whether R2P is an "international legal norm" *de lege ferenda*? Unfortunately, this thesis will not answer this question but will focus in the following lines on the issues raised by the implementation of R2P.

Indeed, the rejection of the wording, "we recognize our shared responsibility to take collective action", is sufficient evidence that States did not clearly want to consider collective responsibility as an obligation.[101] Moreover, States did not specify the normative content of the concept of "responsibility" and the legal sanctions that would follow in case of non-compliance. Thus, R2P formulations remain a "rhetorical trick".

Thus, R2P has not brought a new deal to the competences of the UNSC as it has not created a binding obligation for the action of this council and limited the use of the veto right by the P5. It should be noted that the R2P has an evolutionary and not a revolutionary content. Therefore, in this sense, responsibility cannot be equated with a legal obligation or duty. R2P is "best understood as a reaffirmation and codification of already

98 Mehrdad Payandeh, "With Great Powers Comes Great Responsibility? The Concept of the Responsibility to Protect Within the Process of International Lawmaking", *YF 35*, no. 2, Fall 2009, p.471.

99 Christopher Joyner, "The Responsibility to Protect: Humanitarian Concern and the Lawfulness of Armed Intervention", *Virginia Journal of International Law 47*, 2006-2007, p.698.

100 Aidan Hehir, "The Responsibility to Protect: 'Sound and Fury Signifying Nothing'?", *International Relations 24*, no. 2 (2010) p. 230.

101 Carsten Stahn, "Responsibility to protect: political rhetoric or emerging legal norm?", *Globalization and Common Responsibilities of States*, Routledge, 2017, p. 157.

existing norms" and as a political concept with political effects.[102]However, the implementation of R2P can raise both theoretical and practical legal issues.

3. Implementation of R2P

The international Community have agreed that the contribution of the International Commission on Intervention and State Sovereignty (ICISS) to prevent and stop mass atrocities has been the triple responsibility contained in R2P. These responsibilities are to prevent, to react, to rebuild.

Moreover, the implementation of R2P raises questions on the use of force as a principle in international law and the duties of States and the UNSC under R2P.

R2P has been invoked by either the UN Security Council or the Secretary-General in response to several crises.[103] The Ivory Coast, Central African Republic, Darfur, South Sudan, Yemen, Mali, Syria, DR Congo, Kenya, Kyrgyzstan and Guinea can be mentioned here.

The idea that the state and the international community have a responsibility to protect populations from genocide, war crimes, ethnic cleansing and crimes against humanity was adopted by the GA. The GA specifies the circumstances in which the international community could intervene and declare that it is its responsibility to take preventive action "before crises and conflicts break out".[104]

The big challenge of implementing the R2P concept is the transition from "promise to practice" or from "words to deeds".[105] The importance of the R2P concept does not lie in its ability to turn promise into practice, but

102 Alex J. Bellamy and Catherine Drummond. "The responsibility to protect in Southeast Asia: between non-interference and sovereignty as responsibility", *The Pacific Review 24*, no. 2, 2011, pp. 179-200.

103 Alex J. Bellamy, *"The Three Pillars of the Responsibility to Protect"*, available at http://www.cries.org/wp-content/uploads/2015/09/006-bellamy.pdf., on 13th February 2019.

104 UN, *2005 World Summit Outcome, GA Res. 60/1, UN GAOR, 60th Sess., Provisional Agenda; Items 46 and 120, Supp. No. 49, UN Doc. A/RES/60/1,* 24 October 2005, paras. 138–9. 5 *Ibid.*

105 *UN Doc. A/RES/60/1,* 24 October 2005, paras. 138–9. 5 *Ibid. 6* UN Secretary-General, *"Implementing the Responsibility to Protect: Report of the Secretary-General"*, UN GAOR, 63rd Sess., Agenda Items 44 and 107, *UN Doc. A/63/677,* 12 January 2009, p. 7.

rather in its ability to turn promise into action, i.e. to act. Actions are more important than this process of turning promises into actions.[106] Therefore, the objective of the implementation of R2P is to succeed in the actions of the international community in order to protect populations against 'major' crimes[107]. Thus, R2P is the ability to put words or promises into practice and not just promises.

This chapter will analyze the implementation of R2P according to the three obligations: to prevent (A), to react (B) and to rebuild (C).

A. The "duty" to prevent

In law, "prevention" refers to the "set of measures and institutions designed to prevent, or at least limit, the occurrence of a risk, the production of damage, the carrying out of harmful acts, etc., by endeavoring to eliminate their causes and means".[108]

Thus, the concept of prevention is an all-purpose word. Defining the concept of prevention is not as easy as it seems. The concern here would be to consider the concept in its literal sense and ignore what would be the objective of prevention which is protection.

It is in this context that Emmanuel DECAUX wonders: "*But if justice itself is prevention, should we not admit that everything is prevention? Prevention would be everywhere and nowhere, (...) We would all be doing prevention without knowing it, like Mr Jourdain was writing prose when asking for his slippers! Prevention would be a euphemism and a panacea, a protection that doesn't say its name, with less harm and less cost*".[109] Thus, prevention does not only mean to preserve as stated in the UN Charter. This is only the first part of the definition of prevention and is not the understanding of 'prevention' in the context of R2P, which is broader.

106 Oxford, *International authority and the responsibility to protect, 26.*

107 Gareth Evans, *The responsibility to protect: ending mass atrocity crimes once and for all, Rowman & Littlefield, 2009.*

108 Gégard Cornu, *Vocabulaire juridique,* Paris, P.U.F., 7 Coll. Quadrige - Dicos Poche. 2005. See also Lenaïg Casiez-Piolot, *La responsabilité de prévenir,* PhD diss., Aix-Marseille, 2017.

109 Emmanuel Decaux, Sébastien Touzé and Jean-Paul Costa. "La prévention des violations des droits de l'Homme: actes du colloque des 13 et 14 juin 2013 », *Coll. Publications de l'Institut International des Droits de l'Homme, Sous-Coll. Institut René Cassin de Strasbourg.* Paris, Pedone, 2015.

The Carnegie Commission's report of 1997 provided central concepts on the "prevention". The report distinguished between 'operational' prevention, which is applicable in the context of crisis and 'structural' prevention', which refers to strategies to address the root causes of conflict before or during the conflict.[110] This document served as a reference for ICISS in drafting its report on the R2P in its prevention dimension.

Wording the ICISS report, the responsibility to prevent addresses "both the root causes and direct causes of internal conflict and other man-made crises putting populations at risk". Moreover, the report explains that prevention is the most important element of R2P and concerns both the State concerned and international community.

For the responsibility to prevent three essential conditions are elaborated: knowledge of the situation at risk, the 'preventive toolbox' and the political will.[111] The ICISS did not draw a clear distinction between conflict prevention and the prevention of mass crimes. For the Commission, conflict prevention would also be the prevention of mass crimes, as most of these crimes are committed in times of conflict. Therefore, the conflict prevention tools are associated with preventive tools in the context of R2P.[112] The effectiveness of mass atrocity prevention leads to effective conflict prevention.

However, the distinction between conflict prevention and mass crime prevention in the context of R2P remains important. After all, the two concepts are still not the same, even if they lead to the same thing, namely protection. The clarification here is: The ICISS understanding of prevention needs to be adjusted as it would be a major problem in operationalizing 'prevention' in the understanding of R2P[113], which only focuses on the four crimes. In fact, conflicts can also result in the commission of genocide, crimes against humanity, ethnic cleansing and war crimes, but these crimes can be committed outside of armed conflict. In the meantime, conflict prevention in general is necessary but not sufficient for prevention as an R2P responsibility. This includes a strategy of deterrence of the perpetrators of these crimes. This is the implication of the link between international

110 Carnegie Commission on Preventing Deadly Conflict, *Preventing Deadly Conflict: Final Report,* Washington DC, Carnegie Commission Preventing Deadly Conflict,1997.

111 *ICISS,* a:20.

112 Gareth,*The responsibility to protect,* p.19.

113 Bellamy, "The Three Pillars of the Responsibility to Protect", *available at http://www.cries.org/wp-content/uploads/2015/09/006-bellamy.pdf.,* on 13th February 2021.

criminal law and R2P. This evolution entails the individualization of the principle, as well as a shift towards bias, intrusiveness and coercion.[114]

This evolution has its roots in the international community's focus on the prevention of serious crimes. This has been "a major turning point for the United Nations" in emphasizing the culture of prevention over that of reaction.[115]

This transformation has developed through a consideration of the place of the individual on the international scene to meet the ideal of respect for human dignity. The international community has even built a legal framework to protect individuals in times of peace. This is demonstrated by the adoption of several legal instruments such as the Convention on the Prevention and Punishment of the Crime of Genocide and the Universal Declaration of Human Rights, adopted within a day of each other in 1948, to name but a few.

It is worth noting that the Convention on the Prevention and Punishment of the Crime of Genocide was the first instrument to stipulate the obligation of prevention on the part of States. Thus, the ICJ has repeatedly interpreted the obligation of prevention in the context of genocide[116]. In the Corfu Channel case, the Court condemned the Albanian State for failing to prevent a disaster in the following terms: "nothing was attempted by the Albanian authorities to prevent the disaster".[117] This analysis by the

114 Ruben Reike, "Conflict prevention and R2P", *The Oxford Handbook of the Responsibility to Protect,* Bellamy, Alex and Tim Dunne, (Eds.) Oxford University Press, 2016.

115 Casiez-Piolot, *La responsabilité de prévenir, p.110.*

116 *This was also the case in the United States Diplomatic and Consular Staff in Tehran case (I.C.J., United States Diplomatic and Consular Staff in Tehran,* Judgment, 24 May 1980*)* and Bosnia and Herzegovina v. Serbia and Montenegro (I.C.J., Bosnia and Herzegovina v. Serbia and Montenegro, *Case concerning the application of the Convention on the Prevention and Punishment of the Crime of Genocide,* Judgment, 26 February 2007, para. 430) In addition, courts whose jurisdiction relates exclusively to the protection of human rights are also concerned with obligations to prevent violations of fundamental rights. A case in point is A. v. United Kingdom before the European Court of Human Rights. In this case, the Court was called upon to qualify the responsibility of the State for the abuse of a child by his stepfather (E.D.H. *Court, A. v. United Kingdom,* Judgment, 22 September 1998, para. 22).

117 I.C.J., *Corfu Channel case,* Judgment, 9 April 1949, p. 23.

ICJ judges has led to the groundwork for what can be described as the "*international law [of] prevention*".[118]

The emphasis on prevention as a responsibility under the R2P principle is an evolution in the struggle against atrocities.[119] Indeed, R2P has not seen prevention as a response to ongoing crises, which is the case with humanitarian intervention, but rather as mechanisms developed to prevent atrocities before the crisis even occurs.

Considered preferable than any kind of response to crimes, prevention can take many forms: long-term or short-term structural aid, preventive actions to avert a looming crisis.[120]

To describe the long- and short-term causes and preventive measures, various terms are used such as "structural" or "operational prevention", or "root causes" or "triggers". The identification of long-term causes is often associated with prevention measures that are in fact very short-term. Cold war debts, poor terms of trade and unequal access to markets are identified as root causes of violence.[121]

The importance of the responsibility to prevent stems from two considerations: the logical priority of prevention according to ICISS (i.e. prevention efforts should be pursued before the responsibility to respond and the responsibility to rebuild are considered) (2001a: xi); and the ability of prevention efforts to reinforce the set of actions associated with the responsibility to protect. These actions need to be characterized by collaboration between the international community and the state concerned in order to ensure their effectiveness. The cases of Kenya and Guinea are prime examples of the effectiveness of preventive measures before a conflict breaks out. Several non-coercive measures have facilitated the operationalization of prevention. In both cases, the remarkable collaboration between the UN Secretariat and regional and national actors has made the goal of protecting populations possible.

---

118 Mohamed Bennouna, "Prevention and International Law", *Collected Courses of the Xiamen Academy of International Law*, Volume 4, Brill Nijhoff, 2013, p. 200.

119 Jaclyn Streitfeld-HalL, "The Responsibility to Protect: Can we prevent mass atrocities without making the same mistakes?" *Global Centre for the Responsibility to Protect, 2014, available at*
*https://www.civicus.org_* accessed on 13th February 2019.

120 Jennifer Welsh, "The responsibility to prevent: Assessing the gap between rhetoric and reality", *Cooperation and Conflict 51*, no. 2 (2016): pp. 217-220.

121 Alexandra Bohm and Brown Garrett Wallace, "R2P and prevention: the international community and its role in the determinants of mass atrocity", Global *Responsibility to Protect 13*, no. 1, 2020, p. 65.

Indeed, to avoid any confusion between the responsibility to prevent as a responsibility in R2P and the responsibility to prevent conflicts, the precise actions to be undertaken must be differentiated according to the different attacks, including attacks associated with a government, a rebel group, inter-community or after a regime change, etc. This categorization is sufficient proof that certain crimes can be committed outside of an armed conflict. This is the case of crimes against humanity committed in North Korea (in the absence of an armed conflict), those linked to the Arab Spring in Libya and Syria (before the existence of the conflict) and those committed in the DR Congo.

Moreover, development assistance, democratic capacity building, better trade access, fact finding, economic sanctions, security sector reform, law promotion and peacekeeping operations are the prevention measures suggested by the ICISS.

An example of the effectiveness of economic sanctions as a preventive measure is the European Union's action to prevent massive human rights violations in the DRC. The European Union Economic sanctions have been proven to stop massive human rights violations and to prevent conflict in the DRC.[122]

In addition, the timing of preventive measures is also crucial to protection under R2P.

The theory of response time provided the basis for the distinction between "root cause prevention efforts" and "direct prevention efforts".[123] Thus, "root cause" measures should aim to address the underlying causes of a deadly conflict, and "direct" measures should address the immediate triggers of a conflict in order to avoid recourse to more coercive measures or the third pillar of R2P. Establishing criteria to determine which states are vulnerable and at risk of mass atrocities would facilitate prevention planning. This requires the establishment of an observation list which should be updated each time a situation arises. It is on the basis of this list

122 See DR Congo: EU, US Sanction Top Officials, UN, AU Should Expand Action Against Rights Abusers, Press for Credible Elections, 1st June 2017, available at https://www.hrw.org/news/2017/06/01/dr-congo-eu-us-sanction-top-officials, accessed on 13th February 2019.

123 Eli Stamnes, "The Responsibility to Protect and Root Cause Prevention", in *Norwegian Institute of International Affairs*, 2010, p. 11.

that one can then distinguish which country is at risk and which is not yet or not at all.[124]

However, the interpretation and determination of these criteria are subject to question. While praising the merits of the proposed criteria, this thesis states that the establishment of this watch list must be based on a systematic analysis of data and not on personal observation. This would be effective for crime prevention. For, these prevention measures should normally be measures of results and not of means.

While recognizing the distinction between conflict prevention measures and preventive measures in the context of R2P, this study will focus more on the analysis of preventive measures in the DRC, trying to differentiate between those that are part of the general context of conflict and those that are specific to R2P.

B. The "duty" to react

The duty to react refers to the responsibility to respond when serious crimes are committed in a state that is clearly no longer able or willing to protect its population. This state will be described as a failing state because it has failed in its duties including security and justice. Thus, the responsibility to protect its population will henceforth lie with international society and more particularly with the Security Council, given its primary mission, which is the maintenance of international peace and security. For the international community to redress the situation, coercive measures may be required.

The responsibility to react is divided into two aspects: on the one hand coercive measures, so-called "sanctions", which include political, economic and judicial steps and military action on the other hand. Unlike preventive measures, coercive measures are taken when crimes are already being committed.[125] Political, economic and judicial measures will differ in that some are taken to prevent the commission of crimes (the responsibility to prevent) while others are taken to stop the commission of crimes (the responsibility to respond or to react).

---

124 Barbara Harff, "No lessons learned from the Holocaust? Assessing risks of genocide and political mass murder since 1955", *Genocide and Human Rights.* Routledge, 2017, pp. 329-345.

125 Sandra Fabijanić Gagro, "The Responsibility to Protect (R2P) Doctrine", *International Journal of Social Sciences 3,* no. 1, 2014, p. 67.

Sanctions can be understood as:

- freezing financial assets held outside the country of [a] the national government, [b] regime members in their individual capacity, or [c] those persons designated as key supporters or enablers of the regime.
- suspension of credits, aid and loans available to the national government from international financial institutions.
- denying access to overseas financial markets and especially banks, both to the government and individual designees.
- controlling specific goods that provide power resources to the regime, most especially highly traded and income producing commodities, weapons, computers and communications technologies.
- flight and travel ban on individuals and specific air carriers.
- denial of visa, travel and educational opportunities to those individuals on the designee list."[126]

However, coercive measures have never been the preferred measure in the implementation of R2P. Looking back at coercive measures as a response in the implementation of R2P in Libya, other measures have been taken before the use of force.[127] The international community, i.e. the states in the region and the UN, took measures to stop the violence against the population.

These are the establishment of a ban on all flights to and from Libya, the arms embargo, travel restrictions, negotiations, etc. Wording the Security Council Resolution 1973, the important element for the cessation of hostilities in Libya is the establishment of a ban on all flights except for humanitarian flights, travel restrictions[128] on the individuals and entities listed and the enforcement of the arms embargo against Libya. The UNSC called upon all member states to enforce these measures for the effectiveness of the protection of the population. In addition, the role of the Arab League in the implementation of R2P in Libya was important. Some measures were

126 George A. Lopez, "Mobilizing Economic Sanctions for Preventing Mass Atrocities: From Targeting Dictators to Enablers", *Reconstructing Atrocity Prevention,* S. Rosenberg, T. Galis, & A. Zucker (Eds.) Cambridge: Cambridge University Press, 2016, pp. 389-392.

127 Bagish Chandra Nirmal, "Responsibility to Protect: A Political Doctrine Or An Emerging Norm (With Special Reference To The Libyan And Syrian Crises)", *Journal of the Indian Law Institute, 2015, p. 335.*

128 Travel restriction concerned individuals and entities listed in annex II and extended the assets freeze provision of the 1970 resolution. See *the Security Council Resolution (1970), 2011, adopted by the security council at its 6491 meeting, on Feb. 26, 2011, para 17,* available at http://www.nato.int/nato_staticassets/pdf/pdf_201 1_03/201 10927_1 103, ll-UNSCR-1973.pdf (last visited on June 21st 2022).

taken such as the action plan of 2 November 2011, adopted on 22 January 2012.

The action plan recommended the handover of power to the vice-president as well as accelerating the transition to democracy, the cessation of all forms of violence against the population, the withdrawal of Syrian military and armed forces from towns and villages. After a bitter assessment of the worsening crisis in Syria, the Arab League recommended political dialogue between the government and the population under its auspices. National sanctions imposed by the United States and the European Union in Libya in the beginning of 2011 resulted in an asset freeze on the Gaddafi regime. This thesis agrees that the combination of UN, EU and US targeted sanctions played a considerable role in degrading the regime's firepower[129] and protecting the population in Libya.

The effectiveness of answers on the mass atrocities is based on the role of neighboring countries as well as regional countries.[130] It is important to stress that these organizations should not be seen as supplanting the UN in the fight against atrocity crimes. The importance of regional and sub-regional organizations in preventing and responding to atrocity crimes is well established.[131] Some regional and sub-regional organizations have already proven their capacity to implement R2P. For the measures to be more effective, a healthy cooperation between the UN and these organizations for the operationalization of R2P is recommended. Therefore, the cooperation between African regional and sub-regional organizations and the UN in the implementation of R2P and the effectiveness of interventions in the DRC context will be analyzed.

In general, sanctions should not be used alone to make R2P effective. Sanctions must be part of a package including other measures to achieve the goal of ending mass crimes and ultimately making R2P effective. They must therefore be accompanied by a diplomatic strategy to maximize their

---

129 The fact that the international community cut off Qaddafi's money, denied him to hire mercenaries and import heavy weapons. These constraints meant that the Libyan war would have been longer and deadlier had these sanctions not been successfully imposed and enforced. Tripoli, for example, was not destroyed in an all-out battle like that which has now engulfed Aleppo and Damascus.

130 Karen Smith, "A reflection on the responsibility to protect in 2020." Global *Centre for the Responsibility to Protect, 2020,* available at https://reliefweb.int/report/world/reflection-responsibility-protect-2020., accessed on 13th February 2019.

131 George A. Lopez, "Tools, tasks and tough thinking: Sanctions and R2P." *Global Center for Responsibility to Protect, 2013,* available at https://sanctionsandsecurity.nd.edu › assets ›, accessed on 13th February 2019.

effect. Sanctions must be clear, consistent, well formulated and precise to facilitate their understanding by the target.

Indeed, sanctions often fail to achieve the desired results because more emphasis is placed on the sanctions than on the policies they are supposed to accompany. This was the case with the US and UN sanctions against Iraq in the 1990s, which became a policy rather than a policy tool. To solve the problem here of stopping the commission of atrocity crimes, sanctions must not be excessively punitive and aimed at isolation, they must provide a framework for the possibility of negotiation between the target and those imposing the sanctions. Moreover, "naming and shaming" the perpetrators of crimes can play a role in reducing the severity of mass killing and thus make the protection of populations effective.[132]

Beyond all that has been said, no tool is sufficient on its own, in order to have a fully functional toolbox decision-makers need to know how the tools work (or do not work) in combination to solve (or perhaps exacerbate) a mass killing situation.[133] Future work should focus on the interactions between different tools that slow down or stop the killing.

The absolute commitment to R2P focuses on the rights of vulnerable people. Since there is no such thing as military intervention in a state under international law, the use of force in the context of R2P is an exception to this rule while rejecting "unilateral interference and institutionalized indifference".[134]Hence, any coercive military action must be framed by Chapter VII of the UN Charter.

The UNA-UK Report[135] states that the legitimate use of military force has conditions. First of all, the state has to be manifestly failing to uphold its responsibility to protect civilians from mass atrocity crimes in order for the use of force to be justified. This condition is called "just cause". Moreover, it must be authorized by the Security Council according to the UN Charter. The Report recognizes that military intervention remains the main point

132 Jacqueline HR. De Meritt, "International organizations and government killing: Does naming and shaming save lives?", *international Interactions 38,* no. 5, 2012, p. 599.

133 Matthew Krain, "The effect of economic sanctions on the severity of genocides or politicides", *Journal of genocide research 19,* no. 1, 2017, p. 99.

134 Simon Adams, "The Responsibility to Protect and the Fate of the Rohingya", *Global Responsibility to Protect 11,* no. 4, 2019, p. 445.

135 UNA-UK, *The Responsibility to Protect In detail,* Feb 25, 2022, available at https://una.org.uk/r2p-detail accessed on 18th June 2022.

of discord regarding R2P.[136] These misunderstandings are also based on the link of R2P's pillar III and the humanitarian intervention.

Therefore, the ICISS Report[137] proposed six criteria for the use of force: right authority, just cause, right intention, last resort, proportional means and reasonable prospect.

The Security Council is the "right authority". The Security Council has the "primary" authority to deal with the use of force.[138] However, the Security Council is not the sole or exclusive authority to do so, its authorization must be acquired before proceeding with military intervention. Bodies have been set up to adequately verify the facts that would justify possible military intervention. In order to be effective and in view of the role of the P 5 in crisis management in the world, States should refrain from exercising their veto power.[139]

There is a progress of this call for states not to use their veto rights in the context of R2P. Indeed, the Accountability, Coherence and Transparency (ACT) group was launched in 2013. This group suggests that states should explain why they used their veto power in certain situations and thus, improve the transparency of the UNSC. A "Code of Conduct concerning the Security Council's action against genocide, crimes against humanity and war crimes" was proposed in 2015 by this ACT group. This Code calls on all UNSC member states and in particular, the Permanent Five not to vote against or abstain from any resolution aimed at preventing or stopping mass atrocities.[140] 121 member states, including two permanent members of the Council (France and the UK), and 2 observers signed the Code of Conduct since the first half of 2022.

Therefore, for the effective protection of populations against atrocity crimes, efforts should focus not only on changing the application of the

---

136 *Idem.*

137 *ICISS Report.*

138 *The Responsibility to Protect, 2001,* Report of the International Commission on the Intervention and State Sovereignty, retrieved from: http://responsibilitytoprotect.org/ICISS%20Report.pdf.

139 Cristina Badescu, *Humanitarian intervention and the responsibility to protect: Security and human rights,* Routledge, 2010.

140 Global Centre for the Responsibility to Protect, *Un Security Council And The Responsibility To Protect,* 2 June 2022, available at https://www.globalr2p.org/calling-for-a-unsc-code-of-conduct/., accessed on 13th February 2023.

veto but also and above all, on achieving an institutional balance between the SC and other regional or sub-regional bodies and organizations.[141]

Indeed, there are other alternatives when the SC is unable or unwilling to authorize military intervention. These alternatives were proposed by the 2011 report in point 6. The first alternative is the General Assembly. This assembly can through its special session "Uniting for Peace", influence the Security Council to reconsider its position in favor of military intervention.[142] Another possibility is that undertaken by regional or sub-regional organizations. Indeed, the UN Charter recognizes this possibility of collective intervention by regional or sub-regional organizations.[143]

It would be judicious for this thesis to analyze R2P with respect to the third pillar and the intervention of regional and sub-regional organizations such as the AU, SADC in the crisis in the East of the DRC. Just Cause refers to situations that should justify military intervention. In light of the ICISS report,[144] the basic elements of justification for action are: actions under the 1948 Genocide Convention with the implication of large-scale loss of life; any threat or occurrence of large-scale loss of life; any evidence of "ethnic cleansing"; the occurrence of crimes against humanity and violations of international humanitarian law; the context exposing the population to mass starvation and/or civil war; and situations of natural or environmental disasters threatening the lives of the population. It should also be noted that such intervention can only be legitimate when the State concerned is unwilling or unable to cope with the situation.

Other precautionary principles are necessary to justify intervention. These principles are the so-called "good intention", the "last resort" and the "proportionate means".[145]

The primary purpose of the intervention must be to stop or avoid human suffering. Thus, military action can only be justified when all other non-coercive measures have failed.[146] To ensure proportionality of means, the scale

141 Jennifer M. Welsh, "The Security Council's Role in Fulfilling the Responsibility to Protect", *Ethics & International Affairs* 35, no. 2, 2021, p. 237.

142 *Report on the Responsibility to Protect*,2001, 6.29-6.30

143 *Ibid. 6.31, 6.35-6.36.*

144 *Ibid. 4.19-4.20.*

145 Evans Gareth, "The Responsibility to Protect: Revisiting Humanitarian Intervention", *Foreign Affairs 81 (2002), available at https://www.crisisgroup.org/global/responsibility-protect.*

146 Andrew Garwood-Gowers, "China's "Responsible Protection" concept: Reinterpreting the Responsibility to Protect (R2P) and military intervention for humanitarian purposes", *Asian Journal of International Law* 6, no. 1, 2016, p. 91.

of the action must be proportionate to the act that caused the situation. In addition, the duration, scale and intensity of military action must be the minimum necessary to ensure the protection of populations.

This was unfortunately rejected as a criterion at the annual Security Council retreat in May 2002. The US rejected the idea on the grounds that such criteria could "limit its right to decide when and where to use force".[147] China, the UK and Russia argued that the failure of the SC to authorize military action would undermine the content and purpose of the Charter. However, several African states were in favor of these criteria as, according to them, it would facilitate transparency in the decision-making of the SC when it comes to R2P.[148]

Indeed, this thesis insists that the application of these criteria would be ideal in the protection of populations through the use of force. This, in turn, does not prove the objectivity of these criteria in determining which state is at risk and which is not. The prime example would be "good intent", which is a moral element. As such, determining it is a problematic undertaking. The criterion of "last resort" on the other hand, which would seem to be more factual, is also not immune to subjectivity. Might there be situations for which only the use of force could effectively ensure the protection of the population? Because the longer one waits for the effectiveness of preventive measures, the more serious the consequences would be. The main question at this level would be the authority to identify such situations. Indeed, the UN member states have already answered this question in article 39 of the UN Charter. The Security Council has this responsibility. Thus, many would understand the objection to the criteria not to be limited to the P-5 Council but rather to extend to the wider community of UN member states. The latter having already given the SC the freedom to decide when to use force.

C. The "duty" to rebuild

There is a certain logic to the responsibilities contained in R2P. It is not only the responsibility to prevent people from suffering serious harm, but also to respond when that harm occurs and, last but not least, to rebuild

147 Nico Smit, "The Evolution of the Responsibility to Protect", *E-International Relations*, 2008, p.617.

148 Smit, "The Evolution of the Responsibility to Protect", p. 630.

afterwards. Unfortunately, in most cases, the responsibility to rebuild has not been considered in the same way as the responsibility to prevent and to react.[149] The evidence is that the decision to establish the Peacebuilding Commission (PBC) has no reference on the responsibility to rebuild although this was discussed in its initial form on the World Summit.[150] Therefore, the PBC has played no role in rebuilding operations in the context of R2P.

In fact, PBC should not be confused with R2P as the two are dissociated. The responsibility to rebuild must be seen as an integral component of R2P conceptually, normatively, operationally and institutionally; but also, as an integral component of the responsibility to protect.[151] This is what distinguishes peacebuilding and the responsibility to rebuild in R2P. Peacebuilding is the set of activities undertaken in the absence of conflict to restore the foundations of peace and the responsibility for this is shared by all states. Reconstruction, however, is inseparable from war. The responsibility to rebuild is as much a moral and political responsibility as the responsibility to prevent and respond. It should be noted that the responsibility to rebuild is specific to states undertaking military intervention, while the responsibility to prevent and respond is shared by all states, which, as far as possible, remain committed to achieving stability. However, one should not only think of military intervention but also have a commitment to help rebuild a lasting peace, promote sustainable development and good governance.[152]

Wording the ICISS report, the objective of the post-conflict intervention strategy must be to help ensure that the conditions that prompted the military intervention do not resurface. For that to be possible, the responsibility to rebuild is important. This responsibility is divided into three constituent components: recovery, reconstruction and reconciliation.[153]

These components of the obligation to rebuild are all possible through measures or policies capable of enabling the state in which there has been intervention to reconstitute itself on all levels and to resolve the problems

---

149 Erin Mooney, "The Guiding Principles and the Responsibility to Protect", *Forced Migration Review 1,* 2008, pp. 11-12, available at https://www.fmreview.org/GuidingPrinciples10/mooney., accessed on 13th February 2019.

150 Rob Jenkins, *The UN Peace-Building Commission and the Dissemination of International Norms,* Crisis States Research Centre, 2008.

151 Ramesh Thakur, "Peacebuilding and the Responsibility to Rebuild", *Asian International Studies Review 19,* no. 2 2018, p. 10.

152 Gagro, *The Responsibility to Protect (R2P) Doctrine*, p. 65.

153 *ICISS 2001.*

that led to this crisis situation. Without this, there is a risk that it will become a vicious circle, with the same problems producing the same consequences.

Any military intervention in the context of R2P should encourage market creation, economic growth and sustainable development. Thinking about economic growth in the reconstruction of a post-conflict state has implications for law and order as well as for all areas of the country concerned. However, education and awareness-raising are as important as other measures in reconstruction, which can promote understanding and tolerance within the community.[154] There is also a practice of acts of commemoration and memorials for atrocity crimes committed and elements of transitional justice, are also significant elements of rebuilding a society.

Nevertheless, rebuilding measures highlighted by the ICISS as transitional justice and reconciliation were not in funding priorities from donor governments. This thesis agrees with the ICISS report[155] on the fact that reconciliation is really important, as part of transitional justice, to ensure that conflicts do not re-emerge. The point here would be that the victims and the "perpetrators" will all come together on a new basis in order to develop their country after the conflict.

Furthermore, the prosecution of perpetrators is an important factor in post-conflict reconstruction. Indeed, the obligation to investigate and prosecute perpetrators of genocide, war crimes and crimes against humanity has its legal basis in customary international law. The institution of accountability for past human rights violations and atrocities not only contributes to their prevention but also to strengthening the credibility of institutions.[156]

The emphasis on national ownership of the reconstruction process and the recognition of the responsibility to rebuild as a responsibility to help build the capacity of the state to benefit from it has led to an evolution in the state's understanding of the responsibility to rebuild. This has influenced intervening states to take a more political view of their involvement in post-intervention reconstruction. The example of Cote d'Ivoire and

154 Larry May, "Responsibility to rebuild and collective responsibility: legal and moral considerations", *Normative Pluralism and International Law: Exploring Global Governance,* J. Klabbers & T. Piiparinen (Eds.), Cambridge University Press, 2013, p. 333.

155 *ICISS* para 5(4).

156 *Report of the Secretary-General,* 2013, para. 40.

Libya are most striking as all attempts through standard channels have led to a mess and have made the lives of the people even more difficult.[157]

The practical application of the responsibility to rebuild norm could prove to be unproductive, "as it would primarily serve to allow states that have waged unjust wars to continue unjust occupations of conquered territories".[158] Only close cooperation with the government and the population concerned and the commitment of funds and resources to do so, can ensure sustainable reconstruction.

Ignorance of these two elements in the past has led to inadequate commitment to reconstruction assistance and to mismanagement of the response. This has led to a vicious cycle of problems and countries being caught up again and again in the same problems that gave rise to the intervention.

Recognizing the importance of post-intervention reconstruction for the protection of populations, a range of institutions have been equipped to manage the various aspects of the reconstruction phase of R2P. One of these is the institution created in 2005 by the UN.

This institution has a mandate to facilitate post-conflict recovery, ideally suited to identify the institutional reconstruction and economic aspects of R2P.

There is ample evidence that when parties to a conflict feel that their needs have not been met, the conflict will resume after a brief period of peace. Although there are many examples of conflicts being resolved through peace negotiations, according to the conflict resolution literature[159], the majority of conflicts in the world end in military victory. Evidence shows that in the majority of conflicts that end in military victory, there is a resurgence of violence after a period of 5 to 10 years. Military victories are rarely sustainable. The seeds of future conflict can gradually grow if genuine grievances remain unaddressed.[160] Thus, to reduce the risk

157 Outi Keranen, "What Happened to the Responsibility to Rebuild", *Global Governance: A Review of Multilateralism and International Organizations 22,* no. 3 (2016): 330.

158 Paul Robinson, "Is There an Obligation to Rebuild", *Justice, Responsibility and Reconciliation in the Wake of Conflict.* Dordrecht, Springer Netherlands, 2012, pp.105-106.

159 Herath Dhammmika, "Post-conflict Reconstruction and Reconciliation in Rwanda and Sri Lanka in Post-Conflict", *Social Cohesion,* 31 May 2018, available at https://www.accord.org.za/conflict-trends/post-conflict-reconstruction-and-reconciliation-in-rwanda-and-sri-lanka/, accessed on 13th February 2023.

160 *Idem.*

of violence and ensure reconstruction, all reconstruction efforts must also address the root causes of the conflict and deal with initial and subsequent grievances.

Indeed, the responsibility to rebuild provided a less vague and flexible set of obligations than prevention and response and therefore had no place in the development of the concept. The reluctance to emphasize the reconstruction element of the responsibility to protect has led to a lukewarm commitment on the part of intervening states and is unlikely to lead to sustainable peace.[161] This explains why the responsibility to rebuild has not entered the political discussion. Changing standards for reconstruction missions and state interests have led to the loss of popularity of the responsibility to rebuild.

An evolution of the concept is envisaged as states recognize that states that have been defeated in war have an obligation to rebuild that state. On the basis of the above discussion, it should be understood that for an effective implementation of R2P, a good conceptual and operational approach must be adopted.

R2P has been invoked in several resolutions by both the Security Council and the General Assembly. The R2P concept has also been invoked in resolutions dealing with human rights violations and in other resolutions calling for the fight against atrocity crimes and thus the protection of populations. All the measures of prevention, reaction and reconstruction have proven to be a success in protecting the population at risk. The crises in the DRC and especially those in its eastern part, have already been the subject of this. However, no analysis to date has assessed the consequences of the implementation of R2P in the specific Congolese context. This is what this thesis will address in the following lines. This will lead us to analyze the ins and outs of the implementation of R2P in the DRC. Several authors[162] have discussed the success or failure of R2P in the DRC. This thesis considers the merits of these authors' positions while focusing not on the impact or effectiveness of R2P in the DRC, but rather on the violations of IHL that were committed during the implementation of R2P and who can be held responsible for them.

161 Albrecht Schnabel, "the Responsibility to Rebuild", *Knight*, W. Andy and Frazer Egerton (eds), The Routledge handbook of the responsibility to protect, London, Routledge, 2012.

162 Danielle N. Allyn, "The Promise of Peace: UNSC Resolutions 2098 and 2147 and the Protection of Congolese Civilians", 2015, available at cdr.lib.unc.edu., accessed on 1th February 2020.

4. Relation between Responsibility to Protect (R2P) and International Humanitarian Law (IHL)

Since war is part of "mankind", there is no need to revisit the devastating consequences of war. Thus, thanks to the arsenal of norms, both legal and political, for the conduct and protection of people before, during and after war, the protection of the population is a priority. Among this arsenal are of course IHL, Human Rights, R2P, etc.

This chapter will focus on IHL and R2P. The aim here is not to review the definition of these two concepts, but rather to examine their differences and common features. This will be done in terms of their origins and legal nature(A) and the obligations of States (B) in relation to the applicability of these two concepts to various situations (C).

From the perspective of our work, it is important to know what researchers have already written about the link between R2P and IHL. This will allow us to know how to link R2P and IHL violations committed in the DRC.

A. Analysis by origin and legal nature of IHL and R2P

The first step in comparing R2P to IHL is to review their origins.[163] Modern IHL has its origins in the Battle of Solferino in 1859. Inspired by this battle and in particular the suffering of the wounded, Henri Dunant campaigned for an international agreement on the treatment of the sick and wounded. This led to the creation of the International Committee of the Red Cross (the founding element of the International Red Cross and Red Crescent Movement) and the Geneva Convention of 1864. Since then, IHL has developed to take into account the protection of persons and their property as well as the methods and means of warfare. In addition to the fact that IHL encompasses a range of customary norms, it is also enriched today by the development of jurisprudence of international enforcement mechanisms such as tribunals and courts.

On the other hand, as recently as 2001, the principle of R2P emerged in response to massive human rights violations on one hand, and respect

163 Helen Durham and Wynn-Pope Phoebe, "The relationship between international humanitarian law and responsibility to protect: From solferino to srebrenica", *collections.unu.edu,* 2013, p. 185.

for the principle of non-interference on the other. R2P has developed since the 2005 World Summit. Its objective has been defined and fixed: the protection of populations against crimes. The report of the Secretary General Ban Ki-moon to the General Assembly in 2009 on the implementation of R2P is considered as the main source of this development as it specifies that the three pillars of R2P are equal and sustainable.[164]

Furthermore, although both concepts were originally created for the protection of persons, IHL and R2P have not developed in the same way. The main purpose of creating IHL was to bring heads of state together to establish international rules to guide the conduct of states in situations of armed conflict. The Responsibility to Protect, on the other hand, does not create a new right for States, nor does it contain guiding rules for the conduct of parties to conflict, although it can be implemented in a conflict context. This is where international humanitarian law comes into play in the implementation of R2P in times of armed conflict.

Even though R2P is based on existing legal mechanisms, its added value should not be underestimated.[165] Today, in situations where populations are facing massive violence, reference to R2P becomes automatic. However, R2P remains political, rather than a legal concept with a content that is still controversial.

In addition, the examination of the legal framework of R2P and IHL is also a key to identifying their divergence.[166] At the heart of the normative framework of IHL are the four Geneva Conventions of 1949 and their two Additional Protocols of 1977. The Geneva Conventions focus on the protection of non-combatants and persons who are not or are no longer taking part in hostilities. In 1977, the two protocols were added in response to the increase in attacks on civilians and the internationalization of war. The first protocol deals with limitations and prohibitions on methods and means of warfare and the second with protection during internal armed conflicts. There are also specific IHL treaties and protocols relating to the protection of cultural property. In total, over 90 treaties constitute the legal regime of IHL. To ensure compliance with IHL, several international and

---

164 *The report of the Secretary General Ban Ki-moon to the General Assembly*, 2009.

165 Paul D. Williams, "The R2P, Protection of Civilians and UN Peacekeeping Operations", *The Oxford Handbook of the Responsibility to Protect*, 2016, p.525.

166 Vesselin Popovski, "The Concepts of Responsibility to Protect and Protection of Civilians: Sisters, but Not Twins", *Security Challenges 7*, no. 4, 2011, p.8, available at http://www.jstor.org/stable/26467112.

hybrid mechanisms have been developed. The creation of tribunals and courts to end impunity for violations is part of this approach.

By contrast, R2P has no legal framework of its own.[167] The R2P principle is silent on the perpetrators of atrocity crimes and only refers to existing law such as IHL, the ICC Statute, the Genocide Convention as the legal framework for action. It is more in the obligations to prevent and rebuild that R2P returns to these elements. Thus, IHL is a set of legally binding treaties whereas the R2P principle is not legally binding.

B. States' obligations under IHL and R2P

Wording paragraphs 138,139 and 140 of the 2005 World Summit documents,[168] obligations of states under R2P are enshrined in the so-called "three pillars". First, the primary responsibility to protect populations from genocide, war crimes, crimes against humanity and ethnic cleansing rests with the State concerned; second, it is the responsibility of the international community to encourage and assist States to fulfil their responsibility; finally, when a State manifestly fails to protect its population, the international community has the responsibility to intervene by appropriate diplomatic, humanitarian and other means to protect populations from such crimes and, if necessary, to resort to collective measures in accordance with the UN Charter.

Indeed, state obligations in implementing the R2P principle are only conceivable in the context of the atrocity crimes of war crimes, crimes against humanity, genocide and ethnic cleansing. As set out in the three pillars, States and the international community have an obligation to protect the population through preventive action against mass crimes: States and the international community have an obligation to protect the population through preventive action against mass crimes, to react to put an end to these atrocities and to support States in reconstruction and peacebuilding after each military intervention. It is clear that within the R2P framework, only States and the UN are subject to the three obligations.

167 Australian Red cross, *International Humanitarian Law and the Responsibility to Protect: A handbook,* available at https://www.redcross.org.au/globalassets/cms-migration/documents/about-us/ihl-r2p-responsibility-to-protect.pdf, 2011 accessed on 3th July 2022.

168 *The 2005 World Summit 's document.*

With regard to IHL, however, all parties to an armed conflict are bound by treaty and customary rules of IHL. However, according to the common Article 3 and the Additional Protocol II, organized non-State armed groups are bound by customary IHL rules concerning non-international armed conflict. By means of a unilateral declaration addressed to the depositary, National liberation movements fighting against colonial domination and alien occupation and against racist régimes in the exercise of the right of self-determination of the peoples they represent may undertake to apply the Geneva Conventions[169] and Additional Protocol I.[170] Moreover, IHL applies to peace operations carried out by or under the auspices of the United Nations which are taking part in the conflict through military intervention. It can be an international armed conflict when they are fighting against a State or a non-state armed group supported by a State and a non-international conflict, when they are fighting against a non-state armed group.

In general, the obligation of States parties to IHL instruments is summarized by their commitment to respect and ensure respect for the provisions contained in these instruments. This must be done both in times of conflict and in times of peace.[171] A set of responsibilities and guidelines on how States and non-state actors should conduct themselves in the context of armed conflict is provided by IHL. In fact, it is not only the parties to an armed conflict that have obligations to respect and to ensure respect for IHL.[172] "To respect" refers to the principle of executing treaties in good faith. Therefore, States party to IHL treaties must apply these treaties in good faith. The obligation "to ensure respect", on the other hand, refers to the obligation of States and the international community as a whole to take measures to ensure respect for IHL by all, especially those not involved in the conflict. This obligation is incumbent on all States and the whole international community whether they are party to a conflict or not.[173]

---

169 Article 1, paragraph 4, of *Geneva Conventions.*

170 Article 96, paragraph 3, *of Additional Protocol I.*

171 Marco Sassoli, "Introducing a sliding-scale of obligations to address the fundamental inequality between armed groups and states?" *International Review of the Red Cross 93,* no. 882, 2011, p. 428.

172 Tristan Ferraro, "The ICRC's legal position on the notion of armed conflict involving foreign intervention and on determining the IHL applicable to this type of conflict", *International Review of the Red Cross 97, no. 900, 2015, p. 123.*

173 Rule 139 of the ICRC's study on customary IHL states that the obligation of parties to a conflict to respect and ensure respect also exists in customary IHL.

This is reflected in common Article 1, in the following wordings: "The High Contracting Parties undertake to respect and to ensure respect for the present Convention in all circumstances".[174]

In addition to this obligation to respect and ensure respect, States have a further legal obligation to spread knowledge of the Conventions and their Additional Protocols.[175] Wording Articles 47 and 48 of the First and Second Geneva Conventions respectively read as follows: "The High Contracting Parties undertake, in time of peace as in time of war, to disseminate the text of the present Convention as widely as possible in their respective countries and, in particular, to include the study thereof in their programmes of military and, if possible, civil instruction, so that the principles thereof may become known to the entire population, in particular to the armed fighting forces, the medical personnel and the chaplains."[176] Articles 127 and 144 of the Third and Fourth Geneva Conventions respectively add the obligation to integrate IHL into military education and training programmes.[177]

Indeed, several articles such as common Article 1 to the four Geneva conventions and the Additional Protocol I have recognised the *erga omnes* nature of most IHL obligations.[178] This nature has also been recognized in the case law of the International Criminal Tribunal for the former Yugoslavia (ICTY) *Prosecutor v. Zoran Kupreškić et al.*[179] and in the ICJ Advisory Opinion on the legal Consequences of the Construction of a Wall in the Occupied Palestinian Territory. The ICJ characterized the rules of IHL as fundamental to the respect of human rights and the *erga omnes* nature of these obligations when violated. In this advisory opinion, the ICJ called on the United Nations to take measures to put an end to this situation, which it described as illegal. From the above discussion, it is clear

174 Article 1, paragraph 1, of *Additional Protocol I.*

175 Article 19 of *Additional Protocol II.*

176 Articles 47,48,127 and 144 of the *First Geneva convention, Second, Third and 144 and Fourth of Geneva Conventions respectively.*

177 See Article 83 of Additional Protocol I: "The High Contracting Parties undertake, in time of peace as in time of armed conflict, to disseminate the Conventions and this Protocol as widely as possible in their respective countries and, in particular, to include the study thereof in their programmes of military instruction and to encourage the study thereof by the civilian population, so that those instruments may become known to the armed forces and to the civilian population."

178 Hanna Broslowski, "The Responsibility to Protect and Common Article 1 of the 1949 Geneva Conventions and Obligations of Third States", *Responsibility to Protect: From Principle to Practice,* Amsterdam, 2012, pp. 97-98.

179 *Prosecutor v. Zoran Kupreškić et al., Judgment, IT-95-16-T, 14 January 2000,* 202-203, para. 518.

that the implementation of IHL takes into account collective responsibility for serious violations of IHL. This is in line with what is expressed in Article 89 of Additional Protocol I.[180]

The legal literature has questioned whether the third pillar of R2P, which provides for collective responsibility for the failure of national authorities to protect their civilian population, adds anything to the existing mechanisms of IHL. More than one researcher considers that this is not the case[181], as Article 1 common to the four Geneva Conventions of 1949 and Additional Protocol I of 1977 have provided for this collective obligation. This obligation is incumbent on both the States parties to the conflict and the international community as a whole and also requires the cooperation of all to end violations of IHL.

It may be tempting to confuse them entirely, therefore, the collective responsibilities under R2P and IHL do not appear to be so different from each other. However, as pointed out above, it should be borne in mind that the application of collective responsibility under R2P is limited to a conflict context as it can be envisaged in the case of military intervention, whereas under IHL it extends beyond the rules of IHL, the violation of which amounts to such crimes.

It is appropriate here to also return to the ideas of researchers on the responsibility of states and/or the UN Security Council for violations of IHL and R2P. Responsibility is defined in the sense of positive law as answering for the breach of one's obligations, essentially legal obligations.[182] It therefore refers, in a way, to the of being accountable and taking responsibility for the breach of one's duties and obligations.

Thus, the formula that makes R2P uncomfortable is "protecting is a responsibility".[183]The term "responsibility" inexorably reminds states that their competences are not limitless and that they must be accountable for what they do with them. This concept of accountability contained in the

180 Article 89 of Additional Protocol I, states that States "undertake to act, jointly or individually, in co-operation with the United Nations and in conformity with the United Nations Charter" case of serious IHL violations.

181 Raphael van Steenberghe, "The Notions of the Responsibility to Protect and the Protection of Civilians in Armed Conflict: Detecting Their Association and Its Impact Upon International Law", *Goettingen J. Int'l L. 6,* 2014, pp.98-100.

182 Iger Dekker, "Accountability of international organizations: an evolving legal concept?", Wouters, Jan, Eva Brems, Stefaan Smis and Pierre Schmitt. (eds), *Accountability for human rights violations by international organisations.* Intersentia, 2010.

183 Léandre Mvé Ella, *La responsabilité du Conseil de sécurité en cas de manquement à la responsabilité de protéger,* Civitas Europa 2, 2018, p.119.

R2P principle has even been the basis of the analysis of the legal nature of R2P, because if it is considered as legal norm, what about failures or violations of this norm. Thus, in analyzing the obligations of states in the Israel-Gaza conflict, the main question would be whether genocide, crimes against humanity, war crimes or ethnic cleansing are being faced in order to remind states of their obligations under R2P.[184] This question will also be decisive in the application or non-application of R2P.

Indeed, the responsibility of the Security Council, has its origin in the failure of a state to fulfill its primary responsibility to protect its own population so that the SC has a secondary responsibility to do so. It would be a derivative, no-fault responsibility based on the failure of the state to meet its responsibility. It is in this same logic that the responsibility of the State can also be engaged.

However, the majority of the essentially positivist doctrine refuses to believe in the "responsibility to protect" of real legal obligations and therefore a real obligation for debtors to be held accountable in the event of a breach.

This is why, for reasons of caution, the term "breach" and not "violation" has been used several times in the doctrine. This approach proves the skepticism of the doctrine on the legal value of the obligations missed or violated. To speak of a breach rather than a violation is therefore to voluntarily or involuntarily choose to attenuate the real scope of obligations under R2P.

The law of international responsibility is the general law of fault and governs when an international violation is concealed and the consequences that follow from it.[185] It plays a central role in international law as it even specifies who can invoke a violation of international law and how.

However, as far as IHL is concerned, its violation is considered a violation of the international norm. States have an obligation to prosecute alleged perpetrators when violations of IHL are committed. National and international criminal courts play an important role in the enforcement of IHL. Thus, the prosecution of perpetrators of violations of IHL is a means of limiting violations of IHL. Apart from individuals who may be brought before the courts to answer for violations of IHL they may have committed,

184 James P. Rudolph, "Gaza and Israel–A case for International Humanitarian Law, Not R2P", *Justice in Conflict*, 2014, p.12.

185 Kirsten Schmalenbach, "International responsibility for humanitarian law violations by armed groups", *Inducing Compliance with International Humanitarian Law*, Lessons from the African Great Lakes Region, Heike Krieger (ed), Cambridge University Press, 2015, p. 480.

a State that is also responsible for violations of IHL will be required to make full reparation for the loss or damage caused.[186]

Outside the context of the UN Charter, Chapters VI, VIII and VII, R2P does not prescribe how states or the international community should fulfil their responsibility to protect populations. However, international humanitarian law does prescribe how parties to conflict should fulfil their obligation. This brings us to a discussion of the applicability of IHL and R2P in the following section.

C. Applicability of IHL and R2P

According to the International law and Responsibility to Protect handbook,[187]whereas IHL only applies when a threshold of armed conflict has been reached, R2P applies because of the nature of the crimes and the fact that they can be committed at any time. The latter point, in effect, only deals with prevention and protection against crimes, whereas IHL goes so far as to provide rules for the conduct of hostilities, the protection of persons and their property, limiting the types of military weapons and tactics. It should be noted that R2P would only protect other objects if their destruction constituted a war crime under IHL.

The legal core of IHL is much broader than the scope of R2P.[188] Whereas IHL applies to isolated actions of individual combatants and prohibits not only attacks on people's persons, but also, for example, on their private and cultural property, R2P takes a very different form, focusing instead on civil society, security sector reform, and the implementation of human rights commitments. In this sense, the two standards are distinct in their application and the approach to their implementation is different.

With regard to the protection of civilians as an important element of international humanitarian law, there are situations that would fall under the IHL regime and others under the responsibility to protect.[189] For instance, the protection of civilians threatened by the escalation of an armed conflict

186 *Rule 150 of Customary Law.*

187 Andy W. Knight and Frazer Egerton, (Eds.) *The Routledge handbook of the responsibility to protect,* London, Routledge, 2012.

188 Hugh Breakey and Francis Angus, "Points of Convergence and Divergence: Normative, Institutional and Operational Relationships between R2P and PoC", *Security Challenges 7,* no. 4, 2011, pp. 39–40. http://www.jstor.org/stable/26467115 .

189 Paul D. Williams, "The R2P, Protection of Civilians and UN Peacekeeping Operations", *The Oxford Handbook of the Responsibility to Protect,* 2016, 539.

but without plan of mass atrocities is a situation that would fall under IHL, but not the responsibility to protect. A situation that would fall under the responsibility to protect, but not under IHL, would be, ethnic cleansing or crimes against humanity unrelated to an armed conflict.

On the one hand, the Protection of Civilians in the context of IHL is more restricted than the responsibility to protect. Thus, not all war crimes would fall under the Protection of Civilians because not all war crimes are committed against civilians, yet all war crimes trigger the responsibility to protect. On the other hand, R2P becomes narrower than the protection of civilians because it would apply only to armed conflicts giving rise to planned and committed mass atrocities and not to any armed conflict, which is what IHL does.

It is significant that R2P is not only about war crimes but also about crimes against humanity, genocide and also ethnic cleansing. In the situation where IHL offers no protection to victims of crimes against humanity and genocide because they can be committed outside the context of an armed conflict, R2P offers this protection.[190]

Thus, R2P is considered an extremely useful political and strategic tool for the protection of civilians. It should be added, however, that this tool builds on elements of existing IHL and international criminal law but provides a profound call for a range of actions to make the protection of civilians effective. To this end, the development of an international criminal regime from genocide to crimes against humanity is another important element to be placed alongside R2P and IHL.

Moreover, although the mechanisms by which armed groups are bound by IHL remain controversial, the applicability of IHL by these groups is generally accepted in international law. In contrast, the primary responsibility to protect under R2P can only be assumed by states, not by armed groups.[191] R2P is a concept based on sovereignty. This has made R2P more successful than the notion of humanitarian intervention. The thesis argues that the problem here would be to envisage that in the case of occupation or when armed groups control a large part of the territory, the occupier or armed groups would not be vested with R2P to protect the populations under their control. However, the scope ratione personae of the primary re-

190 Helen Durham and Wynn-Pope Phoebe, "The relationship between international humanitarian law and responsibility to protect: From solferino to Srebrenica", *collections.unu.edu*, 2013, p. 185.

191 Emily Paddon Rhoads and Jennifer Welsh. *"Close cousins in protection: the evolution of two norms"*, international Affairs 95, no. 3, 2019, p.600.

sponsibility to protect under R2P is only available to states and not, at least until now, to armed groups. However, when it comes to the protection of civilians in armed conflict, the responsibility is assumed by all parties to the conflict, i.e. states, armed groups and the UN (peacekeeping). By contrast, several states have made it clear in their declarations that the responsibility to protect civilians in armed conflict lies primarily with states[192], in line with what R2P has proposed.

Many of the activities required for States to fulfil their obligation to respect IHL are the same as those required to prevent the commission of R2P crimes.[193] For example, for IHL protection to be effective, education and training in IHL must be taken seriously by States and their agencies. This would lead to the prevention of war crimes, which is one of the four principles of R2P.

The Secretary-General's 2009 report on implementing R2P outlined measures to support states' obligations to protect populations at risk of R2P crimes.[194] Based on the first pillar of R2P, these measures include: encouraging states to protect their own populations through technical assistance from the international community; assisting states in exercising this responsibility through training, learning and education programmes; confidential or public persuasion; capacity building; and cooperation with regional and sub-regional bodies.

The similarity of these measures is also demonstrated by Article 1 of the Geneva Convention. Activities related to IHL and R2P are similar in these cases. The difference lies in the scope of IHL, which is broader and encompasses many rules and guidelines for the conduct of armed conflict that do not directly concern war crimes.

---

192 See, e.g., *declaration of Ghana ,SC, Verbatim Record of the 6427th Meeting, UN Doc S/PV.6427 (Resumption 1), 22 November 2009, 20 declaration of Belgium on behalf of the European Union ,SC Verbatim Record of the 5781st Meeting, UN Doc S/PV.5781 (Resumption 1);7 (); SC, Verbatim Record of the 6216th Meeting, UN Doc S/PV.6216 (Resumption 1), 11 November 2009, 25- 26; (declaration of France), SC, Verbatim Record of the 6216th Meeting, UN Doc S/PV.6216, 11 November 2009, 15; declaration of Germany SC, Verbatim Record of the 6790th Meeting, UN Doc S/PV.6790, 25 June 2012, 23; and declaration of the United States , SC, Verbatim Record of the 6151st Meeting, UN Doc S/PV.6151, 26 June 2009, 23.*

193 Toni Pfanner, "Various mechanisms and approaches for implementing international humanitarian law and protecting and assisting war victims", *International Review of the Red Cross 91,* no. 874, 2009, p. 300.

194 U.N-Secretary-General, *Implementing the responsibility to protect: report of the Secretary-General,* 2009, available at *https://digitallibrary.un, accessed on 3rd November 2023.*

Firstly, even where certain human rights may be suspended in a public emergency, the prohibition on the commission of crimes under the responsibility to protect cannot be suspended because they are *erga omnes.*

In the same vein, there are many forms of activities that states and the international community can undertake to protect populations. The establishment of effective early warning mechanisms, training and education in the rule of law and human rights, policing, the instillation of good governance and economic development, the effective application of IHL and R2P, etc., are examples.[195]

As the 2005 World Summit document so well emphasized, diplomatic means, public and private pressure, sanctions and, if necessary, the use of force can be undertaken when R2P crimes are imminent. These responses are described by many as far-reaching because they provide a framework that can help prevent the most heinous international crimes and violations of international humanitarian law. Thus, moral outrage, within the framework of international humanitarian law, has fostered the development of the responsibility to protect.

To further this idea, R2P can fill the gap in the limited mechanisms for monitoring the application of IHL.[196] It is true that mechanisms such as international criminal courts and the UNSC for violations of IHL exist, but these sanctions remain limited. Indeed, R2P can be seen as a specification of and counterpart to the protection of civilians, which would confirm the complementarity between the two notions. However, this complementarity and export of R2P in the field of civilian protection has a risk for IHL.

The first would be the politicization of IHL, which is otherwise neutral. IHL is characterized by neutrality and impartiality and provides for the protection of persons independently of the party to the conflict, whereas R2P is a political concept that would undermine the principle of neutrality and impartiality. Another risk is the emergence of two parallel and competing regimes applicable to the protection of civilians in the context of armed

195 Rosenbergand Sheri and Strauss Ekkehard, "A Common Approach to the Application of the Responsibility to Protect", *Operationalizing the Responsibility to Protect A Contribution to the Third Pillar Approach,* Daniel Fiott Robert Zuber Joachim Koops (eds), The Madariaga, Brussels, 2012, p.58.

196 Raphael van Steenberghe, "The Notions of the Responsibility to Protect and the Protection of Civilians in Armed Conflict", p.102.

conflict[197]. On the one hand, there is the "classic" IHL regime, the scope of which concerns the protection of civilians (and also the wounded) and collective responsibility for IHL violations.

Secondly, R2P is considered a "modern" regime, with a more limited scope of application concerning the protection of populations, including civilians, in armed conflicts. This phenomenon could therefore lead to a situation of fragmentation and application of civilian protection rules in the context of armed conflict.

This thesis is in line with the idea of the application of IHL and R2P in the context of the conflict in the DRC. Thus, the examination here is not limited to the protection of civilians but rather to the protection of the population in general, according to the content of the R2P principle. The link between R2P and IHL, in the context of this work, remains at the level of violations of IHL norms during the implementation of R2P in the DRC. In order to better establish this, it is necessary to first clarify the context of the DRC, a context that would imply the use of the R2P principle to protect the population.

---

197 Phoebe A. Wynn-Pope, *The Responsibility to Protect Against Crimes Against Humanity and Genocide: Effective Operationalisation of the Principle*, PhD diss., University of Melbourne, Melbourne Law School, 2008.

Chapter II: Responsibility to Protect in the Specific Context of DRCongo.

For more than two decades now, the DRC has been facing endless conflicts, especially in the eastern part. These conflicts have resulted in several violations of human rights and humanitarian law.[198] To resolve these conflicts, several international and regional actors have intervened, such as the UN, the AU, SADC and the EAC.

The aim of this chapter is not to analyze the interventions of these actors in the general context, but rather their interventions in the specific context of R2P. The analysis of R2P in the context of the DRC refers to the examination of the country's situation in relation to mass crimes, which are crimes for which the R2P principle can be invoked. To this end, the analysis of the three pillars of R2P will allow the examination of the application of the DRC's ' duty ' or obligation, that of the international community and that of the UN under UN Security Council Resolution 2098 in relation to the use of all necessary measures to protect the Congolese population.

1. Crimes in the context of the Responsibility to Protect in the DRC

R2P does not apply to all human rights violations and abuses or to all serious threats to human security in general. Only the four types of mass atrocity crimes of genocide, ethnic cleansing, war crimes and crimes against humanity are covered. Other urgent violations that are not included in the 2005 World Summit Outcome document are addressed by the human rights and international humanitarian law system.

---

198 See several reports by Human rights watch at https://www.hrw.org/africa/democratic-republic-congo , Amnesty international at https://www.amnesty.org/en/location/africa/east-africa-the-horn-and-great-lakes/democratic-republic-of-the-congo/ and others. see also Off. of the U.N. High Comm'r for Hum. Rts. (OHCHR), *Democratic Republic of the Congo, 1993–2003: Report of the Mapping Exercise Documenting the Most Serious Violations of Human Rights and International Humanitarian Law Committed within the Territory of the Democratic Republic of the Congo between March 1993 and June 2003, Aug. 2010, available at https://perma.cc/6SEG-LB2C* [hereinafter DRC: Mapping Human Rights Violations].

Since the legal classification of acts of violence is only permitted in the context of legal proceedings, i.e., before a court of law, the objective here is to establish the nature of these violations and possibly the extent to which they would be covered by a certain classification under international law or human rights law.

A. War crimes

While providing for war crimes as a crime for which the R2P principle could be considered, the R2P document does not provide a definition of war crimes. It goes without saying that the definition of war crime in international law remains a feasible definition in the context of R2P.[199]

The definition of a war crime has raised several questions since the dawn of time. In 1942, already before the International Military Tribunal in Nuremberg, the internationalist jurist Hersch Lauterpacht asked in his memo if there was a definition of war crimes.[200] The most common approach to date defines a war crime as a criminalized violation of the laws of war. From this approach, the definition of the competent jurisdictions to judge these crimes has been more accepted.[201]

Thus, the term "war crimes" generally refers to any serious violation of international humanitarian law. War crimes are primarily found in the Geneva Conventions of 12 August 1949 and their Additional Protocols I and II of 1977, as well as The Hague Conventions of 1899 and 1907 and The Hague Conventions of 1899 and 1907.

Article 8 of the Rome Statute provides the most recent codification of war crimes. The latter are distinguished into four categories:

199 David scheffer, "Atrocity crimes framing the responsibility to protect", *Responsibility to protect: The global moral compact for the 21st century,* New York: Palgrave Macmillan US (2009): 78.

200 Memorandum by Hersch Lauterpacht to the Committee on Crimes Against International Public Order entitled *Punishment of War Crimes* 6, 1942, available at http://diginole.lib.fsu.edu/islandora/ object/fsu%3A547450, accessed 9th 05 2023.

201 Oona A. Hathaway, Paul K. Strauch, Beatrice A. Walton and Zoe AY Weinberg. "What is a war crime." *Yale J. Int'l L.* 44 (2019): 53.

- Grave breaches of the Geneva Conventions committed against protected persons or property in the context of an international armed conflict.[202]
- Other serious violations of the laws and customs applicable in international armed conflict.[203]
- Serious violations provided by Article 3 common to the four Geneva Conventions against persons not taking an active part in hostilities in an internal armed conflict.[204]
- Other serious violations of laws and customs applicable in an internal armed conflict.[205]

From an analysis of this definition in the Rome Statute, it appears that the commission of a war crime requires, in addition to a mental element, proof of four main elements, namely a prohibited act; an act committed against protected persons; this act must be committed during an armed conflict (internal or international) and finally, the existence of a link between the armed conflict and the act committed.[206] In determining the applicable legal regime with respect to war crimes, the qualification of the conflict is an essential element.[207] On this point, the qualification of the conflict in the DRC is necessary because all acts of war crimes allegedly committed in the DRC were committed in the context of an internal armed conflict as well as an international armed conflict.[208]

---

202 Art.8. para.2, sect. a pf the Rome Statute noted crimes such as willful killing, torture, willfully causing serious bodily injury to persons or property, torture, serious injury to body or health, destruction and appropriation of property.

203 sect. b, para. 2 of article 8, crimes such as intentional attacks against the civilian population, rape and sexual slavery, as well as recruitment into armed groups

204 Sect. c, para. 2 of Article 8 provides such as violence to life and person, in particular murder, mutilation, cruel treatment and torture.

205 Sect. e, para. 2 of Article 8 mentioned crimes such as intentional attacks on the civilian population, rape and sexual slavery, conscription and enlistment in the armed forces.

206 Knut Dörmann, *Elements of war crimes under the Rome Statute of the International Criminal Court: sources and commentary, Cambridge University Press, 2003.*

207 *ICTY, The Prosecutor v. Dusko Tadić, Judgment on the appeal by the defence challenging jurisdiction, no. IT-94-1-A,* 2 October 1995, para. 70.

208 Depending on the context, some conflicts in the DRC have been led by foreign countries or by rebel groups supported by foreign countries. See *Case Concerning Armed Activities on the Territory of the Congo (Democratic Republic of the Congo v. Uganda), ICJ, Judgement,* 19 December 2005. See also *DRC: Mapping human rights violations,* 1993-2003 para 479-480 available at https://www.ohchr.org/en/countries/africa/2010-drc-mapping-report

The first crisis from 1993 to 1996 was a regional crisis. In this conflict, described by many as an international conflict because several countries in the region intervened either directly or indirectly, several war crimes were committed. During this same period, ethnic groups clashed over land ownership.[209] As a result, many people were killed and others internally displaced.

For example, the intensity of the violence resulting from the inter-ethnic fighting over land between Hunde and Banyarwanda in Masisi from 1993 onwards was "sufficiently serious to trigger the application of Common Article 3 of the Geneva Conventions, ratified by Zaïre, which applies to non-international armed conflicts".[210] Numerous killings were committed by Hutu and Hunde militias at the time, including the attacks on Mutobo and Bikenge in 1995 and on Osso and Mokoto in 1996. The multiple atrocities committed by the armed Forces of Zaïre (Les forces armées zaïroises: FAZ) against the civilian population during this period can also be qualified as war crimes. This concerns the assassinations and torture committed in 1995 in Masisi and in the context of Operation Mbata in June 1996 in Vitshumbi, Kibirizi and Kanyabayonga.

The second crisis in Congo (1998-2001) or the second war was also characterized by several war crimes, both in the context of internal and international armed conflict. Thus, the systematic killings, rapes and pillaging committed by the RCD (and its various factions), the Mayi-Mayi groups and the ex-FAR/Interahamwe against the civilian population could be considered as war crimes.

In North and South Kivu, this period was marked by large-scale massacres, such as those in Kasika and Makobola. Numerous massacres in Maniema, Katanga and Orientale province have plagued the DRC. The same is true of the killings, rapes and looting perpetrated by Rwandan and Ugandan forces as they advanced from Kitona, Bas-Congo, towards Kinshasa in 1988. Similar crimes were committed by the Angolan Armed Forces (FAA) along the Moanda-Boma-Matadi-Kisantu axis and in Bas-Congo.

Examples include the stopping of the turbines at the Inga dam by elements of the ANC/APR/UPDF, which caused the deaths of many people; the aerial bombardment of Kinshasa by the Zimbabwean Defense Forces (ZDF) in August 1998; the bombing of Businga in August 1998; the use

209 For instance, the MAGRIVI [Mutuelle des agriculteurs du Virunga] and other militias involved in the violence have demonstrated their ability to carry out coordinated attacks on several occasions. See para.483 Mapping Report on the DRC.

210 *Mapping Report on the DRC 1993-2003* para 483-484.

of heavy weapons by the Rwandan and Ugandan armies in the city of Kisangani, a city densely populated by civilians, caused the death of several hundred civilians and the destruction of their property.

From 2001 to 2003, Ituri was the scene of an ethnic conflict between the Hema and the Lendu. These crimes committed against civilians and MONUSCO personnel would constitute war crimes. As the conflict started some time before the withdrawal of the occupying force (Uganda), but continued after its effective withdrawal, it should be noted that some of the crimes were committed in the context of an international armed conflict and others in an internal context. The challenge here would be how to differentiate them over time and with precision.

Can one conclude that, as there are internal and then internationalized conflicts, this specific Ituri conflict was then internalized by knock-on effects?

The ICJ[211] and ICC[212] judges determined the nature of the conflict. In their view, this conflict remains an international conflict because Uganda as an occupying power exercised its authority in Ituri and would be responsible for all acts and omissions in violation of IHL and HR committed by its armed forces on the territory of the DRC.

However, the Mapping Exercise Report cast doubt on the nature of the acts committed on the day the occupying force withdrew, and the conflict continued until several months later.

After analyzing this situation, it would be appropriate to clarify the responsibilities of the occupying force with regards to the scope of IHL. Hence the need to distinguish between acts committed during the occupation and before its withdrawal and acts committed after the occupation, which are beyond the control of the occupying force.

In addition, there was the massacre committed in Kishishe during the occupation of this village by the M23 at the end of November 2022. The death toll from this massacre is estimated at 272, including babies and children and is attributed to the M23 rebel movement that occupied part of the territory of Rutshuru. This massacre has been declared by many to be a war crime.[213]

---

211 ICJ, *Armed Activities on the Territory of the Congo (DRC v. Uganda)*, 19 December 2005, para. 179 and 180.

212 ICC, *The Prosecutor v. Thomas Lubanga Dyilo. Decision on the confirmation of charges*, 29 January 2007, ICC-01/04-01/06

213 DRC: *M23 armed group must stop killing civilians and respect international law on December 2*, 2022 available at https://www.amnesty.org/ ; see also Atrocity Alert No.

Congolese jurisprudence[214] and Several NGO reports[215] prove the existence of other war crimes that continue to be committed in the DRC to this day. The presence of several rebel groups[216] and the conflicts they engage in either against other rebel groups or against the Congolese armed forces and peacekeeping forces always make civilians and people protected by IHL victims.

B. Crimes against humanity

Crimes against humanity are not yet codified in a separate treaty of international law, like genocide and war crimes. First formulated in international law in the Statute of the Nuremberg Tribunal,[217]crimes against humanity have been clearly defined in the Rome Statute of the International Criminal Court.

According to Article 7, Paragraph 1 of the Rome Statute, crime against humanity means acts committed as part of a widespread or systematic attack directed against civilians.[218]

This article lists 11 acts which constitute crimes against humanity:[219] murder; extermination; deportation or forcible transfer of population; torture; rape, sexual slavery, enforced prostitution, forced pregnancy, enforced sterilization, or any other form of sexual violence of comparable gravity;

328, *DR Congo, International Justice and Genocide Victims Day by Global Centre for R2P*, on December 7, 2022 available at https://www.globalr2p.org/publications

214 Jacques Mbokani, "La jurisprudence congolaise en matière de crimes de droit international." *une étude de l'Open society initiative for Southern Africa,* Osisa, 2016.

215 The UN Joint Human Rights Office (UNJHRO) in the DRC documented at least 2,024 civilians killed during 2021 by armed groups in North Kivu, South Kivu, Tanganyika and Ituri provinces.

216 Such as ADF, CODECO, M23 etc see Global Centre for The R2P, Democratic Republic of Congo, 1 September 2021 available at https://www.globalr2p.org/countries/democratic-republic-of-the-congo/ on 6th September 2022

217 Article 6(c) the Nuremberg Charter, see also Roger S. Clark, "History of efforts to codify crimes against humanity: From the Charter of Nuremberg to the Statute of Rome" *Forging a Convention for Crimes Against Humanity,* Cambridge University Press, 2011, p.17.

218 The expression "civilian population" refers to all people who are "out of combat" and those who are no longer taking part in the conflict. See Rosa Ana Alija Fernández and Saura Estapà Jaume, "Towards a Single and Comprehensive Notion of Civilian Population'in Crimes against Humanity", *International criminal law review 17*, no. 1, 2017, p.57.

219 *Article 7 Rome statute*

the crime of apartheid; persecution against any identifiable group or collectivity on political, racial, national, ethnic, cultural, religious or gender grounds; enforced disappearance of persons; any other inhumane act of a similar nature. The latter must be committed with the intention of causing great suffering or serious harm to the body or to mental or physical health.

These elements can only be qualified as crimes against humanity if they are committed in a widespread and systematic manner and not necessarily in the context of armed conflict.

Nevertheless, it should be noted that an isolated act may constitute a crime against humanity if it is part of a larger attack.

Indeed, the widespread nature of the attack is based not only on the number of persons victimized or on the "cumulative effect of a series of inhumane acts" but also on the scale of the act, however unique it may be.[220] Systematicity refers to the framework of a broader policy or plan, in short to the "organised nature of the acts committed and the improbability of their randomness".[221]

It follows from the above that random, accidental and/or isolated acts of violence cannot constitute a crime against humanity.[222]

Between 1992 and 1995, several acts listed in the definition of crimes against humanity were perpetrated against the Kasaian people. These attacks against the Kasaian civilian population were clearly widespread and systematic, including murder, deportation or forcible transfer of the population and other inhumane acts of a similar character intentionally causing great suffering or serious injury to body or mind. These attacks were orchestrated in a calculated manner by the military and political authorities through an anti-Kasaian campaign.[223]

Crimes against humanity were committed against both Hutu and Tutsi populations.

---

220 Charles Chernor Jalloh, "What makes a crime against humanity a crime against humanity." *Am. U. Int'l L. Rev.* 28, 2012, p. 381; See case Kordić and Cerkezs, *ICTY, Appeals Chamber, no. IT-95-14/2-A,* 17 December 2004, para. 94.

221 Darryl Robinson, "Defining crimes against humanity at the Rome Conference", *American Journal of International Law 93,* no. 1, 1999, p.47.

222 Leila Nadya Sadat, "Crimes against humanity in the modern age", *American Journal of International Law 107,* no. 2, 2013, p. 354.

223 Para 493-493 Mapping report.

Between 1997 and 1998, the Secretary General's investigation report in the DRC concluded that the systematic massacre of Hutu refugees by AFDL/APR forces was a crime against humanity.[224]

The widespread nature of this attack is demonstrated by the very high number of serious crimes listed, such as rape, murder, etc. The systematic, planned nature of the attack, on the other hand, is manifested by the repeated attacks on refugee camps and on ethnic Hutus who have been established in the North Kivu region for many years.[225]

While in North Kivu it was attacks against Hutus, in South Kivu it was attacks against the Tutsi population.[226]The authorities, both at the national and local level, called on the population to hunt them down and asked the army to expel them by force:[227]this proves the systematic nature of these attacks. The high number of victims and attacks almost throughout the Republic explain the general nature of the attacks and it should be noted that the authorities did not do everything possible to stop and punish the perpetrators of these crimes at the time.[228]

With the ongoing conflict in the DRC, several attacks have been directed against civilian populations. Here we can cite the attacks committed by the CNDP/M23 between 2006 and today (2022)[229] against the populations of Rutshuru, Bunagana, ... In addition, there were attacks by the ADF against the population of Beni and its surroundings.[230]

These attacks can be qualified as crimes against humanity depending on the context. For example, those committed by the M23 nowadays (2022) in Bunagana would not be considered as crime against humanity but rather a

---

224 *The Report of the Investigative Team of the Secretary General (S/1998/581),* appendix, para. 96.

225 Marie Béatrice Umutesi, "Is reconciliation between Hutus and Tutsis possible?",*Journal of International Affairs,* 2006, p.167.

226 Marina Rafti, "South Kivu: a sanctuary for the rebellion of the democratic forces for the liberation of Rwanda." *Institute of Development Policy and management University of Antwerp, Discussion paper 05,* 2006, p.33.

227 International arrest warrant issued by Examining Magistrate Vandermeersch re. Mr Abdulaye Yerodia Ndombasi, of 11 April 2000.

228 *Mapping Report,* para 498-499.

229 *DRC: UN calls for justice for crimes committed by the M23 and for the repatriation of ex-combatants,* 9 October 2014 available at https://www.ohchr.org/ on 12 September 2022. See also Human Right Watch, *DR Congo: Resurgent M23 Rebels Target Civilians,* 25 July 2022 available at https://www.hrw.org/ on 12 September 2022.

230 Daniel Fahey, "Congo's 'Mr. X' The Man who Fooled the UN", *World Policy Journal 33,* no. 2, 2016, pp. 91-100. See also Oxford Analytica, "Congo's Beni crisis may become more complex", *Emerald Expert Briefings oxan-db,* 2019.

war crime because they were committed during the occupation. In fact, the town of Bunagana has been occupied by the rebel group since June 2022.

C. Ethnic cleansing

The term ethnic cleansing emerged in the context of the 1990s conflict in the former Yugoslavia. It has been used in UN Security Council and General Assembly resolutions but has also been recognized in the judgements and indictments of the International Criminal Tribunal for the former Yugoslavia.

Although ethnic cleansing has not been recognized as an independent crime under international law, it can be defined as a systematic policy of forced population transfer, based on the identification of target groups by ethnic, national and religious characteristics.[231]

In the Interim Report of the UN Commission of Experts on Violations of International Humanitarian Law in the Territory of the Former Yugoslavia, ethnic cleansing is defined as "the rendering of an area ethnically homogeneous by the use of force or intimidation to drive out persons belonging to particular groups".[232] Accordingly, it must then be a policy designed by one ethnic or religious group to drive the civilian population of another

231 Marie-Janine Calic, "Ethnic Cleansing and War Crimes, 1991–1995", *Comparative Southeast European Studies 55,* no. 1, 2007, p.76.
Todd A. Salzman, "Rape camps as a means of ethnic cleansing: Religious, cultural and ethical responses to rape victims in the former Yugoslavia", *Human Rights Quarterly 20,* no. 2, 1998, p. 368.
Herbert F. Weiss and Georges Nzongola-Ntalaja, *Decentralization and the DRC–an overview,* New York, Social Science Research Council, 2013.
Wairagala Wakabi, "Ntaganda Convicted at ICC for Rape, Sexual Violence and Murder", in*ternational Justice Monitor,* 2019, last modified July 8, 2019 available at https://www.ijmonitor.org/2019/07/ntaganda-convicted-at-icc-for-rape-sexual-viole nce- and-murder.
Todd A. Salzman, "Rape camps as a means of ethnic cleansing: Religious, cultural and ethical responses to rape victims in the former Yugoslavia", *Human Rights Quarterly 20,* no. 2, 1998, p. 368.
Herbert F. Weiss and Georges Nzongola-Ntalaja, *Decentralization and the DRC–an overview,* New York, Social Science Research Council, 2013.
Todd A. Salzman, "Rape camps as a means of ethnic cleansing: Religious, cultural and ethical responses to rape victims in the former Yugoslavia", *Human Rights Quarterly 20,* no. 2, 1998, p. 368.

232

ethnic or religious group from certain geographical areas. These deliberately planned acts must be done by violent and terror-inspiring means.

These acts may include murder, torture, arbitrary arrest and detention, forcible displacement and deportation of the civilian population, extrajudicial executions, rape and sexual assault, serious physical injury to civilians, rendition, use of civilians as human shields, deliberate military attacks or threats of attacks against civilians and civilian areas, destruction of property and theft of property from persons and attacks on civilian objects.[233]

In the last years of the Mobutu dictatorship, following the abandonment of the policy of appointing non-natives to local or provincial administrative posts, ethnic conflicts developed. Between 1992 and 1994, ethnic cleansing took place in Katanga, where almost one million "Kasaïens" were victims. This ethnic cleansing took place at the instigation of the then governor of Katanga.[234]

Based on UN Security Council Resolution 1820 of 2008, there is a direct relationship between the systematic use of sexual violence as an instrument of conflict and the fact that mass rape is used as a weapon of war, genocide and ethnic cleansing. This is the case of rape and sexual violence in several conflicts, notably in the eastern DRC. Often ordered by certain rebel leaders,[235] these acts have led certain ethnic groups to abandon their land.[236] The nature of the rapes committed in the DRC has been linked by many to the ethnic cleansing plan in Bosnia and Herzegovina.[237]

According to the UN, there was a risk of ethnic cleansing in central DRC in 2017.[238] Massacres committed by various armed groups in the Kasai region could result in "a process of ethnic cleansing on a larger scale". Indeed, the report alleges that the Kawmina Nsapu militia uses children aged between 7 and 13 in its attacks and has used girls, called "Lamama", in

---

233

234 Herbert F. Weiss and Georges Nzongola-Ntalaja, *Decentralization and the DRC–an overview*, New York, Social Science Research Council, 2013.

235 Wairagala Wakabi, "Ntaganda Convicted at ICC for Rape, Sexual Violence and Murder", *International Justice Monitor*, 2019, last modified July 8, 2019 available at https://www.ijmonitor.org/2019/07/ntaganda-convicted-at-icc-for-rape-sexual-viole nce- and-murder, accessed on July 8, 2023.

236 Anna Maedl, "Rape as Weapon of War in the Eastern DRC? The Victims Perspective", *Human Rights Quarterly 33*, no. 1, February 2011, p.137.

237 Robin Kennedy, *The Prevalence of Sexual Violence in the Context of Armed Conflicts: the Case of the DRC*, 2020.

238 United Nations, "DRC: Victims' harrowing accounts indicate Government complicity in ethnic-based massacres in Kasai" *UN report*, 4 August 2017 available at https://www.ohchr.org/en/press-releases.

rituals where they had to drink the blood of victims to make their groups invincible. Another militia called Bana Mura is said to have carried out beheadings and summary executions. This militia is accused of burning their victims alive in their homes.

According to the report, both militia and government forces are responsible for executions in the region.[239] In this conflict, two UN experts monitoring the regime of sanctions were assassinated.[240] In 2022, 51 people were convicted for this assassination.

From 2003[241] to the present day, there have been many claims that the killings and decapitations of the Nande people in Beni would qualify as ethnic cleansing. In fact, since the "cutthroats" have been massacring the population in Beni and Lubero, several sources have asserted that the aim is to frighten this Nande ethnic group and to encourage them to abandon their fields and villages. Another fact that would confirm the ethnic cleansing is that after the flight of the victims, these people are replaced by another unidentified group.[242]

D. Genocide

The definition of the concept "Genocide" has been in force since 1948 in the Convention on the Prevention and Punishment of the Crime of Genocide in its Article 2.[243]This definition was taken up by the Rome Statute in Article 6. The latter defines genocide as: "any of the following acts committed with intent to destroy, in whole or in part, a national, ethnical, racial or religious group, as such".

The Rome Statute also lists the acts that are likely to constitute genocide with this intent in Chapter 6: killing members of the group; causing serious

239 Radio-Canada, *Risque de nettoyage ethnique en République démocratique du Congo, selon l'ONU,* on 4 August 2017, available at https://ici.radio-canada.ca/ 14 Septembre 2022.

240 UN, *Murder of UN experts in DRC,* 16 August 2017 available at https://news.un.org/ on 14 September 2022.

241 Etienne Rusamira, "La dynamique des conflits ethniques au Nord-Kivu: une réflexion prospective", *in Afrique contemporaine 207,* no. 3, 2003, pp. 150-152.

242 Pacifique Makuta Mwambusa, Emmanuel Kandate, Léon Irenge, Pascal Kaboy, Didier Munguakonkwa and Justin Matete. "*Acteurs de la vie politique et violences identitaires à Beni, RDC* ", *Research Initiatives for Social Development,* RISD, 2021.

243 Nehemiah Robinson, "The genocide convention", *Case W. Res. J. Int'l L.* 40, 2007, p. 7.

bodily or mental harm to members of the group; deliberately inflicting on the group conditions of life calculated to bring about its physical destruction in whole or in part; imposing measures intended to prevent births within the group; forcibly transferring children of the group to another group.[244]

The 1948 Convention also provides that not only the acts themselves are punishable, but also conspiracy to commit genocide, direct and public incitement to commit genocide, the attempt to commit genocide and complicity in genocide.[245] In addition, the victims of this crime are targeted because of their actual or presumed membership in one of the four protected groups. Thus, where these acts are committed against only part of the group, genocide may be possible if that part of the group is identifiable and "substantial".[246]

It is the specific intent to destroy an identified group, in whole or in part, that distinguishes the crime of genocide from a crime against humanity.

Since proof of specific intent, a "dolus specialis", is an important element in the establishment of a crime, in genocide the inference of intent to destroy a group in whole or in part must be made with great care.[247]

The ICTY has stated that "a defendant can only be found guilty of genocide if such intent is clearly established"[248] and the existence of intent "must be the only reasonable possibility in light of the evidence gathered".[249]

Given that in genocide the destruction of an ethnic group can be limited to a particular geographical area and constitute genocide,[250] it is plausible that the destruction of part of the Hutu population in Rutshuru (30 October 1996) and Mugogo (18 November 1996) was genocide.[251]The attacks

---

244 Article 6, *Rome statute.* See also International Criminal Court (ICC), *Elements of Crimes,* 2011, ISBN No. 92-9227-232-2.

245 Article 3 of the *Convention on the Prevention and Punishment of the Crime of Genocide.*

246 Claus Kreß, "The Crime of Genocide and Contextual Elements: A Comment on the ICC Pre-Trial Chamber's Decision in the Al Bashir Case", *Journal of International Criminal Justice 7,* no. 2, 2009, p.230.

247 Kai Ambos, "What does 'intent to destroy'in genocide mean ?" *International Review of the Red Cross 91,* no. 876, 2009, p.843.

248 *Krstić decision, ICTY, Appeals chamber, no. IT-98-33-A,* 19 April 2004, p. 134.

249 *Ibid,* para 41.

250 *ICTY, Trial chamber, 1 September 2004,* para. 703; *Krstić, ICTY, Trial chamber,* 2 August 2001, para. 590

251 *Mapping Report,* para 514.

against other Hutus who were not refugees seem to confirm that all members of the Hutu community were targeted.[252]

During the second war in DRC, it has been estimated that any Christians protestants pastors, catholic bishops, priests, nuns or seminarians were killed in 1998 because of their membership in the Christian churches. This could be qualified as genocide.[253]

In 2003, more than 60,000 members of the Hema and Lendu ethnic groups were killed or died as a result of the conditions imposed to destroy all or part of the targeted groups in the Ituri district.[254] A UN report explains that they were killed because of their membership of these groups.[255]

Although some authors believe that there is a "genocide" against the Banyamulenge populations,[256] this thesis considers that the facts alone would prove the existence of either a crime against humanity or war crime rather than genocide. Indeed, mens rea is difficult to prove genocide against Banyamulenge populations.

In fact, as indicated in the jurisprudence of the ICTY[257] and ICTR[258], *mens rea* can be inferred from repetition, planning, development of plans and strategies.

Thus, for example, the rallying of a large number of members of the targeted group, the destruction of the essential foundations of social life, etc. are among the strategies.

These elements are missing in the killing of the Banyamulenge, as there is no evidence of serious planning so far. It should also be mentioned that the intention to destroy this group in whole or in part has not been proven.

Although proof of men's rea would not focus solely on particular circumstances in order to conclude whether or not there was an intention to

---

252 Filip Reyntjens, *The great African war: Congo and regional geopolitics 1996-2006,* Cambridge University Press, 2009.

253 Bayolo H. Hemdi, "L'Eglise profane" *chronique des violations des droits du clergé pendant la guerre d'agression,* 1998–2000.

254 Jean Migabo Kalere, "Genocide in the African Great Lakes States. Challenges for the International Criminal Court in the Case of the Democratic Republic of Congo." *International Criminal Law Review 5,* no. 3, 2005, pp. 473-474.

255 United Nations, "Special report on the events in the Ituri", *Security Council January 2002– December 2003,* New York, 16th July 2004, p. 32. S/2004/573.

256 Delphin Ntanyoma Rukumbuzi and Helen Hintjens. "Expressive Violence and the Slow Genocide of the Banyamulenge of South Kivu", in *Ethnicities 22,* no. 3, 2022, p. 378.

257 See *ICTY, Jelisic case.*

258 See *ICTR, Akayesu case.*

destroy in whole or in part, sufficient evidence would be required in any case to determine the plausible existence of genocide.[259] This approach is reflected in the ICJ's analysis of the cases Application of the Convention on the Prevention and Punishment of the Crime of Genocide (Bosnia-Herzegovina v. Serbia and Montenegro) and Application of the Convention on the Prevention and Punishment of the Crime of Genocide (Croatia v. Serbia). In both cases, the ICJ relied on the intent criterion either to reject Croatia's claims in their entirety (judgment, I.C.J. Reports 2015 (I), p. 154, para. 524) or to conclude that the serious and widespread atrocities committed in Bosnia-Herzegovina were not perpetrated with the specific intent to destroy, in part, the Bosnian Muslim group (judgment, I.C.J. Reports 2007 (I), p. 194, para. 370).

The conflict in the DRC has caused many direct and indirect victims. Since the beginning of the conflict, more than 10 million people have been killed (5.4 million between 1998 and 2003 alone), more have been raped and many thousands have been displaced or made refugees. This conflict keeps the DRC in a critical situation and blocks its development process. It is therefore appropriate to examine the DRC's obligation to protect its population in the following section.

2. The "Duty" of DR Congo under Responsibility to Protect

According to the 2005 Word Summit document, the primary responsibility for protection lies with the state concerned. This seems logical as this responsibility is an element of the state's sovereignty and its ability to assert its internal sovereignty. Internal or (domestic) sovereignty refers to the supreme power that the state has over its national territory in order to ensure the continuity and cohesion of the society.[260] This sovereignty also implies tasks such as protecting its national territory, asserting the authority of the state over the whole of this territory and protecting people and their property against all kinds of violations.

259 *Separate opinion of Judge ad hoc Barak, Application of the Convention on the Prevention and Punishment of the Crime of Genocide in the Gaza Strip*, (South Africa v. Israel), Document Number 192-20240126-ORD-01-05-EN, 26.01.2024 at https://www.icj-cij.org/node/203452, accessed on 1rst may 2023.

260 Andrew Arato and Jean Cohen. "Banishing the sovereign? Internal and external sovereignty in Arendt", *Constellations* 6, no. 2, 2009.

Thus, the DRC's obligation under R2P is summarized in the content of the principle itself. It is the state's obligation to prevent mass crimes, to intervene and also to reconstruct.[261]

This state responsibility to prevent mass atrocities is the foundation of the R2P doctrine.[262] This is also echoed by the 2009 report on implementing the responsibility to protect, in which the UN Secretary General reiterates the importance of the first pillar of R2P by stating that this state obligation to protect its population remains fundamental to the very existence of the state in relation to its sovereignty.[263]

Beyond the operational aspect of the implementation of R2P by the State, this report recommends a methodological approach to facilitate the implementation of this responsibility through the incorporation of international legal norms for the protection of human rights into national legislation and the criminalization (in domestic law) of mass crimes. In addition, the report recommends that special attention should be paid to the prevention of sexual violence.[264]

In domestic life, the DRC has taken certain measures to ensure the protection of its population. Although not fully effective, these measures do exist.

The DRC is party to the main human rights treaties. These include the International Covenant on Civil and Political Rights (ICCPR), the Convention on the Rights of the Child (CRC) and the Convention on the Elimination of All Forms of Discrimination against Women (CEDAW). The Congolese government must therefore comply with its obligations as a State to respect, fulfil and promote human rights.[265]From the above-mentioned treaties, it follows that the State must use all necessary means to prevent, stop and punish human rights violations.

Even in conflict situations, the DRC has an obligation to protect its population. This is based on the fact that DRC is also one of the States Parties to the Geneva Convention and the Rome Statute of the International Criminal Court, to name but two.

---

261 Sandra Szurek, "La responsabilité de protéger : du principe à son application. Quelques remarques sur les enjeux du law making process en cours", *dial.uclouvain.be,* 2014.

262 *UN Doc. A/63/677,* 12 January 2009.

263 INT'L COAL, *For the Responsibility to Protect, a toolkit on the Responsibility To Protect 25,* available at https://perma.cc/P3UW-Q9H2 on 18 September 2022.

264 UN "Implementing the responsibility to protect", *Report of the Secretary-General UN Doc. A/63/677, 12* January 2009.

265 Article 2(1) *of International Covenant on Civil and Political Rights.*

It is in this context that the DRC has incorporated in its constitution of 18/02/2006 as amended to date, the sanctity of human life and all other human rights by dedicating a fundamental nature to them.[266] Several laws have been passed and promulgated to ensure the protection of the population against sexual violence,[267] the competence of national civil courts to judge mass crimes,[268] the law on security reform in the DRC.[269]

Despite some notable efforts by the Congolese government to protect its population from massive human rights violations, the country, especially in its eastern region, remains a place where civilians are exposed to mass atrocities on a daily basis, targeted by armed groups and sometimes by the Republic's armed and security forces.

The situation of civilians in the DRC highlights the challenges faced by the state in the security domain. The lack of control and transparency of arms and ammunition, corruption and the culture of impunity encourage

266 See Tite II of the Constitution de la République Démocratique du Congo du 18 février 2006 telle que modifiée par la loi n° 11/002 du 20 janvier 2011 portant révision de certains articles de la constitution de la République Démocratique du Congo du 18 février 2006, *Journal officiel*, Kinshasa numéro spécial, 5 février 2011.

267 Loi n° 06/019 et 06/018 du 20 juillet 2006 modifiant et complétant le Décret du 06 août 1959 portant Code de Procédure Pénale Congolais, in *Journal officiel de la République Démocratique du Congo*, numéro spécial du 20/07/2006.

268 Loi n° 15/023 du 31 décembre 2015 modifiant la Loi n° 024-2002 du 18 novembre 2002 portant Code pénal militaire, in *Journal officiel de la République Démocratique du Congo*, numéro spécial du 18 novembre 2002.

269 Loi n°13/011-B du 11 avril 2013 portant organisation, fonctionnement et compétences des juridictions de l'ordre judiciaire, in *Journal officiel de la République Démocratique du Congo,* 54ème année, numéro spécial, 04 mai 2013. Under Congolese law, mass crimes such as crimes against humanity and genocide are nowadays punishable in the ordinary courts for civilians, in the first instance the courts of appeal and in the second instance the courts of cassation, in accordance with article 91 of organic law no. 13/011-B of April 11, 2013 on the organization, functioning and jurisdiction of the competent judicial courts. As far as military personnel are concerned, the military courts remain competent by virtue of law n°024-2002 of November 18, 2002 on the military penal code. The President of the Republic and the Prime Minister are justiciable before the Constitutional Court under organic law n°13/026 of October 15, 2015 on the organization and functioning of the Constitutional Court. The Affaire Kimbanguistes (MP et PC c. Kumba et consorts), TGI/ Kalamu 17.12.2011 laid the groundwork for this novelty in the jurisdiction of Congolese civil courts. The civil judge of the Tribunal de Grande Instance of Kalamu was faced with the dilemma of applying the Rome Statute on the definition of the group in the constituent elements of Genocide. The Lubumbashi CA followed suit in the case of Genocide and crimes against humanity involving Bantus and Pygmies in August 2015.

the commission of serious violations of human rights and humanitarian law.[270] In general, the absence of a solid judicial system and the culture of corruption have not permitted the effective protection of the population.

In the light of the Congolese context and of this interminable conflict, it should be noted that the DRC seems to be failing to protect its population. This has been echoed by several human rights reports that mention violations that require the effective involvement of the DRC to protect its population.[271]

The calls for intervention made by the DRC to the regional and international community[272] are also sufficient proof that the DRC's efforts to protect its population have not been successful. Therefore, the second pillar of R2P, which is the intervention of the international community, is most welcome to protect the Congolese population.

Several measures have been adopted by the countries of the region and even the United Nations in order to solve the DRC problem.

It is therefore necessary to analyze the measures taken by the actors in relation to the three pillars of the responsibility to protect: the "duty" of the international community. A specific analysis will be made of the intervention of the Regional, in the present case African Organizations, the European Union and the United Nations through several resolutions.

3. *The "Duty" of the International Community*

The second pillar of R2P specifies that other states have a responsibility to protect populations threatened by or vulnerable to mass crimes. The intervention of the international community can be considered differently in three situations. Depending on whether it is a well-governed state, or a state with the goodwill and society to fulfil this obligation to protect but with undue means, or finally, an "ill-intentioned" state that has no consideration for the protection of its population.[273]

---

270 Françoise Joly, *The responsibility to protect: from doctrine to practice 'R2P'and protection of civilians: case study: DRC*. PhD diss., Dublin City University, 2015.

271 Global Centre for R2P, *Democratic Republic of the Congo* ,1 September 2022 available at https://www.globalr2p.org/ accessed on 14 September 2022.

272 Martha Mutisi, "SADC Interventions in the Democratic Republic of the Congo." *Conflict Trends 2016*, no. 3, 2016, p. 29.

273 Szurek, "*La responsabilité de protéger*", p. 26.

The *modus operandi* of the international community's intervention in R2P is also necessarily different depending on the context. In situations of peace, tension, internal and/or internationalized armed conflict.[274]

In this section, we will not examine whether the DRC is well governed, has a good will to protect civilians or is an ill-intentioned state, but rather the nature of the international community's R2P intervention in the DRC. Thus, the analysis of the intervention of the African Union, International Conference on the Great Lakes Region, the European Union, the International Criminal Court and that of the UN will form the structure of this section.

It should be noted here that the intervention of the international community must initially be of non-military nature, as military intervention is conditional on the failure of other means and is therefore a last resort.

A. Regional intervention

Within the African Union framework, the responsibility to protect is also organized. Indeed, the content of Article 4(h) of the Constitutive Act of the AU provides for R2P. Although not explicitly enshrined in this concept, the AU's right to intervene should therefore be analyzed as a legal instrument for implementing R2P.[275] This is because Article 4(h) presents the same thresholds for intervention as R2P except that it does not incorporate the concept of 'ethnic cleansing' into its formulation. There is a difference between the wording of R2P and that of Article 4(h).[276] Whereas the implementation of R2P takes place "through the Security Council", the AU Act is silent on the authorization of the Security Council. Even though R2P could be considered a political concept, Article 4(h) of the AU Constitutive establishes a legal obligation to intervene.

As the details of this debate are not part of this analysis, this section will analyze the practical intervention of the AU and other organizations in the region under the responsibility to protect in the DRC crisis.

274 Dorota Gierycz, "From humanitarian intervention (HI) to responsibility to protect (R2P)", *Criminal Justice Ethics 29,* no. 2, 2010, p. 120.

275 Dan Kuwali, The African Union and the Challenges of Implementing the "Responsibility to Protect", *Policy Notes 2009/4,* The Nordic Africa Institute, March 2009.

276 Valérie Soma, "Le Droit d'intervention de l'Union Africaine", *Sciences Juridiques et Politiques 1,* no. 1, 2017.

The African Union quickly endorsed the concept of R2P in a declaration called the Ezulwini Consensus. Released in March 2005, the Ezulwini Consensus is a declaration by African states in relation to the challenges and level of threat posed to the United Nations in pursuit of its goal of international peace and security.[277] While stressing the importance of allowing regional organizations to act directly, as in most cases UN bureaucracy causes delay in action, this declaration embodies the AU's endorsement of the concept of the responsibility to protect (R2P).

Although the AU's direct intervention to resolve the conflicts in the DRC has not been fully visible and thus criticized by many, its attempts through mediation and negotiation in the political processes are not to be overlooked.

On each occasion, the AU has reminded member states of what they have agreed to in the treaty, in line with its objective of providing the means for stability to member states. It is within this framework that the AU Panel of the Wise has been regularly deployed in the DRC in each electoral process such as November 2011, etc.[278]

Following the political crisis linked to the legality and legitimacy of Joseph Kabila's regime, which led to massive human rights violations, the AU sent former Togolese Prime Minister Edem Kodjo to mediate in the crisis in January 2016. This mediation, requested by the DRC, was supported by the SADC and the International Conference on the Great Lakes Region (ICGLR). Unfortunately, the conclusions of this mediation, which led in October 2016 to an agreement between the political actors, were criticized for not being inclusive. Indeed, this agreement excluded most of the opposition.[279]

Although the AU did not intervene directly in the peace process that led to the signing of the Final Act of the dialogue by the parties to the inter-Congolese dialogue in Sun City on 2 April 2003, it welcomed the process in its Decision on the DRC peace process.[280]

277 AU, Decisions, declarations and resolution, Jul 5, 2005.

278 Tatiana Carayannis and Aaron Pangburn, "AU and UN Cooperation in Peace Operations in the Democratic Republic of Congo", *African Politics, African Peace,* Paper n0 14, june 2016.

279 Africa Center for Strategic Studies, *The Role of External Actors in the DRC Crisis*, January 12, 2017, available at https://africacenter.org/spotlight/role-external-actors-drc-congo-crisis-sadc-au-icglr-un-eu/, accessed on 19 July 2022.

280 *Decision on the peace process in the Democratic Republic of the Congo doc. ex/cl/42 (iii) e, Executive council third ordinary session, 4 - 8 July 2003,* Maputo (Mozambique) ex/cl/dec. 20 - 74 (iii).

It urges the states in the region to respect the embargo measures and to stop supplying arms and ammunition to armed groups in the region and condemns the massacres of the population.

In 2007, following the resurgence of the conflict with the presence of Laurent Nkunda's CNDP rebel group, the AU organized a summit in Nairobi, under the aegis of the United Nations, dedicated to the crisis in the east of the Democratic Republic of Congo. The summit was "dedicated to the fighting" in the eastern DRC and solutions to try to "resolve this crisis". In the agreement of 9 November 2007, resolutions were taken, including an immediate ceasefire, the possibility of recourse to Chapter VII of the UN Charter and the disarmament of militias.[281] Unfortunately, all these attempts failed and in 2008 the rebel group CNDP took the town of Goma.

The African Union helped lay the groundwork for peace, security and cooperation in the DRC and the region, leading to the Addis Ababa Framework Agreement of 24 February 2013. Signed in Ethiopia by the leaders of the DRC, Angola, Burundi, Central African Republic, Republic of Congo, Rwanda, South Africa, South Sudan, Tanzania, Uganda and Zambia, as well as the UNSG, the agreement refers to the "recurrent conflicts and persistent violence perpetrated by national and foreign armed groups" and the need to pool all efforts in order to resolve the conflict both in the eastern DRC and in the entire Great Lakes region.[282] The agreement calls for regional engagement, while reminding States Parties of the prohibition on harboring and providing protection of any kind to persons accused of war crimes, crimes against humanity, acts of genocide or crimes of aggression, or to any person under the UN sanctions regime.[283]

In addition, this agreement laid the groundwork for the establishment of a neutral intervention force to address and resolve the issue of rebel forces operating in eastern DRC. Although seen as an important step in resolving the crisis in eastern DRC, the agreement has also been criticized for its unclear action plan.[284]The challenges for the African Union in its intervention in the DRC are both internal and external. Based on the situation in the

281 Roland Pourtier, *Le Kivu dans la guerre: acteurs et enjeux*, EchoGéo, 2009.

282 Gberie Lansana, *La brigade d'intervention : fin de la guerre en RDC ?Une dimension nouvelle des opérations de maintien de la paix*, Août 2013, available at https://www.un.org/africarenewal/fr/magazine/ao%C3%BBt-2013/la-brigade-d%E2%80%99intervention-fin-de-la-guerre-en-rdc, accessed on 31 October 2022

283 *Peace, Security and Cooperation Framework for the Democratic Republic of Congo and the Region*, available at http://www.peaceau.org/uploads/scanned-on-24022013-125543.pdf, accessed on 31 October 2022

284 Joly, "The responsibility to protect", p.169.

DRC, which is sui generis. The organization has not taken the time to study the actors in the conflict and those who should be involved in the peace process. This makes mediation almost impossible because, as many have pointed out, the success of mediation depends on its inclusiveness.

The nature of the conflict in the DRC is a major challenge. The actors in this conflict are internal, the states of the region but also multinationals. Thus, all attempts at peace have failed because the states participating in the negotiations want to integrate their agendas into the agreements in an official or unofficial manner.[285] Unfortunately, the AU and other actors in the process have not yet considered this element as very important in the resolution of the conflicts in the DRC.

Another major challenge is the lack of neutrality of the AU's intervention. This is most noticeable in the AU's reluctance to oppose the governments in power.[286] It should also be added that the fact that the African Union's intervention was only envisaged after the DRC's call for action is a major challenge for the effectiveness of the intervention. There is a certain unpreparedness in the activities, which leads to the ineffectiveness of the intervention.

Not limiting oneself to certain participants in the peace process such as state political parties and rebel groups, but rather integrating civil society would be a strategy for conflict resolution in the DRC, as many conflicts are ethnic.[287] In fact, there is a need for a thorough analysis in identifying rebel groups because in the DRC, there are rebel groups who identify themselves as loyalists protecting ethnic interests and who, unfortunately, are hardly involved in this process.

Furthermore, conflict resolution in the DRC should not be based on existing resolution models. It has been shown that these models can be seen on a theoretical basis, but that they are not sufficient for sustainable peace. Each conflict is unique and the conflict in the DRC involves almost all neighboring states and even the whole of Africa. This requires a way of resolving the conflict by focusing on 'using a more inclusive concept of peace, the starting point of which must be the emancipation of African

285 Marc-André Lagrange, "Les mécanismes de paix régionaux dans les Grands Lacs : des outils incapables de promouvoir la démocratie ?", *Revue Tiers Monde 2016/4*, n° 228, 2016, p. 151.

286 Miriam Abaya, "No Place for Immunity: The Arguments against the African Criminal Court's Article 46BIS", *Temp. Int'l & Comp.* LJ 30, 2016, p. 189.

287 Nzongola-Ntalaja, G., *The Congo: From Leopold to Kabila: A People's History*, London, Zed Press, 2002.

humanity.[288] Strengthening the diplomacy and capacity of the AU can resolve the conflicts in the DRC and therefore protect civilians from mass atrocities,[289]as the most important actors in this conflict are members of this organization.

B. The Intervention of the European Union (EU)

Referred to as the "Petersburg tasks", EU external operations are the essential contribution of the EU to one of the major objectives it has assigned to its Common Foreign and Security Policy, namely the maintenance of peace and the strengthening of international security.

Long considered as primarily an economic and political organization,[290] the EU has nevertheless begun to intervene in the field of security in line with its aspirations to be a "global security actor and peace builder".[291] It is within this framework that the EU's intervention in the DRC takes place.

Indeed, the EU has not only developed cooperation with the DRC in terms of humanitarian assistance and state reconstruction, but also civilian and military missions to protect civilians against mass crimes.

Thus, the EU's intervention can be categorized among the obligations of states and the international community under R2P in terms of the obligation to prevent, react and rebuild. This intervention is done either through the European Commission or the European Council.

Through its Commission, the EU has developed the Country Strategy Paper for the DRC to budget funds for infrastructure, governance and security issues.[292]

To this end, the European Commission is providing millions of euros through the 10th European Development Fund (EDF). EU humanitarian aid is mainly directed towards the eastern provinces of the DRC, which

288 Patricia Daley, "Challenges to peace: Conflict resolution in the Great Lakes region of Africa", *Third World Quarterly 27,* no. 2, 2006, p. 305.

289 Getrudah Sidi Kirenge, *An Assessment of African Union's Application of the Responsibility to Protect Doctrine,* PhD diss., United States International University-Africa, 2017.

290 Meike Froitzheim and Fredrik Söderbaum. "Building peace from the outside': the role of the EU in the Democratic Republic of Congo", *Globalization and Development,* Routledge, 2013, p. 201.

291 European Union, *A Secure Europe in a Better World - European Security Strategy.* Brussels, 2003.

292 European Commission , *EU Relations with Democratic Republic of Congo*", 2010.

are still suffering from the horrors of war. In addition, several EU Member States are intervening individually through donations for the reconstruction of the state and the protection of the population against mass violations. These are mainly: Belgium, Germany, the UK, France, Sweden and the Netherlands.[293]

The Council of the European Union has also intervened in the DRC through civilian and military missions.

The first military mission, codenamed Artemis, was launched in 2003. It aimed to help stabilize the security and humanitarian situation in Bunia where the Lema and Lendu ethnic groups were fighting. Authorized under Chapter VII of the U.N. Charter, the deployment of a French-led Interim Emergency Multinational Force to enforce peace in Bunia took place on May 30, 2003, by U.N. Security Council Resolution 1484. The mandate of the operation was to stop the massacre of civilians, prevent mass atrocities in Bunia, protect civilians under imminent threat of physical violence, re-establish security in the town and improve humanitarian conditions.[294]

Although the Artemis intervention cannot be considered an EU mission related to R2P because it was undertaken before the principle was even recognized internationally, the success of this intervention could help other possible interventions by the international community in the fight against mass crimes and the protection of civilians.

Indeed, the mission prevented and ended an ethnic cleansing in Bunia.[295] Thus, Operation Artemis can be considered a positive experience of solidarity and cooperation between the UN and the EU in the fight against mass atrocities. As a matter of fact, this operation was successful because of its well-defined mission and its highly qualified and well-trained troops.[296] The latter is an aspect that is often lacking in UN operations[297] and which, if really taken into account, would lead to the success of the UN intervention in the protection of the populations in the DRC.

---

293 *L'Union Européenne et la République démocratique du Congo*,at https://www.eeas.europa.eu/republique-democratique-congo/lunion-europeenne-et-la-republique-democratique-du-congo_fr?s=94 on 1st Novembre 2022.

294 *UNSC Resolution 1484 of 30 May 2003, UN Doc. S/RES/1484, 2003*, available at http://daccess-ddsny.un.org/doc/UNDOC/GEN/N03/377/68/PDF/N0337768.pdf?OpenElement, accessed on 01 November 2022.

295 Katarina Engberg, *The EU and military operations: a comparative analysis*, Routledge, 2013.

296 Engberg, *The EU and military operations, 295.*

297 Mugombozi, *Examination of the impact of the United Nations Security Council Resolution 2098 on the protection of civilians in North-Kivu, 140.*

The fact that the EU intervenes within the framework of the UN would lead us to confirm once again that military intervention as part of R2P can only be envisaged through the UN applying Chapter VII. This, although it predates the concept itself, would be a good example of the application of the third pillar of R2P in the protection of populations against mass crimes.

In 2005, a civilian police mission was deployed to assist the Congolese national police in maintaining order as part of their role during the election period. This mission, called EUROPOL-Kinshasa, remained in place until 2007. In July 2007, this mission was replaced by the EU Police Mission for the DRC, which extended the mission's scope to other parts of the DRC, such as the provinces of North and South Kivu. The main objectives of the mission were to "contribute to the restructuring of the Congolese police by supporting the establishment of a professional and human rights compliant civilian police force" and "to help improve the interaction between the police and the criminal justice system...".[298]

In a second mission in 2005, the EU set itself the objective of helping the Congolese authorities to rehabilitate an army capable of guaranteeing security throughout the country. This mission was called the EU Advisory and Assistance Mission for SSR in the DRC (EUSEC RD Congo).[299]

Another mission, of a military nature, called EUFOR RD Congo, was launched from June to November 2006 to support the United Nations Organization Mission in the Democratic Republic of Congo (MONUC).[300]

Since the restoration of the rule of law and development also requires fair and equitable justice, a program called the Restoration of Justice in Eastern Congo Program (REJUSCO) was implemented by the European Commission in 2010. This program, implemented in cooperation with Belgian, Dutch, French and Swedish development agencies, aimed to fight impunity and crime; and restore justice in Eastern Congo.

In an effort to resolve the conflict in the DRC and make the DRC a livable place, a position of EU Special Representative (EUSR) for the Great

298 Thierry Mayamba Nlandu, "Mapping Police Services in the Democratic Republic of Congo: Institutional Interactions at Central, Provincial and Local Levels." *IDS Research Reports 2012*, no. 71, 2012, p.73.

299 Marta Martinelli, "Helping transition: the EU police mission in the Democratic Republic of Congo (EUPOL Kinshasa) in the framework of EU policies in the Great Lakes", *European Foreign Affairs Review 11*, no. 3, 2006.

300 Major Claudia, "EU-UN cooperation in military crisis management: the experience of EUFOR RD Congo in 2006" *European Union Institute for Security Studies*, Vol. 72, 2008.

Lakes Region (GLR) was created within the Commission. The mandate of the EUSR-GLR has evolved over time from recognizing the nature of the conflict, assisting countries in resolving the regional conflict, to coordinating activities on the ground by providing political guidance to the Heads of Mission.[301]

In response to human rights violations and the obstruction of the 2016 electoral process, the EU Council has taken individual restrictive measures against state and non-state actors such as members of the DRC government and armed forces and security services.[302]

These EU sanctions measures include the freezing of assets and the prohibition of entry for certain individuals to European soil and a ban on EU persons and entities making funds available, directly or indirectly, to listed individuals. In December 2021, the Council maintained its sanctions because it considered that the situation at the time could not guarantee that human rights violations would not be committed.[303]

Indeed, the possibility of considering these sanctions measures as being related to R2P is relevant because, as a result of the situation in the DRC, human rights violations were widespread throughout the Republic. Some reports even estimated at the time that if nothing was done, a crime against humanity would be committed in the DRC[304], a crime that is part of the R2P framework.

Therefore, these measures have been considered by many to be effective in reducing the commission of violations, as they have played both a deterrent and a preventive role.[305]

The EU's intervention in the DRC faces a major challenge that is linked to the organization itself, which is masked by internal conflicts between the

301 Schneider, Catherine. "Les opérations extérieures de l'Union européenne en Afrique." *1er Symposium international sur la sécurité en Afrique, La sécurité en Afrique: Défis et perspectives, 2010.*
Engberg, *The EU and military operations*, 290.

302 Council of the EU, *Democratic Republic of the Congo: EU adopts sanctions against a further 9 people, Press release,* 29 may 2017 available at https://www.consilium.europa.eu/en/press/press-releases/2017/05/29/rdc-sanctions/, *accessed on* on 31 October 2022.

303 TV5 Monde, *RDC : l'Union Européenne maintient ses sanctions contre le camp Kabila, sans surprise,* 24.12.2021 at https://information.tv5monde.com/afrique.

304 FIDH, *Slaughter in Kasai: Crimes against humanity perpetrated to create chaos,* Report 20/12/2007 available at https://www.fidh.org on 31 October 2022.

305 See the statement by Aldo Ajello, *The EU Special representative for Africa's Great Lakes Region,* Brussels, 17 September 2003, available at http://www.irinnews.org/Report/46206/DRC-EU-calls-Artemis-operation-a-bigsuccess on 31 October 2022.

Commission and the Council, leading to inconsistent action and lack of coordination.[306]

In sum, the EU is almost reluctant to implement R2P in the DRC. Some have characterized the EU as being absent from the worrying situation in the DRC. Some authors[307]even believe that the EU is still not able to take great risks when it comes to intervening in a state that is not a member. The present author is of those who think that the effective involvement of the EU in the protection of populations would be an asset and not the least suitable measures to solve the problem of the DRC.

This being the case, it is imperative to analyze the intervention of the UN in the DRC, an intervention that dates from the very beginning of the independence of this country.

C. United Nations' intervention

UN intervention in the DRC is as old as the DRC itself. The organization has been present in the DRC since the early 1960s. From then on, the UN has always tried to resolve conflicts and protect the population through peacekeeping and/or peace enforcement missions, State building or through its good offices during negotiations, etc.

The first UN mission was created by UN Security Council Resolution 143 of July 14, 1960, the ONUC (United Nations Organization in the Congo) and was mandated to assist the government in overcoming the presence of Belgian soldiers.[308] Through Resolution 161 of 21st February 1961, the ONUC was authorized to take all necessary measures to prevent a civil war in the Congo and to use force if necessary.[309]

As a result of the genocide in Rwanda in 1994, the eastern part of DRC faced a security crisis leading to regional instability and security risks. Several countries in the region were involved in this conflict. During this time, in 1999, the United Nations Organization Mission in the Democratic Republic of the Congo (MONUC) was established by resolution 1279 with

306 Lisbeth Aggestam and Francesco Anesi, *The Security Development Nexus,* Stockholm, Swedish Institute for European Policy Studies, 2008.

307 Meike Lurweg, "Coherent Actor or Institution Wrangler? The European Union as a Development and Security Actor in Eastern Democratic Republic of the Congo", *African Security 4,* no. 2, 2011, p. 106.

308 *S.C. Res. 143,* July 14, 1960.

309 *S.C. Res. 169, November 24, 1961.*

the initial mandate of observation of the ceasefire and disengagement of forces. The mandate of MONUC was later extended by resolution 1291 (2000) and to include supervision of the implementation of the Lusaka ceasefire Agreement.[310] MONUC played a role in the political, military, capacity-building of the DRC. Among other examples was the organization of democratic elections in 2006 after 46 years.

Despite several peace and ceasefire agreements aimed at resolving the conflict and establishing political stability, violence continued throughout the 2000s. For example, the official armed forces of neighboring countries such as Rwanda and Uganda were accused of committing war crimes and crimes against humanity during their military activities on Congolese soil.[311] Therefore, the Security Council attempted to stem the violence with Resolution 1493 in July 2003 and strengthened MONUC's mandate by permitting "all necessary measures" to "protect civilians and humanitarian workers under imminent threat of physical violence and imposed an arms embargo on rebel militias. Even with MONUC's new mandate, the political instability and conflict in the DRC continued, to the point that in June 2004, the International Criminal Court, at the request of the DRC, opened an investigation into war crimes and crimes against humanity committed in the DRC. Contrary to other authors who believe that R2P has not been included in the resolutions concerning the situation in the DRC,[312] the present author believes that it was only a matter of time. Indeed, only four months after the adoption of R2P at the 2005 Summit and four days after the January 2006 attack by the Lord's Resistance Army (LRA) that led to the death of eight MONUC personnel, the Security Council adopted Resolution 1653 referring for the first time to the concept R2P in the situation in DRC. The Resolution invoked the DRC's Pillar I obligation to protect its citizens and condemned the attack. The resolution states: "the "government in the region have a primary responsibility to protect their populations, including from attacks by militias and armed groups."[313] Thus, Pillar II of R2P can also be found under these lines.

Indeed, during the open debate preceding the adoption of resolution 1653, some member states insisted on the first pillar of R2P, which concerns the DRC. Others, in fact, recalled the obligation of the international com-

---

310 *S.C. Res. 1291, February 24, 2000.*

311 The Kisangani war, commonly known as the six-day war, from June 05 to 10, 2000. See *DRC: Mapping Human Rights Violations*, supra note 170, at 31, 463–64. The U.N.

312 Joly, *The responsibility to protect, p.123.*

313 *S.C. Res. 1653,* at p 10, January 27, 2006.

munity to fulfil its obligations under R2P because the conditions were met.[314]

In 2008, widespread attacks persisted in the DRC, particularly in its eastern and western parts. These attacks led to several assassinations, rapes, looting and even the burning of villages. Not the least of these attacks was the CNDP (Congrès pour la Nation du Peuple) attack on Goma, the capital of North Kivu. The MONUC has been unable to protect civilians during all of these attacks, whether in villages or in towns. Some even report that looting and even the raping of women has been committed within a few meters of the MONUC base.[315] As a result, through Resolution 1856 (2008), the UN Security Council decided to make the protection of civilians the priority mandate of MONUC and it became the first UN operation with this priority.[316]

In its concern to protect civilians from mass crimes, the Security Council held a meeting on the situation in the DRC on November 26, 2008. The President of the Council recalled the responsibility of the international community and in particular of the Security Council, to protect those who suffer the consequences of the violence in the Democratic Republic of Congo.[317]

In 2010, the Council changed the name of MONUC to the United Nations Organization Stabilization Mission in the Democratic Republic of Congo (MONUSCO). By resolution 1925, MONUSCO is mandated to protect civilian, humanitarian and human rights personnel from the imminent threat of physical violence, atrocity crimes and support the DRC government in its stabilization efforts.[318]

Accordingly, this Thesis agrees with Genser[319], that the resolution invoked the DRC's first pillar responsibility to protect its population and, through the Security Council, the international community's second and third pillar obligations under R2P.

314 *U.N. SCOR, 61st Sess., 5359th mtg. at 18, U.N. Doc. S/PV.5359, Jan. 27, 2006.*

315 Lydia Polgreen, "A Massacre in Congo, Despite Nearby Support", *N.Y. TIMES, Dec. 11, 2008,* available at http://www.nytimes.com/2008/12/11/world/africa/11congo.html on 31 October 2022.

316 Julie Reynaert, "NONUC/MONUSCO and civilian protection in the Kivu's", *terns and Volunteers series,* IPIS, 2010, p.16.

317 *UN. DOC S/PV.6024,* 26 November 2008.

318 *S.C. Res. 1925, May 28, 2010.*

319 Jared Genser, "The United Nations Security Council's Implementation of the Responsibility to Protect: A Review of Past Interventions and Recommendations for Improvement", *Chi. J. Int'l L. 18,* 2017, p. 420.

The first pillar is revealed in its preamble which states: " (...) stressing the primary responsibility of the Government of the Democratic Republic of the Congo for ensuring security in its territory and protecting its civilians (...)".[320] The second pillar can be analyzed insofar as the resolution calls on MONUSCO to support the DRC government in establishing democratic, accountable and professional judicial and national security institutions.[321] Furthermore, the third pillar is stated by mandating MONUSCO to use "all necessary means" to "ensure the effective protection of civilians.[322] However, all interventions by MONUSCO forces were intended to support DRC forces.

Even after the deployment of MONUSCO with its stronger mandate than MONUC, the commission of mass crimes has not stopped. In 2012, the UN dispatched a group of experts to investigate the existence of an internal armed conflict internationalized by the fact that Rwanda and Uganda were arming and supporting the M23 rebel group[323] operating in the region and committing war crimes.[324] In response to this situation, the EU and some states have taken individual sanctions against Rwanda.[325] The US and the UK cut latter military aid to Rwanda.[326]Unfortunately, these sanctions were not very persuasive because in November 2012, the M23 rebel group took over the city of Goma in the face of MONUSCO's inaction, which was unable to engage. This proved once again the ineffectiveness of MONUSCO in protecting the population against mass crimes.

This situation has led the UN Security Council to take robust measures to once again address this recurring crisis in eastern DRC. It is with this in mind that Resolution 2098 was adopted and established a rapid intervention force called the Brigade. This Resolution will be analyzed in the following point.

---

320 *SC. Res. 1925 Pmbl,* May 28, 2010.

321 *Id., at p 6ii-iii,* May 28, 2010.

322 *Id., at pmbl.,* p 11–12.

323 Louis Charbonneau and Michelle Nichols, "Exclusive: Rwanda, Uganda Arming Congo Rebels, Providing Troops—U.N. Panel", *REUTERS,* Oct. 17, 2012, available at https://perma.cc/Z5YY.

324 *HUM. RTS. WATCH, DR Congo: M23 Rebels Committing War Crimes, Sept. 11, 2012,* available at https://perma.cc/X2YU-49H8.

325 Jason K. Stearns, "Helping Congo Help Itself: What It Will Take to End Africa's Worst War", *Foreign Aff. 92,* 2013, p. 99.

326 Stephanie Burchard and Stephen Burgess, "US training of African forces and military assistance, 1997–2017: Security versus human rights in principle–agent relations", *African Security 11,* no. 4, 2018, p.359.

Nevertheless, several other resolutions have referred to the Responsibility to Protect in the DRC context. This is the case of resolution 2777 of March 30, 2016, which recalls "the primary responsibility of the Government of the DRC to protect civilians from crimes against humanity and war crimes and urges the government to strengthen its judicial system and thus hold accountable all those who have committed war crimes, crimes against humanity, or genocide.

With the situation still not stable, a year later, the UN Security Council adopted another resolution 2360 on the situation in the Democratic Republic of Congo (DRC) on June 21, 2017. Resolution 2360 emphasizes the primary responsibility of the DRC authorities to protect the populations on their territory from crimes against humanity and war crimes and condemns the killings of civilians around Beni and in the Kasai region. This resolution renews the sanctions regime with the objective that it will take effect.

4. The UNSC resolution 2098 (2013)

The adoption of Resolution 2098 was welcomed by many. In accordance with its mandate, the rapid reaction force had the blessing of the member states of the Security Council to use all necessary measures to put an end to the crisis in the eastern part of the DRC (North- and South- Kivu), which was so desired.

In this section, it will be imperative to first analyze the context of the adoption of this resolution (A). Here, the author will not insist on the historical context, as it has already been taken up in the previous section, but rather on the contours of the adoption of this resolution. Then, an analysis of the content of the resolution will be made (B) followed by the question of the nature of this resolution. Can it be considered as a measure taken within the framework of R2P or simply as a robust peacekeeping mandate (C)? Finally, the implementation of this resolution (D) will be dealt with in order to allow for a deep analysis of its impact on International Humanitarian Law.

A. Background to the Resolution 2098

In order to grasp the full extent of the significance of Resolution 2098, some pertinent political and legal aspects and to some extent historical elements shall be briefly outlined at this point.

As MONUC became the United Nations Stabilization Mission in the Congo (MONUSCO) in 2010, the protection of civilians remained the mission's top priority. It should be noted, however, that MONUSCO's mandate to prevent the breach of the peace by armed groups was not clear in resolution 1925. In its operationalization, the resolution did not provide for the possibility of preventive action to interfere with the military capacity of armed groups to protect civilians.[327] The striking example here is the Kibua-Mpofi crisis. Located 30 km from the conflict, MONUSCO was unable to intervene and protect the populations of thirteen villages, which were attacked by armed groups such as the Maimai Cheka, FDLR and undisciplined elements of FADRC. Indeed, in this example among many others, at least 303 civilians were victims of gang rape for several days (from July to August 2010)[328] because the attackers cut off all communication (road) with the outside of the villages.

Another challenge faced by the MONUSCO in the protection of civilians in North-Kivu was the lack of training. For example, in Kibua, where a MONUSCO Company Operational Base (COB) was deployed, the peacekeepers were not familiar with the situation and had no special training in the protection of civilians. In carrying out its mission, MONUSCO has faced several internal and external challenges.[329]

All of these challenges for MONUSCO to protect civilians have prevented the Mission from protecting civilians in an effective and efficient manner. In order to address these challenges, on the proposal of the SG, the "Addis Ababa Framework Agreement" was signed on 24 February 2013. This agreement was signed by 11 countries of the region (South Africa, Angola, Burundi, Uganda, Central African Republic, Democratic Republic of Congo, Republic of Congo, Rwanda, South Sudan, Tanzania and Zambia), the AU, ICGLR, SADC and the UN SG. It should be noted here that Kenya and Sudan also became signatories to the Framework Agreement on January 31, 2014. The main objective of the agreement is to address the underlying causes of the conflict and to ensure that a lasting peace is achieved in the country in particular, and the region in general.

---

327 Jean Reynaert, "ONUC/MONUSCO and civilian protection in the Kivus", *Interns and Volunteers series, IPIS, 2010.*

328 *Report issued by the Joint Human Rights office, September 2010.*

329 For more details on this point, read Thomas F. read Copeland, "Civilian protection in the Eastern DRC: Evaluation of the MONUSCO Peacekeeping Operation" *Naval Ppostgraduate School Monterey ca dept of national security affairs,* 2012.

While taking into account the context of the conflicts in the region, the states committed themselves to resolving the problem by respecting the sovereignty and territorial integrity of their neighbors through non-interference in their internal affairs; non-assistance of any kind to the groups; respecting the legitimate concerns and interests of their neighbors by refraining from harboring or protecting persons accused of war crimes, crimes against humanity, genocide or aggression, or persons under UN sanctions; and facilitating the administration of justice by encouraging judicial cooperation in the region. Emphasis was placed on the principle of "*aut dedere, aut judicare*" with a view to prosecuting all alleged perpetrators of mass crimes in the region, irrespective of the territory of the State in which they are located.

From these commitments, the present author reads the root causes of the interminable conflicts in the region. Thus, if actions are taken in relation to each specific area as reflected in the commitments of the states of the region, peace will no longer be an ideal sung but not lived. Rather, it will be a reality.

For the implementation of this agreement, governance mechanisms have been established. Called the "11+4" mechanism after the 11 signatory States and 4 organizations (the AU, UN, International Conference on the Great Lakes Region (ICGLR) and the Southern African Development Community (SADC), the governance mechanisms of the Framework Agreement are chaired by the AU and the UN. These governance mechanisms are divided into two structures: The Regional Oversight Mechanism (ROM) and the Technical Support Committee (TSC).[330]

As a result of this security situation and all the information regarding the involvement of neighboring countries in the conflict, on November 20, 2012, the Security Council adopted resolution 2076 requesting the SG to report on the humanitarian situation in eastern DRC and on the follow-up to the Expanded Joint Verification Mechanism established by the ICGLR to monitor the border between Rwanda and DRC. The SG's report should present options for the Security Council to improve MONUSCO.[331]

On February 27, in his special report to the SC, the envoy communicated the steps taken with all the states in the Great Lakes region and presented recommendations related to the need and nature of UN intervention to address the underlying causes of the conflicts.

---

330 *Regional Oversight Mechanism available at https://ungreatlakes.unmissions.org/regional-oversight-mechanism-rom,* accessed on 31 October 2022.

331 *SC Res 2076 of 20 November 2012,* preamble and para 9.

It is within this framework that the SG presented to the SC the need for the creation of the Special Intervention Brigade within MONUSCO. In fact, this was only possible after consultation with the guarantors of this agreement, which are the AU, SADC and the International Conference on the Great Lakes Region (ICGLR), who had already proposed that a peace enforcement force be deployed to deal with the threat posed by armed groups in the DRC and in the region.

This brigade would "perform peace enforcement functions consisting of preventing the expansion of armed groups, neutralizing them and disarming them".[332]

It is clear from this paragraph that the installation of the Brigade would be based on Chapter VII of the UN Charter. Indeed, the legal provisions that authorize UN peace operations to use military force to protect civilians could be based on Article 2. Article 2 (4) prohibits the use of force by the UN and its members to act against "the territorial integrity or political independence of any state". However, paragraph 7 of the same article authorizes "the application of coercive measures under Chapter VII". The UN can therefore interfere in the internal affairs of states when it applies coercive measures under Chapter VII, which is at the heart of the UN's collective security mechanism. In this context, mass crimes may constitute a threat to international peace and security and thus lead to the application of Chapter VII by the Security Council.

In addition, in his letter of March 4, 2013, the SG insists that the Brigade would help the FARDC have more time to fulfill its primary responsibility.[333] This, as stated in the Doctrine, is an element of state sovereignty. It is clear from this paragraph that the SG tacitly acknowledges that the Brigade could act either with the FARDC or alone in cases where it is necessary to protect civilians in eastern DRC. Whether alone or in collaboration with the armed forces of the Republic, the Brigade's interventions would be aimed at the restoration of state authority and the establishment of lasting stability in the eastern DRC.

This resolution was more than welcome. In its June 20, 2013, communiqué, the African Union praised the UN's efforts in conflict resolution and civilian protection. Indeed, the organization believes that the adoption of

332 UN, *Special report of the Secretary-General on the Democratic Republic of the Congo and the Great Lakes Region, UN Doc S/2013/119*, para 60-64.

333 Letter dated 4 March 2013 from the Secretary General to the President of the Security Council S/2013/131.

Resolution 2098 and the appointment of a special envoy of the Secretary General for the Great Lakes is a major step in the restoration of peace in the region.[334]

The opportunity of Resolution 2098 also depends on the security context in Kivu. Indeed, a general in the national army (FARDC) has said that it is time for the United Nations to reorient its approach to intervention in the DRC. Faced with well-organized rebel groups, a robust measure is needed; "for great evils, great remedies," he said.[335]

To support the objectives of the PSC Framework Agreement, the Security Council unanimously adopted Resolution 2098, which came into being one month after the receipt of the Secretary General's letter and a few months after the capture of Goma, in the face of MONUSCO's inaction. France, the author of the text of resolution 2098, has specified that the tasks entrusted to the intervention brigade in no way hinders the ultimate mandate of MONUSCO, which is the protection of civilians.

Thus, the Brigade was created to support and reinforce the peace mission in the East of the DRC, as it is considered the first "offensive" combat force whose mission is to neutralize the rebel groups present in the DRC and more precisely those operating in the East of the DRC. In addition, this Brigade would operate under the command of the MONUSCO force, which has not been the case for previous peace enforcement missions carried out by non-UN forces.[336] The present author will return to this debate later in the analysis by examining whether the resolution can be seen as a measure taken under R2P or whether it is simply seen as a reinforcement of MONUSCO's mandate.

B. Scope of Resolution 2098

While recalling all the other resolutions from 1925 of 2010 establishing MONUSCO, to 2078 of 2012 addressing the security situation in the DRC,

334 African Union, *Communiqué of the 381st meeting of the Peace and Security Council (5-7)20 June 2013,* available at https://www.peaceau.org/, accessed on 9 November 2022.

335 Mugombozi, *Examination of the impact of the United Nations Security Council Resolution 2098 on the protection of civilians in North-Kivu,* p.90.

336 Müller, Lars. "The Force Intervention Brigade—United Nations forces beyond the fine line between peacekeeping and peace enforcement", Journal *of Conflict and Security Law 20,* no. 3, 2015, pp. 359-380.

in particular the sanctions regime, Resolution 2098 reaffirms the commitment of the Security Council to the goals of the United Nations. Indeed, the SC insists that the logic of Resolution 2098 does not impede in any way the sovereignty, independence and integrity of Congolese territory.[337] In the preamble to the Resolution, the principle of non-interference remains a sacrosanct principle in international relations. Derogation from this principle is only possible in accordance with the spirit of Chapter VII of the United Nations Charter, that is, in the case of a threat to international peace and security, obviously including the framework of R2P.

The Security Council, having then determined that the situation in the DRC was a threat to peace and security in the region, adopted the resolution under Chapter VII.

From the very first paragraphs of the resolution, the Security Council praises the efforts made by the DRC and the countries of the region in resolving the conflicts in eastern DRC and in the region. Indeed, the SC welcomes the signing of the Framework Agreement on Peace, Security and Cooperation for the DRC and the Great Lakes Region, which, at least for the SC, is of paramount importance for the long-term stability of the Eastern DRC and the Region.[338]

Thus, the SC recalls the principle of good faith execution in the execution of international treaties and agreements in mentioning the non-execution of commitments by all parties to this agreement.[339] In fact, the Doctrine notes that the principle "*pacta sunt serwanda*"[340] contained in the Vienna Convention of 1969 is a guiding principle of treaties. A principle which, when not applied, could render ineffective or almost impossible the execution of a treaty. This has been the case with the Addis Ababa Framework Agreement, where the non-fulfilment of obligations by the States Parties has rendered ineffective all the efforts made for peace in the region.

In addition, the resolution condemns all forms of violence committed by the rebel groups, naming among others: The Movement of 23rd March (M23), the Forces Démocratiques de Liberation du Rwanda (FDLR), the (ADF), the National Force of Liberation (FNL), the APCLS, the Lord's Resistance Army (LRA) and all other armed groups. In this paragraph, the

337 Preamble, *SC resolution 2098, 2013.*

338 *UNSC resolution 2098,* para 1-5.

339 *UNSC resolution 2098,* para 6.

340 *Art 25 Vienna Convention 1969.*

Security Council calls for an immediate cessation of hostilities and reiterates that the prosecution of members of the rebel groups for all crimes they have committed, including violations of human rights and international humanitarian law, must be effective.[341]

An important point in this endorsement is the non-integration of these forces into the national security forces. Indeed, this has always been a constitutive point of the rebel groups' demand to leaders in DRC. Applied in 2008, this practice has not been a solution to the problem of the presence of rebel groups in the DRC. Called "Brassage", this practice consisted of integrating members of rebel groups who laid down their arms into either the FARDC or the National Police in order to form a republican army.[342] This was not a bad idea, as the country was coming out of a strong political and security crisis and reforming the army was a necessity. Unfortunately, this was more of a burden than a benefit for the DRC, which faced several problems of non-training and instruction of these troops, the insecurity in which these forces were deployed and so on. This prohibition in resolution 2098 was informed by the chaotic context of past experience.

Thus, the resolution decides to create the intervention brigade under the direct command of MONUSCO and mandates it to "use all necessary measures" in order to achieve the four main tasks.[343] The phrase "use all necessary measures" would be directly understood as an authorization to use force to disable these rebel groups. This authorization will have an impact on the nature of this intervention force, which is different from the regular military component of MONUSCO. Even where other missions have had robust mandates with the phrase "to use all necessary measures", none have been explicitly authorized to use force against parties to the conflict as the Brigade has. The author believes that the application of international humanitarian law to this brigade is based on the authorization contained in the resolution.

The first task of the Brigade is the protection of civilians who are under imminent attack of physical violence. This protection must take place before, during and even after the military intervention. In addition, the Brigade must protect the United Nations personnel, their equipment and facilities.

341 *UNSC resolution 2098,* 2013 para 8.

342 Roger Thamba, "Financement des groupes armés et gouvernance démocratique en République démocratique du Congo", in *Africa Development/Afrique et Développement 44,* no. 2, 2019, p. 78.

343 *UNSC resolution 2098,* 2013, Para 12.

Secondly, the Brigade has the mandate to neutralize armed groups. The SC stresses the importance of "neutralizing all armed groups" in relation to the worrying security situation in eastern DRC. The interpretation of the concept "neutralize" can be broad or narrow. A broad interpretation of "neutralize" could mean a range of permissible actions that can range from capture to murder, whereas the narrow one, according to the dictionary, would simply mean to render ineffective.[344]

The broader reading would be more consistent with the philosophy of the resolution, as it refers to other concepts such as "offensive" and "targeted". Indeed, on a deeper reading of the resolution, given the historical context of the resolution itself and the nature of the rebel groups as parties to the conflict, all moves would be permitted to the brigade to end the existence of the rebel groups. The proof is that this brigade is considered by many as a peace enforcement force with all that follows.

Accordingly, the Rules of Engagement (RoE) of the Response Brigade should reflect military doctrine for war fighting and therefore contain more traditional RoE elements. Hence, the use of certain military concepts such as hostile force and non-hostile attack, would be clearer. As the MONUSCO ROE is not publicly available, there is still some doubt about a specific document for the Brigade, as some believe that all UN missions use one set of ROE.[345]

Third, the Brigade shall monitor the implementation of the arms embargo. This Monitoring is the monitoring and reporting of the flow of military personnel, arms or related materiel across the eastern border of the DRC. All of this must be done in relation to the elements of resolutions 2078 (2012) and 1533 (2004). Finally, the fourth mandate is to support national and international judicial processes. The effectiveness of this mandate will depend on the cooperation of all states in the region, including the fulfillment of their commitments under the Addis Ababa framework agreement. The resolution specifies support and work with the government of the DRC to arrest and bring to justice those responsible for war crimes and crimes against humanity in the country, including through cooperation with regional states and the ICC.

---

344 NATO, *NATO Glossary of Terms and Definitions*, AAP-06, 2013, ed. Brussels, Belgium, 2013.

345 Sheeran, Scott and Stephanie Case, *The Intervention Brigade: Legal issues for the UN in the Democratic Republic of the Congo.* New York, International Peace Institute, 2014. See also Bruce Oswald, "The Security Council and the Intervention Brigade: Some Legal Issues", *American Society of International Law Insights 17,* No. 15, June 6, 2013, available at *www.asil.org/insights*.

This paragraph would not mean that only the alleged perpetrators of these two crimes are prosecutable. A good analysis of the resolution would not attempt to interpret the paragraph in its singularity, but rather to place it in the general context of the resolution. This means that, in accordance with the preamble, which is an integral part of the resolution, the prosecution here will concern all crimes for which the ICC is competent. Furthermore, given the context of conflict in the DRC, it would be appropriate to simply say the prosecution of all violations of human rights and international humanitarian law.

The Brigade's mandate has been renewed several times, following the renewal of MONUSCO's mandate in the DRC. It should be noted that on August 5, 2020, the SADC expressed its concern about the unilateral reconfiguration of the Brigade by the United Nations.[346] The DRC, the object of the implementation of this resolution, was surprised with the SADC, the organization where the troops come from, on this particular issue.

This brings us back to the study of the nature of resolution 2098 creating the Intervention Brigade.

C. Resolution 2098: "R2P measure" or "robust peacekeeping mandate"?

The adoption and implementation of resolution 2098 has raised many questions about the nature of an ordinary peace mission as well as legal issues. In its operationalization, this resolution has raised questions about the very guiding principles of peace missions such as the consent of concerned State, neutrality, impartiality and the non-use of force (except in self-defense and defense of the mandate).[347]

However, the analysis of the nature of resolution 2098 would require this thesis to determine whether this resolution is a measure taken under the principle of the Responsibility to Protect or whether it would only be considered as a reinforcement of the mandate of the Protection of Civilians. In addition, it will be important to determine whether there is a difference

346 SADC, *Communiqué of the Virtual Organ Troika Summit Plus Force Intervention Brigade - Troop Contributing Countries (FIB - TCC) and the Democratic Republic of Congo (DRC),* August 5, 2020, Para 7, available at https://www.sadc.int/latest-news, on November 12, 2022.

347 For details on "capstone doctrine", see De Coning, Cedric, Julian Detzel and Petter Hojem. "UN Peacekeeping Operations Capstone Doctrine." *Norwegian Institute of International Affairs,* 2008.

between military intervention under R2P and that under the peace enforcement mandate. This section will examine this issue based on the content and context of the resolution.

With Resolution 2098, the Security Council broke with tradition and authorized the creation of a Force Intervention Brigade (FIB), with a mandate to "conduct targeted offensive operations (unilaterally or jointly with the FARDC)" with the aim of neutralizing armed groups and stabilizing eastern DRC in a sustainable manner.

According to many, Resolution 2098 is a resolution that did not transform the mandates of MONUSCO, but rather strengthened it in order to protect civilians.

In paragraph 9 of the resolution, the phrase "on an exceptional basis and without creating a precedent or any prejudice to the agreed principles of peacekeeping" may lead some to believe that the intent of the resolution was not to change MONUSCO's mission but rather to strengthen its mandate to protect civilians. The SC recognizes that this resolution is an exception to the guiding principles of peace missions, but at the same time, the Council insists that it is not outside the peacekeeping context. In addition, and as a refresher, the Security Council places the Brigade under the command of MONUSCO in order to avoid "precedents".

The integration of the Brigade Force into MONUSCO would lead one to believe that this force is included in the peacekeeping framework. However, this analysis would be erroneous because it is important to distinguish between a peacekeeping force and a peace enforcement force.

The peacekeeping force is characterized by two essential elements. On the organizational level, these missions are considered as subsidiary organs of the Security Council and are placed under its command, in accordance with Article 29 of the UN Charter. The other characteristic is related to the principles that govern these missions, 'the principles of capstone'. These principles allow for a clear distinction between peacekeeping and coercive action as modes of operation. Unlike peace enforcement, peacekeeping is not intended to achieve its objectives through the use of force.

The Brigade cannot be considered a peacekeeping mandate and should not be treated as such. It is a peace enforcement mission in accordance with its mandate under the resolution, specifically to neutralize armed groups. Although placed under the command of MONUSCO, which is generally a peacekeeping mission, the Brigade has a different mandate than that of MONUSCO. Indeed, placing a peace enforcement mission under the command of a peacekeeping mission has brought more challenges in the operationalization and application of the principles of neutrality, impartiality and non-use of force. These challenges would also be related to the distinction between the civilian and ordinary military personnel of MONUSCO and the Brigade.

It is within this framework that the author echoes the idea of former Secretary General Boutros-Ghali described in the context of the UN missions in Somalia (UNOSOM I and II) that "when peacekeepers are deployed, they endeavor, through peaceful persuasion, to bring about a cessation of fighting between the belligerent parties or to carry out other aspects of their mandate; they do not force belligerents to cease hostilities".[348] In fact, the Brigade's mandate was to force armed groups to cease hostilities.

Indeed, the difference in the language of resolution 2098 and that of other resolutions that explicitly refer to R2P would lead many to believe that R2P remains a strengthening of MONUSCO's mandate. However, the Security Council has had a strong and explicit commitment in the resolutions concerning the situation in Libya and Cote d'Ivoire. In its resolution 1973 the SC provided for the establishment of a no-fly zone and the freezing of assets of certain Libyan authorities. It also authorizes member states to "take all necessary measures to protect civilians and civilian populated areas under threat of attack ...".[349] In turn, member states are authorized to "use all necessary means to carry out its mandate to protect civilians under imminent threat of physical violence...", in resolution 1975, regarding Cote d'Ivoire.[350] It is difficult, however, to find such direct and clear language in resolution 2098. While the latter only clearly takes up the first pillar of R2P, the other two resolutions take up the responsibility of the international community, i.e. pillars II and III, in the most precise way.

Given these differences, it could be argued that a different interpretation of responsibility by the international community, followed by a different resolution or mandate based on the third pillar of the R2P principle, could affect the scope of authorized measures but also the nature of the resolution.[351] Thus, in a narrow interpretation, resolution 2098 would be a strengthening of MONUSCO's mandate by establishing a peace enforcement mission.

---

348 Boutros-Ghali, *Introduction, in United Nations, The United Nations and Somalia 1992-1996*, 1996, cited in Bothe, Michael and Thomas Doerschel, (Eds.) *UN Peacekeeping: A Documentary Introduction.* BRILL, 2021.

349 *UNSC resolution 1973*, 2011, para 3.

350 *UNSC resolution 1975*, 2011.

351 Michelle de Vries, *The Resposibility to Protect in the DRC conflict,* Master diss. Radboud University, (2017).

Indeed, there is a relationship between the R2P principle and UN peace missions. This link goes back to the genesis of the R2P concept itself in the face of the inability of peace missions to protect civilians in Rwanda and Bosnia. Thus, the R2P concept and UN Protection of Civilians (POC) operations are conceptually linked.

Although related, the concepts remain distinct in their scope of application. POC is broader than R2P in that it applies to the protection of civilians from all violations of international humanitarian law and human rights law in situations of armed conflict, whereas R2P is limited to the four crimes at all times, i.e., in peacetime and in wartime.

Even when the protection of civilians in times of armed conflict is the overlap between R2P and POC, their operationalization requires different preconditions and strategies.

In his first annual report, the SG recommended that "R2P objectives" be "integrated into the priorities" of UN peacekeepers and peacemakers and identified the roles of peacekeeping missions in the second and third pillars.[352]

In addition, R2P was referenced multiple times as it articulated the peace operation's protection strategy in relation to each of the three R2P pillars. Linkages began to be made by the Secretariat and the UNSC between POC in peace operations and R2P since 2006.

For example, the resolution authorizing the UNAMID mission in Darfur-Sudan included a preambular paragraph "recalling [resolution] 1674 (2006) on the protection of civilians in armed conflict, which reaffirms, inter alia, the provisions of paragraphs 138 and 139 of the 2005 UN World Summit Outcome Document. With regards to the situation in the DRC, already with the adoption of resolution 1856, which made the protection of civilians a priority for the UN mission in Congo (MONUC) and later for MONUSCO, the states of the UNSC at the time declared that this mandate was part of the R2P concept.[353]

Meanwhile, although reference to R2P has become an essential element of many UN Security Council resolutions and presidential statements, while the protection of civilians has become an integral component of many UN peacekeeping mandates, these resolutions are not often issued

352 UN, *A New Partnership Agenda: Charting a New Horizon for UN Peacekeeping.* New York, DPKO/DFS, 2009, paragraphs 40, 55, 68.

353 UN (2009a). *SC Verbatim Records: 6066th Meeting, UN Doc S/PV.6066 (Resumption 1),* January 14, 2009.

under the coercive Chapter VII of the UN Charter. UN Security Council Resolution 2098 (March 28, 2013) authorizing the establishment of a "Force Intervention Brigade" in the Democratic Republic of Congo is one of the few resolutions expressly adopted under Chapter VII.[354]

This resupply is not exclusively justified for the purposes of the POC, even though the Security Council envisioned the FIB as "contributing to the objective of reducing the threat posed by armed groups to state authority and the safety of civilians in eastern DRC and making room for stabilization activities" and thus protecting civilians.

Indeed, efforts to implement R2P in practice have consistently identified peace operations as a possible avenue. For example, the Secretary-General has identified United Nations (UN) peacekeeping missions as an appropriate instrument to operationalize R2P. The normative status of R2P is more accurately described as a set of norms that intersect with and sometimes build upon other norms, regimes and programs.[355]

However, those seeking to advance R2P have also become more cautious about where, when and how they have linked it to the work of peace operations. For example, the SG's 2012 report on the third pillar of R2P downplayed the role of peace operations in rapid and decisive responses. Mentioned in only one paragraph of the report, later in the delineation: UN peacekeeping missions are based on the principle of consent and are generally deployed in support of and with the general consent of the host state. As such, they fall under the second pillar and are to be distinguished from third pillar tools.[356]

Thus, interpretation of the resolution is a key element in determining whether a resolution is within the context of R2P.

Interpreting the language of Security Council mandates is not an easy task as it is often vague. This has also led to some disagreement about what exactly constitutes a "reference" to R2P in a UNSC resolution.[357] Thus,

354 Ramesh Thakur, "The responsibility to protect at 15." *International Affairs 92,* no. 2, 2016, pp. 415-434.

355 Charles T. Hunt, "The responsibility to protect and the protection of civilians in UN peace operations: interaction, feedback and co-evolution",, *Constructing the Responsibility to Protect: Contestation and Consolidation,* Charles T. Hunt and Phil Orchard. Abingdon, Oxon, (eds) Taylor and Francis. 2020, pp. 89-112, available at https://doi.org/10.4324/9780429352430-5.

356 Ban Ki-moon. 2012a, *Responsibility to Protect: Timely and Decisive Response. Report of the Secretary-General, UN Doc. A/66/874–S/2012/578,* July 25.

357 Jess Gifkins, "R2P in the UN Security Council: Darfur, Libya and beyond", *Cooperation and Conflict 51,* no. 2, 2016, p. 158.

would the absence of an explicit reference to the concept of R2P mean that the resolution does not refer to it?

The clarity of this reference would somehow raise the question of what would exist between R2P and Responsibility to Protect within peace operations framework.

One can then say at this level that the interpretation of resolution 2098 necessarily refers to the operationalization of R2P in missions to protect civilians. As some think: MONUSCO represents a test for the operationalization of the responsibility to protect.[358] At this level, one can even confirm that it comes down to the first, second and third pillars. While the first pillar is clearly stated in the resolution[359], the second and third pillars are not explicitly mentioned.

In the second pillar, the resolution proposes to assist in the reform of the justice system and to work in conjunction with the FARDC and call all states in the region to respect their commitments under the PSC Framework.[360] The third pillar is where the Brigade can act alone as needed and is not accountable to the FARDC.[361] The third pillar again becomes manifest, inasmuch as the decision to allow the FIB in the DRC to neutralize armed groups (M23, ADF, FDLR, various Mai-Mai groups, etc.) is an example of where it was deemed unnecessary to obtain the consent of these non-state parties to the conflict. In addition, as mentioned above, the reorganization of the Brigade by the Security Council without first consulting SADC and DRC,[362] the country concerned, is sufficient proof that the consent aspect was not relevant.

As a matter of fact, the SC can always refer to the R2P without saying it clearly.[363] This is the case of resolution 2098, which, because of its context of adoption and its content, does not prevent the use of R2P from being confirmed. Based on this analysis, it is then necessary to explicitly recognize the "... need to overcome the prevailing tendency to consider R2P as disconnected from related activities in conflict prevention, peacebuilding,

---

358 Danielle N. Allyn, "The Promise of Peace: UNSC 2098 and 2147 and the Protection of Congolese Civilians", *Global Africana Review*, Volume 1, Issue 1 Spring 2017, 2017, p. 14.

359 See Preamble of the resolution 2098 and paragraph 10.

360 See Preamble of the resolution 2098.

361 Paragraph 12 (b) of the resolution 2098.

362 *La RDC s'oppose à la reconfiguration d'une brigade spéciale de la force onusienne, 'DRC opposes the reconfiguration of a special UN force brigade',* available at https://www.lemonde.fr/afrique/article/2020/08/06/ on 06 August 2020.

363 Alex J. Bellamy, *Responsibility to protect: a defense, Oxford, OUP Oxford, 2014.*

protection of civilians, protection and empowerment of women and girls and international criminal justice".[364]

It is accepted that for the implementation of the responsibility to protect in conflict areas, the involvement of humanitarian actors is necessary.[365] This should not lead to confusion between R2P and other humanitarian actions, even if both concepts have the same objective, that of protecting civilians. The above analysis implies that it is not the fact that a resolution refers directly to R2P that is important for it to be considered as such. What is important here is the analysis of the objectives assigned in the resolution and its implementation on the ground. The actors involved in this implementation will, of course, be different depending on whether R2P is in its first, second or third pillar. Thus, in the following section, we will analyze the implementation of Resolution 2098 as a R2P measure on the field.

D. Implementation of the Resolution 2098

In accordance with resolution 2098, the Force Brigade has four main tasks: the protection of civilians, neutralization of armed groups, monitoring of embargo measures and supporting the national and international justice process.

This section will focus on the first and second mandates. Indeed, all missions are linked because the main objective is the protection of civilians. However, the neutralization of armed groups will be analyzed in this section because it gives the opportunity to understand the direct intervention of the Brigade on the ground against the rebel groups named and not named in the resolution in a bid to protect civilians against mass atrocities. An essential element here is not to confuse MONUSCO's operations with the Brigade's operations. There are military operations by MONUSCO to protect civilians that are different from those of the Intervention Brigade.

For this reason, this section will focus only on Brigade operations, the Brigade in cooperation with the FARDC und also on joint operations

---

364 Ban Ki-moon, *Responsibility to Protect: State Responsibility and Prevention. Report of the Secretary-General, UN Doc S/2013/399,* July 9, 2013a.

365 Jaya Murthy, "Mandating the protection cluster with the responsibility to protect: a policy recommendation based on the protection cluster's implementation in South Kivu, DRC", *Journal of Humanitarian Assistance,* 5 Oct. 2007, available at https://sites.tufts.edu/jha/archives/55., on 06 August 2020.

between the Brigade and MONUSCO regular forces carrying the mandate of resolution 2098. This section will focus on the operations of the Brigade from its deployment in 2013 until September 2022.

Adopted in March 2013, the resolution authorized the ceiling of 19815 men, including the Brigade which was composed of three infantry battalions, an artillery and a company of special forces and reconnaissance.

Placed under the direct command of the MONUSCO force commander, whose headquarters is in Goma, the Brigade was composed of troops from three African countries, namely Tanzania, South Africa and Malawi. Deployed in 2013 in the vicinity of Goma, this brigade was provided with attack and technical means to make its mandate effective.[366] The first operations were launched against the M23 rebel group. These operations were strong in nature and led to the neutralization of the M23 rebel group in 2013. After the defeat of the M23, the MONUSCO Force Commander, who is also the Brigade Commander, relocated the area of operations to Beni where there was a need to track down but also to deal with the ADF group. This relocation had consequences in the organization of the Brigade.

According to MONUSCO's Force Command, the brigade was reorganized for one main reason: to adapt the forces to the nature of the conflict.[367] Operations against the M23 required a very specific method of warfare, different from that against the ADF. Indeed, with the M23 group, which was located in the vicinity of the town of Goma, a body-to-body approach was required in order to limit the damage, whereas with the ADF group, a more holistic approach and much more air means were required because the rebel group, for a longer period of time, lived in the middle of the forests without road access. This is why soldiers, called special soldiers, from Kenya, Nepal, Tanzania and South Africa, joined the Brigade in 2019. Thus, several operations were conducted against the ADF. For example, on 13 November 2018, a joint operation between the brigade and the FARDC was launched in Beni. Called "Usalama", this operation aimed to destroy the ADF rebel camps from which they launch attacks against the civilian

366 *Le déploiement de la Brigade d'intervention est imminent,* 21.04.2013, available at https://www.radiookapi.net/nations-unies/magazine-un, on 06 August 2020.

367 Interview with LTG Marcos Affonso da Costa, Force Commander & Head of the Military Component of MONUSCO in Goma held on 24th January in Goma at the MONUSCO headquarter.

population. As a result, the strategic ADF stronghold of Kididiwe was recaptured by the FARDC.[368]

On 14 May 2021, the Brigade conducted an aerial bombardment against an ADF camp, authorized by the commanding force.[369] In August 2021, another operation by the Brigade and the FARDC in localities where the ADF rebels had been established for several months was initiated. These operations were conducted in the areas of the confluence of the Lusilubi, Nzelube, Semuliki, Talya, Mwalika valley.[370]Today, the Brigade has an area of operation in Sake and Beni with its largest operation against the ADF. According to paragraph 12 of resolution 2098, the neutralization of named rebel groups and the possibility to attack unnamed ones was the main objective. However, according to an interview with the MONUSCO Force Commander, who is also the Brigade Commander, it was difficult for the Brigade to conduct operations against all these rebel groups, so they focused on the well-organized rebel groups.[371]

Only the operationalization document for resolution 2098 could shed light on this research into the understanding and implementation of paragraph 12 of resolution 2098. Unfortunately, the document is not publicly available. The understanding of paragraph 12 remains an important point in the analysis of the effectiveness of resolution 2098 and its impact on the protection of civilians, as it is not only well organized rebel groups that put the population at risk of crimes and abuses.

This, in turn, would also be an additional argument in the understanding of resolution 2098 as a measure in the context of R2P, as the idea would be to identify those rebel groups that are, depending on the context, likely to put the population at risk of mass crimes. In implementing resolution 2098, the Brigade has faced some challenges. The first challenge is bureaucracy. Indeed, the brigade as a military component faces bureaucracy and its slowness in executing the command's requests. A striking example is the request made by the Force Command for heavy artillery to respond to the

368 *RDC : Deux otages retrouvés après bombardement de plusieurs campements des rebelles ADF à Beni,* December 1, 2018, available at https://actualite.cd/2018/12/01/rdc., on 06 August 2020.

369 *L'état de siège a-t-il amélioré la sécurité dans l'est de la RDC ?* on juin 10, 2021, available at https://blog.kivusecurity.org/fr/tag/brigade-dintervention, 13th January 2023.

370 *Opérations contre les ADF : L'appui de la MONUSCO aux FARDC est conséquent* , 18 August 2021 available at https://peacekeeping.un.org/., on 06 August 2020.

371 Interview with LTG Marcos Affonso da Costa.

M23 that has been emerging since June. This request was made in early June 2022 but as of 24 January 2023 nothing has been done.[372]

One recommendation would be to institute a 100% military mechanism in the implementation of resolution 2098. That is, the Command Force should have its own budget that would facilitate rapid responses to the commission of mass crimes by rebel groups. Indeed, when a request is made to meet a military need, the approval to raise the funds should be direct. This is the way to make this resolution effective. Another challenge is an operational one, as the UN has no military, but rather that of its member states, there is a challenge of combat doctrine.[373] Each member country has its own combat doctrine. This makes it very easy for the members of the brigade to disagree on any given approach in the field. A consequence of the diversity of the military's origins is also the diversity of languages. Thus, communication is still not easy between the members in the field. In the first operation against the M23, this was not experienced because almost all the contributing countries speak English. The challenge was in communicating with FARDC elements during joint operations. From the above, it is worth noting that the Brigade has been effectively engaged in combat. Thus, it is important to analyze the violations of international humanitarian law in implementing the R2P under resolution 2098.

372 *idem.*
373 *idem.*

Title II: Legal Implications of Applicability of IHL in the Implementation of R2P in the DRCongo.

Chapter I: Applicability of IHL in the Implementation of R2P Under Resolution 2098

There is no need to recall again that there is a link between international humanitarian law and the principle of R2P. Both norms have as their goal the protection of populations.

Indeed, in the third pillar of R2P, which also implies the use of force, it is definitely clear that certain rules must be respected, including International Humanitarian Law.

However, in order to identify the rules of IHL that apply to the situation in the DRC and to the implementation of R2P, it is necessary to qualify this conflict (1). It will also be important to know the legal consequences of the application of IHL to the implementation of R2P through Resolution 2098 (2). Finally, an analysis will be made of the cases of IHL violations committed during these R2P operations on the ground (3).

1. Qualification of the conflict in the Democratic Republic of the Congo

Rather than reviewing the conflict situation in the DRC since the first United Nations intervention in the DRC after its independence in 1960, this section will analyze the nature of the conflict that led to the adoption and implementation of Resolutions 2098 and 2147. The latter are considered to be the resolutions that have made direct use of R2P in its third pillar. Thus, the important element here would be the application of International Humanitarian law in the implementation of resolution 2098. To this end, it will be imperative for this research to determine the nature of the conflicts in which the Brigade was engaged and the legal consequence of these operations.

According to Resolution 2098, the UN forces, referred to here as the Brigade, become party to the armed conflicts between the Congolese Armed Forces (FARDC) and rebel groups.

In the light of paragraphs 8 and 12 of resolution 2098, the Brigade Force, alongside the FARDC, intervenes in clashes against named and unnamed rebel groups.

These include M23, FDLR, ADF, APCLS, LRA, the National Force of Liberation (FNL), Mayi Mayi groups in all its forms and all other armed groups. The list of these rebel groups in the resolution under review contains both national and foreign rebel groups. Indeed, the nature of a group has an impact on the nature of the armed conflict under IHL. It is therefore imperative to analyze the nature of the conflict when it is an armed conflict between the FARDC, the Brigade and a national or foreign rebel group.

According to the typology of conflicts in International Humanitarian Law, there are two kinds of armed conflict: Non-International Armed Conflict (NIAC) and International Armed Conflict (IAC). It should be noted here that the conflict formerly known as internationalized internal armed conflict falls into the basket of international armed conflict.

However, without denigrating the importance of the distinction between the two types of conflict in determining the applicable law, as long as human beings are involved, this distinction between the applicable rules will be called into question. Thus, certain rules of the law of international armed conflict will apply in the context of an internal armed conflict. For example, the rules on "grave breaches" of IHL that were once considered possible only in IACs will also be considered possible to be committed in the context of internal conflict. The point made by the United States of America in their *Amicus curial brief* to the ICTY in the Tadic case is that the rules on "grave breaches" to the GCs are applicable to internal as well as international conflicts.[374]

Indeed, the frequency of civil wars, the consequences of internal armed conflicts which have become more devastating than those between States and the development of international human rights law are the reasons for questioning this categorization of armed conflicts. In the Nicaragua case, the judge recalled that considerations of humanity applicable under customary law must be dominant in an armed conflict, regardless of how the conflict is categorized.[375] This reasoning can be deduced from that of the judge in the Tadic case, which held that, depending on the content and the obligation to respect Article 3 common to the Geneva Conventions, the nature of the conflict is irrelevant.[376]

The notion of non-international armed conflict in humanitarian law is mainly taken up by Article 3 common to the Geneva Conventions of

374 Presse Release. *Communiqué de presse, CC/PIO/015-E, the Hague, 10.08.1995, Case no IT-94-I-T/defendant: Mr. Dusko Tadic,* available at https://www.icty.org/en/press/case-no-it-94-i-tdefendant-mr-dusko-tadic, on 23 August 2020.

375 *Nicaragua case,* para. 218

376 ICTY, *The Prosecutor v. Dusko Tadić, IT-94-1-AR72, Appeals Chamber, Decision,* 2 October 1995, Para 97

1949 and the article of Additional Protocol II of 1977. Indeed, article 3 applies only to armed conflicts not of an international character and sets a minimum standard of treatment for persons not directly taking part in hostilities.[377]

Non-international armed conflict can then be defined as a conflict between state forces and one or more-armed groups.[378] In this conflict, one of the parties must not be a state actor.

This first criterion is met. It is indeed a conflict between several rebel groups and the DRC. Resolution 2098 praises the efforts of the DRC and all states in the region to eradicate the conflicts in the eastern part of the DRC.[379] This part alone refers to more than 120 armed groups.[380]

However, a distinction must be made between armed conflicts and other forms of violence such as internal tensions, riots and isolated acts, as IHL does not apply to the latter.

Thus, to speak of a non-international armed conflict, the situation must reach a level that distinguishes it from all the other forms of violence mentioned above. The following criteria must be met: the intensity of the violence and the organization of the parties.[381]

The intensity of the violence would be characterized by the means the state puts in place to combat the threat of these armed groups. The state, unable to restrain violations, will resort to its army and other forces and to more coercive measures. In addition, the occupation and territorial control of rebel groups, human rights violations and displacement of populations are also elements to be taken into account in determining the intensity of the situation.[382]

377 Article 3(1) commun to *Geneva Conventions.*

378 Nicholas Tsagourias and Morrison Alasdair, *International humanitarian law: cases, materials and commentary,* Cambridge University Press, 2018.

379 Para 11 of the *UNSC resolution 2098.*

380 *Baromètre Sécuritaire du Kivu, La cartographie des groupes armés dans l'Est du Congo, opportunités manquées, insécurité prolongée et prophéties auto-réalisatrices, Février 2021. (Mapping armed groups in eastern Congo, missed opportunities, prolonged insecurity and self-fulfilling prophecies) Translated,* available at https://kivusecurity.nyc3.digitaloceanspaces.com/reports/39/2021%20KST%20rapport%20FR.pdf, on 06 August 2020.

381 Daniel H.Lawrence, "A Government-Based Framework for Conflict Classification", *Texas Law Review 101.1, 2022.*

382 Miloš Hrnjaz and Janja Simentić Popović, "Protracted Armed Violence as a Criterion for the Existence of Non-international Armed Conflict: International Humanitarian Law, International Criminal Law and Beyond", *Journal of Conflict and Security Law 25.3,* 2020, p. 483.

There is no need to go back over the intensity of the violence in the eastern part of the DRC. Several human rights reports have documented the impact of the violence in this region. Several parts of the territory have been under the control of rebel groups,[383] with massive violations of human rights and international humanitarian law[384] resulting in massive displacement.[385] A further element to prove the intensity of the violence is the qualification of the situation as a first African world war[386] but also as a situation threatening international peace and security in the region.[387]

As the intensity of violence criterion is not sufficient to determine a NIAC, the organizational criterion, in addition, requires that the armed group be structured, be under command and have the power to coordinate the different operations of its units.[388] Additional Protocol II of 1977 also applies to non-international armed conflicts and adds another element to the organizational criterion. Indeed, Article 1(1) of Protocol II states that the armed group must exercise control over a portion of territory, from which they organize continuous and concerted operations and that they must be capable of implementing this Protocol.

This organizational criterion raises a number of legal issues in the context of the implementation of Resolution 2098. Indeed, the resolution authorized the use of force against all rebel groups without exception. Wording the paragraph 12(b), the brigade must use all necessary measures: "(...) to prevent the expansion of all armed groups, neutralize these groups and to disarm them in order to contribute to the objective of reducing the threat posed by armed groups on state authority and civilian security in eastern DRC and to make space for stabilization activities; (...)". But according to

383 Erick Kennes and Ninah Wilén, *Multi-Layered Violence in the DRC: Is History Repeating Itself ?*, 27.01.2023 available at https://www.institutmontaigne.org, on 06 August 2020.

384 *Democratic Republic of the Congo, Populations at risk*, 28.02.2023 available at https://www.globalr2p.org/countries/democratic-republic-of-the-congo/, on 09 August 2020.

385 *Democratic Republic of the Congo, Human Rights Report 2022*, 23.03.2023 available at https://www.state.gov/wp-content/uploads/2023/03/415610, on 26 August 2020.

386 Christopher Williams, "Explaining the Great War in Africa: How Conflict in the Congo Became a Continental Crisis", *The Fletcher Forum of World Affairs*, Vol. 37, No. 2, Summer 2013, p. 91.

387 Preamble the *UNSC resolution 2098.*

388 Tilman Rodenhäuser, *Organizing rebellion: Non-state armed groups under international humanitarian law, human rights law and international criminal law*, Oxford University Press, 2018.

IHL, the rules of the NIAC will only apply to conflicts involving organized armed groups.[389]

However, not all rebel groups mentioned in resolutions 2098 and 2147 reach the threshold of Organized Armed Groups (OAGs) as they do not meet the above criteria under IHL.[390] The insecurity situation created by these non-organized armed groups will be qualified as internal tensions, isolated cases, guerrilla warfare, etc. It should be noted that the latter situations are not covered by the Geneva conventions and their additional protocol.

Thus, in the context of the DRC, the United Nations intervenes in a NIAC when it undertakes operations against OAGs, but also in internal tensions when the Brigade intervenes in an internal situation. The latter raises the issue of the rules applicable in this situation and the principle of non-interference in the internal affairs of a state. This intervention further reinforces the thesis that Resolution 2098 is a measure of R2P because the objective is to protect the population, regardless of the legal qualification of the context that puts populations at risk of mass crimes. This study will not focus on whether a "non-organized" armed group may be able to create a situation that puts populations at risk in the context of R2P. It would be useful if other researchers would look at this question as the Congolese context and the implementation of Resolution 2098 are *sui generis.*

What will be of interest to the research is the implementation of the resolution against OAGs, since it is only then that one will be able to determine IHL violations in the implementation of R2P. In practice, however, the Brigade has only intervened against "well-organized" rebel groups.

According to the Brigade Force Commander, it is more appropriate to launch offensives against organized groups like the M23, LRA and the ADF.[391] So far, the majority of interventions have been launched only against these three groups.

Indeed, many would like to know the criteria on which the Brigade bases its determination that armed group X is organized while armed group Y

389 Nils Melzer, "Interpretive guidance on the notion of direct participation in hostilities under international humanitarian law", *International Committee of the Red Cross*, 2009, p. 27.

390 Scott, Sheeran and Stephanie Case, *The Intervention Brigade: Legal issues for the UN in the Democratic Republic of the Congo.* New York: International Peace Institute, 2014, p.5.

391 *Interview with LTG Marcos Affonso da Costa.*

is not.[392] As the answer to this question is not clear, the recommendation is that if there is a guiding principle, it should be the same across all missions to ensure coherence of UN actions. This will allow the public to understand the UN's missions in the protection of populations. In the territory of Rutshuru, for example, where the Brigade intervened, many wondered about the understanding of the Brigade's mandate contained in Resolution 2098. Indeed, this territory has witnessed several other mass human rights violations such as the burning of villages, killings, kidnappings (even of humanitarians), just a few meters from the Brigade's base without any reaction from them.[393] All this on the grounds that the armed groups involved in these attacks are not "well organized".

It should be noted that these two criteria (intensity and organization) are *sine qua none* conditions for the qualification of an NIAC and any situation, regardless of the objective of the parties to the conflict, that does not meet these conditions would be assimilated to other forms of internal violence that IHL does not cover, or at least, that common Article 3 does not cover.[394] Whether it is common Article 3 or Additional Protocol II, NIAC's jurisdiction *ratione loci* is limited to the territories of the High Contracting Party.

Furthermore, as mentioned above, the Brigade engages in conflicts against foreign rebel groups such as the Forces Démocratiques de Libération du Rwanda (FDLR), The Allied Democratic Forces (ADF), The Lord's Resistance Army (LRA) and Forces nationales de libération (FNL). It is not the foreign character of a rebel group that can change the nature of a NIAC into an IAC. For this conflict to be considered as an IAC, there is one criterion that must be met: Overall control.

Overall control is defined as the role of a foreign state in the organization, coordination or planning of military actions by an armed group. This control also includes the financial support, training, equipment and/or

392 Ashley Deeks, "How Does the UN Define 'Direct Participation in Hostilities'?" *Lawfare (blog)*, October 21, 2013, available at www.lawfareblog.com/2013/10/how-does-the-un-define-direct-participation-in-hostilities/, on 06 August 2020.

393 Mugombozi, 77.

394 The International Criminal Tribunal for the former Yugoslavia, in the Limaj case, recalls that the two criteria of intensity and organisation of the parties are mandatory and exhaustive in determining the existence of an armed conflict and this "regardless of whether the objective of the armed forces was limited to committing acts of violence", For more details see ICTY, *Limaj Case, Judgment of 30 November 2005*, para. 170.

operational input of the armed group by the foreign state.[395] However, the fact that the foreign state does not directly direct, through specific orders, all operations of the rebel group would not hinder the existence of an IAC.[396]

Indeed, there is no evidence to date that Rwanda, Uganda and Burundi have overall control over the FDLR, ADF, LRA and FNL respectively. There is no evidence on the ground that would lead researchers to believe that these rebel groups are acting in the names and on behalf of their home states.[397] As proof, both countries have even signed agreements with the DRC to neutralize these groups. For instance, on 26.11.2021, the president of DRC authorized the deployment of Ugandan armed forces to fight ADF.[398]Rwanda has intervened legally in the eastern part of DRC in order to fight and destroy FDLR.[399]

Meanwhile, the nature of the M23 rebel group raised questions about the nature of the conflict as well. In the light of the facts on the ground and several other sources, the M23 rebel group is said to be acting on behalf of Rwanda. Here, it is necessary to distinguish between two different armed conflicts triggered by the M23 group. One, in 2012, was even the basis for the adoption of resolution 2098 and the other was triggered 10 years later, in 2022.

The cessation of fighting in the first conflict in 2013 was the very result of the implementation of resolution 2098, as the rebel group had been defeated and deposed by the Brigade in collaboration with the FARDC. It is worth noting that even though Rwanda has always been accused, rightly or wrongly, of supporting the M23, the latest clashes in 2022 and early 2023 would lead many to reflect on the overall control that Rwanda would exercise over this latter group.

---

395 ICTY, *Tadić (Appeals Chamber), Judgment of 15 July 1999,* at paras. 131, 137.

396 Gabor Kajtar, "An overall critique of the overall control test", *Gabor Kajtar: An overall critique of the overall control test,* Zsuzsanna Csapó (Ed.), Emlékkötet Herczegh Géza születésének 85, 2018, p. 87.

397 The ICTY judges in the Tadic case noted that the rebel group must be acting on behalf of a state to establish an IAC.International Criminal Tribunal for the former Yugoslavia (ICTY), *Tadic Case, Judgment of 15 July 1999,* para. 84

398 Romain Gras, *DRC allows Uganda's army to enter Congolese territory to fight the ADF,* 02.12.2021 available at https://www.theafricareport.com/151989/drc-allows-ugandas-army-to-enter-congolese-territory-to-fight-the-adf/, on 29 August 2020.

399 *DR Congo: A comprehensive strategy to disarm the FDLR,* 09.07.2009 available at https://reliefweb.int/report/democratic-republic-congo/dr-congo-comprehensive-strategy-disarm-fdlr, on 29 August 2020.

In December 2022, the Group of Experts of the United Nations reported on the existence of "substantial evidence" of "direct intervention by the Rwandan defence forces" in the DRC alongside the M23 rebels between November 2021 and October 2022. In its letter to the UN Security Council dated 6 December 2022, the Group of Experts identified the nature of Rwanda's intervention in two main points: First of all, the direct intervention of the Rwandan Defence Force on the territory of the Democratic Republic of the Congo, either to reinforce the M23/ARC or to conduct military operations against the Forces Démocratiques de Libération du Rwanda (FDLR); and secondly the supply of arms, ammunition and uniforms to the M23/ARC.[400]

Several other sources confirm the direct intervention of Rwandan armed forces alongside the M23 in the clashes that took place on Congolese territory in late 2022 and early 2023.[401]

From all of the above discussion, some would be tempted to conclude that the conflict between the FARDC and the M23 is an IAC, described by the Congolese government as an "act of war". Hence, the Brigade intervened in an IAC. This is confirmed by the fact that the brigade's command force has been requesting arms supplies from the Security Council since June 2022 to fight the M23 group[402], which they have described as a "modern army".[403]

Beyond the above points, even though some authors believe that the mere intervention of the UN in a conflict would change the nature of an NIAC into an IAC[404], this thesis is opposed to this argument. Indeed, IHL and international law in general provide for two situations that can change

400 *S/2022/967, Mid-term report of the Group of Experts pursuant to paragraph 6 of resolution 2641,* 2022, 16 December 2022, available at https://documents-dds-ny.un.org/doc/UNDOC/GEN/N22/757/87/PDF/N2275787.pdf, accessed on, 26th September 2024.

401 *DR Congo: The atrocities of the Rwandan-backed M23 rebellion*, 06.02.2023 available at https://www.hrw.org/fr

402 Interview with LTG Marcos De Sa Affonso Da Costa.

403 Antonio Guterres stated in September 2022, shortly before the opening of the 77th session of the UN General Assembly in New York that: the M23 is today a modern army, with heavy equipment that is more advanced than the equipment of MONUSCO and that equipment comes from somewhere. "They were not born in the forest", available at https://www.dw.com/en/congo-crisis-in-focus-at-un-general-assembly/a-63196552, accessed on, 26th September 2024.

404 Ray Murphy, "United National military operations and international humanitarian law: What rules apply to peacekeepers?", *Criminal Law Forum*, vol. 14, 2003, p. 183. See also Ashley Deeks, *How Does the UN Define 'Direct Participation in Hostilities'?*,

an NIAC into an IAC. These are the situations in which non-state actors are fighting on behalf of a state and the situation of what treaties/customs call territorial entities.[405]

Thus, until now, International Law has not provided for the intervention of an international organization as capable of distorting the qualification of a conflict. In the current state of affairs, IACs take place between states either directly or by proxy. Since the UN is neither a state nor an armed group, its intervention, regardless of its objective, does not distort the conflict. It is therefore clear that the Brigade, through resolution 2098, intervened in non-international armed conflicts and in an international armed conflict. Situations that imply the applicability of IHL.

2. Legal consequences of applicability of IHL to the implementation of resolution 2098

The applicability of IHL to a given situation has implications. Although these implications depend on the IAC to the NAC, the protection of those who are not or no longer participating in combat remains a priority of this branch of law. To this end, IHL elaborates principles such as distinction, necessity and proportionality to better protect individuals. The Geneva Conventions, the Additional Protocols and the customary rules on the conduct of conflicts confirm these principles. International criminal tribunals have returned to the practicality of these principles.

Indeed, from the moment UN forces participate in hostilities, which may be qualified as a conflict by IHL, these forces become a party to the conflict or a combatant as the case may be. The concept of "party to the conflict" refers to parties taking part in a non-international armed conflict. While the concept of combatant refers to parties taking part in an international armed conflict. A combatant is a person who is authorized to use force in situations of armed conflict and not to be punished for the use of such force as long as it is in conformity with IHL. Such use of force is permissible under international law not when it is the result of an individual decision, but

21.10.2013, available at https://www.lawfaremedia.org/article/how-does-un-define-direct-participation-hostilities, accessed on, 26th September 2024.

405 Marko Milanovic, "What Exactly International izes an Internal Armed Conflict?" *Blog of the European Journal of International Law,* May 7, 2010, available at https://www.ejiltalk.org/, accessed on, 26th September 2024. See also Natia Kalandarishvili-Mueller, "Transforming a Prima Facie NIAC into an IAC: Finding the Answer in IHL", *Israel Law Review 53.3*, 2020, pp. 334-354.

rather of a chain of command. In accordance with the Geneva Conventions and their First Additional Protocol of 1977, combatants are members of the national army or organized groups under the effective control of those forces. From this definition, it can be directly understood that only forces belonging to States or acting for and on behalf of a state can be considered as combatants. In the third Geneva Convention, the notion of combatant refers directly to the notion of prisoner of war in IAC.

Additional Protocol 1 specifies in Article 43 (2) that combatants are armed forces of a party to the conflict with the exception of medical personnel and chaplains.[406] This definition equalizes the regimes of protection and responsibility to all those participating in the conflict. While the distinction between civilians and combatants is maintained, the second Additional Protocol reverts to the protection of both categories. The nature of civilians participating in the conflict is also regulated by Additional Protocol 2. Although the combatant cannot be punished for using force in an armed conflict, he or she can be prosecuted before international and national courts for violating the rules of IHL by committing war crimes, crimes against humanity, genocide and other violations of IHL.

It should be noted that the concept of "combatant" has been used in both international and national armed conflicts.[407] In the latter case, it is used only in its usual context, recalling only that those who participate in conflicts lose their protection and not in its practical sense, as this would only be possible in IAC contexts.

It should also be noted that this definition of a combatant in the Geneva Convention and its Protocol has acquired a customary character.[408] Several States have adopted this definition in their national legislation and reiterated their commitment to its respect.[409]

406 Article 43 (2) API.

407 UN General Assembly, *Res. 2676 (XXV)*, 9 December 1970, preamble and para. 5; see also *Cairo Declaration, paras 68-69 and Cairo Plan of Action*, para 82, both adopted at the Africa-Europe Summit under the auspices of the Organisation of African Unity and the European Union, 3-4 April 2000.

408 *Commentary on Rule 3, IHL Databases,* available at https://ihl-databases.icrc.org/fr/customary-ihl/v1/rule3

409 The German and US military manuals indicate that there may be other non-combatant members of the armed forces in addition to medical and religious personnel. The German military manual indicates that combatants are persons who may take a direct part in hostilities. For this manual, direct participation in hostilities means participation in the use of a weapon or weapon system by performing an indispensable function. Thus, there may be persons who are members of the armed forces

However, the main instruments of IHL such as the Geneva Conventions and their Additional Protocols have not provided for peacekeeping activities and in particular, for peacekeeping forces. These peacekeeping activities were not foreseen because in the formal conception, it was almost inconceivable that peacekeepers would be considered parties to the conflict because their involvement did not affect the qualifications of the conflict. However, practice on the ground has shown that the actions of peacekeepers are not different from those of persons qualified as parties to the conflict. As one of the objectives of IHL is the equal treatment of all parties to a conflict, clarification of the status of peacekeepers was necessary.

Indeed, the discussion on the respect of IHL by peacekeeping forces is not recent. In the 1960s, recommendations were made to the UN in regards to the applicability of and compliance with the rules of IHL by these forces. These include the resolutions adopted at the 20th International Conference of the Red Cross,[410] the 52nd Conference of the International Law Association (ILA)[411] and the resolution on the "Conditions of the Application of Humanitarian Rules of Armed Conflict to Hostilities in which United Nations Forces May Be Engaged," of 1971.[412]

Even when the UN was resistant in its capacity as a party to the Geneva Conventions and their Additional Protocols, the organization recognized the application of IHL to peacekeeping operations decided under Chapter VII of the UN Charter. The UN General Assembly appears to have recognized this in the 1994 Convention on the Safety of United Nations and Associated Personnel.[413]

In addition, the UN recognizes the mandatory nature of these rules in its operations through agreements signed between the UN and host states or troop contributing countries.

---

but who do not have a combat mission, such as judges, civil servants and manual workers. The latter are then non-combatants. *Germany,* Military Manual (cited in Vol. II, Ch. 1, para. 587).

410 The Resolution of 1965 is reproduced in handbook of the international red cross and red crescent movement, 13th ed., 1994, p.748.

411 Paul C. Szasz, "UN Forces and international humanitarian law", *International Law Studies 75,* no.1, 2000, p.3.

412 Keiichiro Okimoto, "The Legal Protection of Personnel of United Nations Peacekeeping Operations in Times of NIAC", *international Humanitarian Law and Non-State Actors: Debates, Law and Practice, 2020, p.100.*

413 *Convention on the Safety of United Nations and Associated Personnel,* 1994, available at https://www.un.org/law/cod/safety.htm, accessed on, 26th September 2024.

Thus, for example, the SOFA states that:

"Without prejudice to the mandate of [force acronym - hereafter UNX] and its international status: (a) the United Nations shall ensure that UNX conducts its operations in [host State] in full compliance with the principles and spirit of the general conventions applicable to the conduct of military personnel. These international conventions include the four Geneva Conventions of 12 August 1949 and their Additional Protocols of 8 June 1977, as well as the UNESCO Convention of 14 May 1954 for the Protection of Cultural Property in the Event of Armed Conflict. (b) The Government undertakes to treat UN military personnel at all times in full compliance with the principles and spirit of the general international conventions applicable to the treatment of military personnel. These international conventions include the four Geneva Conventions of 12 August 1949 and their additional protocols of 8 June 1977. The UNX and the Government will therefore ensure that their respective military personnel are fully aware of the principles and spirit of the above-mentioned international instruments."[414]

The obligation of peacekeepers to respect IHL was provided for in the Secretary-General's Bulletin entitled "Respect for International Humanitarian Law by United Nations Forces" (hereinafter "Bulletin") of 6 August 1999.

While making it clear that it is not exhaustive in relation to the rules of IHL applicable to peacekeeping forces in armed conflict, the Bulletin states that peacekeepers are obliged to respect IHL, either because their home States are bound by these instruments or as customary rules.[415]

The scope of this Bulletin is limited to operations under the command and control of the UN. It should be noted here that all other operations not under direct UN control, although authorized under Chapter VII, are not covered by the Bulletin.[416] The contingents in these operations are subject to the rules of IHL binding their respective States with other parties to the conflict.

414 Section 3 of the Secretary,General's Bulletin provides that in SOFAs the United Nations will ensure that its forces fully respect "the general conventions applicable to the conduct of military personnel", These obligation still biding even in the absence of SOFA. That states the situation of Peace enforcement operations which may occurs without former consent of the State and that its forces be fully acquainted with these principles and rules. It is further stated that the same obligations are to apply even in the absence of a SOFA.

415 Article 2 of the Bulletin.

416 Article 5 of the Bulletin.

Indeed, in addition, the Bulletin provides that IHL is applicable to UN forces when they are actively engaged in an armed conflict as combatants for the duration of their engagement.[417] This first article of the Bulletin admits that the Blue Helmets can be considered as a party to the conflict for a given period of time in relation to their active engagement in the fighting. This latter analysis does not meet the IHL applicable to the NIAC, which specifies that the status of party to the conflict is to be maintained in relation to the duration of the conflict. There is no need to recall that the Brigade is a force authorized by UNSCR 2098 and is placed under the direct command of MONUSCO which is a UN mission. The nature of the Brigade would not pose any problem in relation to the applicability of IHL by these forces, as foreseen by the Bulletin.

The creation of the Brigade by resolution 2098 has resulted in a new understanding of the applicability of IHL to UN forces in relation to their participation in the conflict. It is worth noting that it is with the Brigade that, for the first time, the United Nations General Secretariat has publicly acknowledged that peacekeeping forces can become parties to conflicts in the DRC.[418]

Indeed, the context of the Brigade's intervention on the ground prompted the UN Legal Counsel to recognize that MONUSCO would be considered a party to the conflict given its new mandate to use all necessary measures, including force to neutralize rebel groups.[419]

This was new to the UN view that peacekeepers are "world policemen" as they use force to maintain international peace and security on behalf of all humanity in the international community.[420] This understanding has, for many years, confirmed the view that forces working for international peace could not be considered a party to the conflict.

---

417 Article 1 of the Bulletin.

418 Patricia O'Brien, "Respecting IHL: Challenges and Responses", *statement made at 36th Roundtable on Current Issues of International Humanitarian Law,* San Remo, Italy, September 5, 2013, available at http://legal.un.org/ola/media/info_from_lc/POB-San-Remo-36th-Roundtable-5-September-2013.pdf, accessed on, 26th September 2024.

419 Patricia O'Brien, *statement by the under-secretary-general for Legal Affairs and UN legal counsel delivered to the International Law Commission,* Geneva, May 23, 2013, available at http://legal.un.org/ilc/sessions/65/Statement%20byTheLegal%20Counsel.pdf.

420 Devon Whittle, "Peacekeeping in conflict: The Intervention Brigade, MONUSCO and the application of international humanitarian law to United Nations forces", *Geo. J. Int'l L. 46,* 2014, p. 837.

Since 2013, the UN's legal position has publicly referred to the possibility of peacekeeping forces becoming a party to the conflict.[421]

Even though the UN is not a party to the Geneva Conventions and other IHL instruments, it is accepted that the rules of IHL are applicable to the UN and its forces. The Brigade will not then make an exception.[422] Indeed, although Resolution 2098 did not provide for the status of the Brigade force, it did provide in paragraph 12(b) that the Brigade will respect the rules of IHL.

In accordance with this paragraph, the Brigade must take robust measures in strict compliance with international law in general and international humanitarian law and human rights law in accordance with the policy on UN-support to non-UN forces (HRDDP).[423]

Thus, when the Brigade engages in combat against the rebels, it must respect all the rules and customs of IHL. Indeed, the Brigade must respect the principles of IHL contained in the Geneva Conventions and their Additional Protocols such as: the principle of distinction, humanity, necessity, precaution and proportionality. Although some of these principles, such as the principle of precaution, have not been taken up by Additional Protocol II in relation to non-international armed conflicts, the doctrine argues that respect for this principle would be mandatory by virtue of its customary nature.[424] In the Kupreskic case, the International Criminal Tribunal for the former Yugoslavia reconsidered the precautionary principle and its content in the context of non-international armed conflict.[425] This thesis will elaborate on these principles later in the analysis of the Brigade's responsibility for IHL violations in the implementation of R2P.

---

421 UN Office of Legal Affairs (OLA) representative Mona Ali Khalil, panel discussion, "Humanitarian Law, Peacekeeping/Intervention Forces and Troop-Contributing Countries: Issues and Challenges", *Asian-African Legal Consultative Organization (AALCO),* United Nations, New York, August 21, 2013; and Mona Ali Khalil, "Peace Forces at War", *panel discussion at the annual general meeting of the American Society of International Law,* April 7–12, 2014.

422 United Nations, *Report of the Special Committee on Peacekeeping Operations and its Working Group on the 2007 Resumed Session, UN Doc. A/61/19 (Part III),* June 12, 2007.

423 Para 12, *UNSC resolution 2098,* 2013.

424 Jean Marie Henckaerts and Louise Doswald-Beck, *Droit international humanitaire,* Bruylant, CICR, 2 vol. 2006, available at https://www.icrc.org/fre/assets/files/other/icrc_001_pcustom.pdf.

425 ICTY, *Prosecutor v. Zoran Kupreskic et al, judgment,* 14 Jan. 2000, § 49 and 132.

In addition, in view of the fact that the Brigade is actively engaged in the conflicts in the DRC, it would be appropriate to expect the Brigade to adhere to and respect the Copenhagen Process Principles and Guidelines on the Application of International Humanitarian Law in Situations of Armed Conflict. These principles, although not binding, provide a general safeguard clause to ensure the continued applicability of international law to military operations conducted by states, international organizations or non-state actors.[426] It should be noted that these principles apply in situations of NIACs.

Beyond the obligations of parties to conflicts in general, IHL also offers "benefits" to combatants. A theory of what might be termed a "right to kill" remains one of these advantages in an international armed conflict. Indeed, IHL recognizes the right of parties to attack "military objectives" even when this would result in civilian or collateral damage, where this is proportional to the military advantage.[427]

Thus, as long as the Brigade has the right to attack the military objectives of rebel groups, it will also be considered a target by those groups. In the implementation of resolution 2098, the Brigade's forces have the status of combatant and party to the conflict: combatant through their participation in an international armed conflict and party to the conflict through their participation in a non-international one. In both cases, this results in the Brigade losing its usual protection under IHL.

Indeed, UN forces enjoy special protection under international humanitarian law. This protection is enshrined in several international and national legal instruments, as well as in customary rules of IHL. The Fourth Geneva Convention and Additional Protocol I of 1977, for example, contain articles that protect humanitarian activities. Many believe that as these provisions do not apply to military operations, this would not apply *mutatis mutandi* to peacekeepers.[428]The protection contained in Article 63 of the IV Geneva Convention would apply to UN organizations such as UNICEF, UNHCR, UNOCHA as it only covers non-military activities.[429]

426 Michael Matheson and Djamchid Momtaz, *Rules and Institutions of International Humanitarian Law Put to the Test of Recent Armed Conflicts*, Brill/Nijhoff, 2011.

427 Brig-Gen. James Mwakibolwa Aloizi, "NGOs Concerned about New DRC Intervention Brigade." *IRIN News*, May 31, 2013, available at www.irinnews.org/report/98140/ngos-concerned-about-new-drc-intervention-brigade, accessed on, 26th September 2024.

428 Szasz, *UN Forces and international humanitarian law*, 6.

429 Art 63, *Geneva Convention IV.*

In the meantime, in accordance with UNSC resolutions, peacekeepers can have both military and humanitarian missions. The mandates of the UN forces are generally divided into 3 but with a fourth possibility, which is more practical than doctrinal.[430]

One distinguishes between the mandates of peace keeping, peacemaking, peace building and solely humanitarian tasks. Although the latter mandate has been observed in the support of peacekeepers for other international and national organizations in the framework of humanitarian assistance, in recent practice, peacekeepers intervene directly and on their own in humanitarian actions. This is the case, for example, of MONUSCO in the DRC, which, in addition to accompanying non-governmental organizations in humanitarian activities, has intervened independently in the distribution of food, the construction of displaced persons' fields, medical assistance to displaced persons and the wounded during conflicts and the organization of protection convoys for humanitarian operations.

From all the above, this thesis would argue that Blue Helmets can benefit from the protection provided by the IV Geneva Convention and the Additional Protocol I, when they have a humanitarian mission. This protection, in fact, would be granted to them, not in relation to their nature but rather in relation to their activities. Thus, for example, an attack on a UN force in the midst of a humanitarian activity, regardless of its nature (created by a GA, ECOSOC or SC resolution), would be in violation of the Fourth Geneva Convention and Additional Protocol I.

This would be the case of attacks on the cohorts of humanitarian organizations convoyed by blue helmets. Such attacks, at least in the opinion of this research, will be considered as prohibited attacks under the Fourth Geneva Convention.

The protection of peacekeeping forces is directly addressed in Rule 33. This rule provides that it is prohibited to launch an attack against personnel and material employed in a peacekeeping mission in accordance with the Charter of the United Nations, provided that they are entitled to the protection of civilians or civilian objects under international humanitarian law.[431] Similarly, in accordance with Regulation 7, equipment used in a

430 Lise Morjé, Howard and Dayal, Anjali Kaushlesh, "The use of force in UN peacekeeping", International *Organization 72.1,* 2018, p. 83.

431 Rule 33, *Customary Law.*

peacekeeping operation is considered civilian objects and as such protected from attack.[432]

This idea is in line, moreover, with the protection of UN forces as provided for by the 1994 Safety Convention and that provided for by the 1993 Bulletin. Indeed, the 1994 Convention provides that UN Forces enjoy special protection like civilians.[433] This has been rejected by the Bulletin in that its promulgation will not affect the status of the protectors of members of peacekeeping operations under the Convention as they are associated with civilians under IHL.[434]

The protection of UN forces is further provided for by the Protocol on Prohibitions or Restrictions on the Use of Mines, Booby-Traps and Other Devices as amended on 3 May 1996. Indeed, in accordance with Article 12 para 2(i) and (ii), peace missions and all other UN missions decided under the UN Charter are protected. Missions established under Chapter VIII of the Charter are also covered.[435]

Thus, any attack on peacekeeping forces and their installations would constitute a war crime. This formulation has been used by international criminal tribunals such as the Statute of the Special Court for Sierra Leone[436] and the ICC Statute.[437]

For example, the Rome Statute stipulates in Article 8 the elements of the definition of "war crimes" as any attack : Intentionally directed against personnel, installations, material, units or vehicles involved in humanitarian assistance or a peacekeeping mission in accordance with the Charter of the United Nations, as long as they are entitled to the protection given to civilians or civilian objects under the intonational law of armed conflict,

432 Rule 7, *Customary law.*

433 José Doria, Hans-Peter Gasser and Cherif M. Bassiouni, (Eds.) *The legal regime of the International Criminal Court: essays in honour of Professor Igor Blishchenko,* Vol. 19, Brill, 2009.

434 Paragraph 1.2 of the Bulletin, Arts 8(2)(b)(iii) and 8(2)(e)(iii), *Elements of Crimes, ICCSt.; Judgment, Sesay, Kallon and Gbao,* ('RUF') (SCSL-04-15-T), *Trial Chamber I, 2 March 2009 (RUF Trial Judgment),* Para 215.

435 Article 12, *Protocol on Prohibitions or Restrictions on the Use of Mines, Booby-Traps and Other Devices as amended on 3 May 1996 (Protocol II to the 1980 Convention as amended on 3 May 1996).*

436 *Statute of Sierra Leone Tribunal, art. 4, al. 1 b) (ibid., par) 217-239.* See also Wharton, Sara. "The Evolution of International Criminal Law: Prosecuting'New'Crimes before the Special Court for Sierra Leone", *International Criminal Law Review 11,* no. 2, 2011, pp. 217-239.

437 *Statut de la CPI (1998)*, art. 8, par. 2, al. b) iii) et art. 8, par. 2, al. e) iii) .

whether these take place in an "international armed conflict" or in an "armed conflict not of an international character.

In ICTY[438] and ICTR[439] jurisprudence, individuals have been either charged or convicted for perpetrating attacks against peacekeepers, the latter being considered as civilians.

The prohibition and condemnation of attacks on UN forces in general and peacekeeping forces in particular has also been reflected in the legislation of States[440] and international organizations.[441]In Congolese law, an attack against peacekeeping forces and those of the African Union is a constitutive element of a war crime.[442]

In addition to the above, all of the above-mentioned texts are limited to the protection of peacekeeping forces as long as they do not take part in conflicts. These instruments do not cover missions decided exceptionally under Chapter VI[443] and generally under Chapter VII of the UN Charter. Indeed, the implementation of peace enforcement mandates leads, in most cases, to UN forces becoming parties to the conflict. This would lead them to be considered as combatants and thus fall under the Third Geneva

438 *Decision on Appeal from Denial of Judgment of Acquittal for Hostage Taking, Karadzkic (IT-95-5/ l8-AR73.9), Appeals Chamber,* 11 December 2012 (*Karadzkic*).

439 In the case Decision on the Prosecutor's Motion to Withdraw the Indictment, *Ntuyahaga (ICTR-98-40-T), Trial Chamber I, 28 September 1998,* Bernard Ntuyahaga was accused of murdering 10 Belgian peacekeepers as part of a widespread and systematic attack against a civilian population, but the Prosecution decided to withdraw the charges. However, in the case The Prosecutor v. Augustin Ndindiliyimana, François-Xavier Nzuwonemeye and Innocent Sagahutu, ICTR-00556-A,27.02.2014, Nzuwonemeye and Sagahutu were convicted for killing of Belgian Peacekeepers as serious as a serious violation of Art. 3 common to the Geneva Conventions and of Additional Protocol II in the Military II case. *Judgment, Ndindiliyimana et al. (ICTR-00-56), Appeals Chamber, 11 February 2014 (Military II Appeals Judgment),* para 323.

440 See for example Germany, Law Introducing the International Crimes Code, 2002, Article 1, § 10(1)(1). This Law punishes anyone who directs an attack against personnel, installations, material, units or vehicles involved in a peace-keeping mission in accordance with the Charter of the United Nations.

441 Several UN resolutions have reiterated the obligations of all parties in relation to the protection of peacekeeping forces and the condemnation of attacks against them. UN Security Council, Res. 819, 16 April 1993, preamble and § 10, UN Security Council, Res. 1592, 30 March 2005, preamble and § 2, UN Security Council, Res. 837, 6 June 1993, preamble, ect.

442 *Section 3, Article 223.2 (c) of Law No. 15/022 of 31 December 2015 amending and supplementing the Decree of 30 January 1940 on the Criminal Code (Translated).*

443 This would be the case of a peacekeeping mission, which may, for reasons of self-defense and within the limits of their mandates, resort to force.

Convention. The Brigade, although a UN force, will not benefit from this protected status under IHL, as it will be considered as a combatant. Since the adoption and implementation of resolution 2098, an increase in attacks against MONUSCO forces has been observed. Some would consider this to be a consequence of the nature of these Brigade Forces as possible targets for attack by rebel groups. Indeed, when the Security Council created the Brigade, it did not, in legal terms, separate it from MONUSCO. Although the Brigade has a specific mandate that is not that of MONUSCO in general, this force is an integral part of MONUSCO.

In accordance with paragraph 9 of Resolution 2098, the Brigade is placed under the same command force as the other regular MONUSCO forces.[444] Both forces use the same UN emblem and blue helmets,[445] share the same military base,[446] the same logistical means and sometimes the same areas of operation. MONUSCO has three sectors plus the Brigade: The Northern sector operates in Ituri, the Central sector in North Kivu and the Southern sector in South Kivu. However, the Intervention Brigade, in accordance with its mandate and the positioning of the rebel groups, operates in all sectors.[447] Another element that demonstrates this mixture between the Brigade and MONUSCO is found in paragraph 12 of the resolution 2098, which authorized MONUSCO to fulfil the mandate included in the resolution by its regular forces and the Brigade if necessary.[448]

In the implementation of the resolution, moreover, several joint operations have been conducted by the Brigade and MONUSCO regular forces. This necessarily has an impact on the ground as it will be difficult to distinguish who is likely to be a military target and who is not.

Furthermore, MONUSCO has three categories of personnel: civilian personnel with peace-building activities, non-brigade military personnel and brigade forces. When all these forces are lumped together, confusion arises in relation to the applicable rules of IHL. Where MONUSCO civilian and ordinary military personnel would benefit from protected status under

444 Paragraph 9, *UNSC Resolution 2098*, 2013.

445 see comments of the Intervention Brigade force commander in "NGOs Concerned about New DRC Intervention Brigade", IRIN News.

446 Although one can identify the base of the Brigade, Goma and Beni, however, the Brigade and MONUSCO use the same military base. See also Tristan Ferraro, "The applicability and application of international humanitarian law to multinational forces", *International Review of the Red Cross 95*, no. 891-892, 2013, p. 566.

447 Interview with LTG Marcos Affonso da Costa.

448 Paragraph 12 (b).

IHL, Brigade personnel would be considered as combatants. But in the implementation of Resolution 2098, ordinary MONUSCO forces undertook joint operations with the Brigade. In this specific case, these forces lose their protection because they participate directly in the hostilities. This was noted in the 2014 report on MONUSCO.[449]

However, other military forces not directly involved in the conflict remain in an unclear situation.[450]This ambiguity has been noted even by some troop-contributing countries. Pakistan, one of the troop-contributing countries to MONUSCO and manager of Sector South, has insinuated that the Security Council's failure to separate the mandate of MONUSCO from that of the Brigade creates confusion in the applicable rules of IHL. This is because one enjoys special protection under IHL and the other does not. The country then revealed its fears in relation to the safety of its troops within MONUSCO without an offensive mandate.[451] This fear was also raised by other states, such as Rwanda, which felt that this confusion would lead directly to attacks on civilian personnel and all UN installations.[452]

During the Brigade's first offensive operations against the M23 rebel group in May 2013, one of the group's leaders stressed that it was difficult for them to apply the principle of distinction between civilians and a military objective within MONUSCO on the ground. Indeed, he had proposed that the fields of operation, or even the uniform of the Brigade and that of MONUSCO's regular forces, should be distinct.[453]

From all the above, after analysis of the first field operations, the position of the ICRC as well as that of the UN Office of Legal Affairs is that all the military components of MONUSCO are parties to the conflicts. This

---

449 *United Nations Mission in Democratic Republic of Congo Must Transform into 'Robust, Flexible, Highly Mobile' Entity, Security Council Told,* 14.03.2014 available at https://press.un.org/en/2014/sc11316.doc.htm, August 29, 2019.

450 Pacholska, Magdalena. "(Il) legality of killing peacekeepers: the crime of attacking peacekeepers in the jurisprudence of international criminal tribunals." *Journal of International Criminal Justice 13,* no. 1, 2015, pp. 43-72.

451 Whittle, *Peacekeeping in conflict, 840.*

452 *UN Security Council, Press Statement on Democratic Republic of Congo, UN Doc. SC/11108,* August 29, 2013.

453 "NGOs Concerned about New DRC Intervention Brigade", available at https://reliefweb.int/report/democratic-republic-congo/ngos-concerned-about-new-drc-intervention-brigade, *accessed on Jun 2020.*

conclusion can be read into the UN's reluctance to condemn the attacks and killings of MONUSCO forces by the M23 as a violation of IHL.[454]

Another analysis is linked to paragraph 12 (a)(iii) and (b) of Resolution 2098.[455]These two sections of this paragraph, in fact, stipulate that the Brigade in particular and MONUSCO in general, must collaborate with the FARDC, with a view to neutralizing rebel groups. This collaboration takes two forms. Firstly, it can be direct, i.e. the forces intervene alongside the FARDC and secondly, it is indirect through logistical and tactical support. While the first form does not pose a problem for the IHL status of MONUSCO forces participating directly in hostilities, the second form does raise questions about the status of these forces as parties to the conflict. This research considers that by providing direct military logistical support to a party to the conflict, the source of the support becomes a party to the conflict *mutatis mutandis*. In this case, as the FARDC is already a party to the conflict, MONUSCO becomes one through its support for the FARDC. Therefore, MONUSCO forces and installations can rightfully be considered as military targets and susceptible to attack.

The other and not the least impact of the application of IHL to the implementation of Resolution 2098, is the possibility for Brigade forces to detain detainees and POWs on the one hand and to be considered as POWs on the other. Indeed, although there are rules in IHL concerning the detention and transfer of detainees, there is no clear understanding in peacekeeping operations.

There is a body of law within the UN that sets out the conditions for the treatment of persons captured during and outside of conflict without detailing this treatment when UN forces are actively involved in the conflict. The Secretary-General's Bulletin and the UN-SOP (Standard Operating Procedure) are examples. Some might also add the Copenhagen Principles as an instrument relevant to the treatment of prisoners by international military forces, including peacekeeping forces.[456] However, the present thesis is in fact aligned with those who believe that it is not so clear that these

454 The killings may, however, be violations of national law of the DRC. See "Martin Kobler, Head of MONUSCO, Strongly Condemns the Killing of UN Peacekeeper by M23", *MONUSCO Press Release*, August 28, 2013.

455 Paragraph 12, *UNSC resolution 2098*, 2013.

456 Fred Nkusi, "Legal Implications of Shifting Paradigm: Intervention Brigade - MONUSCO's Enforcement Action in the DRC", *Berkeley Journal of International Law (BJIL)*, Vol. 2, No. 2, 2013, Available at SSRN: https://ssrn.com/abstract=2326376, accessed on 20th Jun 2020.

principles apply directly to UN forces.[457] Aware of this controversy over the application of the Copenhagen Principles to UN forces, a specific SOP for the implementation of Resolution 2098 has been developed. Furthermore, based on the experience of the implementation of interim SOPs by mainly MONUSCO and other UN missions such as MINUSMA and MINUSCA, a new Standard Operating Procedure on the Handling of Detention in United Nations Peacekeeping Operations and Special Political Missions has been adopted since January 2021 to replace the interim SOP.[458] This new SOP seems to take into account the challenges related to the application of the general rules and principles of detention contained in the Third[459] and Fourth[460] Geneva Conventions in the Secretary General's Bulletin. Indeed, these principles did not seem to fit the context of MONUSCO, which would be faced with the capture of persons who are members of armed groups and not of the Armed Forces, on the one hand and the time limit for the detention of captured persons, on the other. Thus, the MONUSCO SOP includes provisions for the detention of captured persons and their detention cannot be effective until "they cease to pose an imperative threat to the security of United Nations personnel, civilians or the DRC national authorities".[461]

---

457 Scott Sheeran and Stephanie Case, *The Intervention Brigade: Legal issues for the UN in the Democratic Republic of the Congo,* New York, International Peace Institute, 2014, Read also *The Copenhagen Process on the Handling of Detainees in International Military Operations: Principles and Guidelines,* 2012 available at http://um.dk/en/~/media/UM/English-site/Documents/Politics-d, accessed on 20th Jun 2020.

458 See *Standard Operating Procedure the handling of detention in united nations peacekeeping operations and special political missions 2021,* available at https://peacekeeping.un.org/en/standard-operating-procedure-handling-of-detention-united-nations-peacekeeping-operations.

459 The Third Geneva Convention applies during the period of IAC and harmonises the detention of members of the Armed Forces and their mercenaries until the end of hostilities.

460 Articles 42, 43 and 78 of the IV Geneva Convention deal with the conditions of treatment of detainees and their release. These articles, concerning civilians, do not seem to be appropriate to the context of the Brigade in the implementation of Resolution 2098.

461 Statement by Mr. Miguel de Serpa Soares Under-Secretary-General for Legal Affair on the 40th Annual Seminar for Diplomats on International Humanitarian Law jointly organized by the International Committee of the Red Cross and New York University School of Law available at https://www.un.org/ola/sites/www.un.org.ola/files/documents/2023/03/15032023-mss-ihl-icrc-nyu-seminar-speech.pdf, accessed on 20th Jun 2020.

In addition, another collaboration document was signed between the UN and the DRC as a rider to the SOFA in relation to ensuring the treatment of captured persons when they are handed over to DRC authorities.[462]

In the implementation of Resolution 2098, we note the captures during the clashes against the Mayi Mayi NDC (Nduma Defense of Congo) on 2.07.2014 in Banyampuli[463] and the "SOKOLA 1" (clean up in the local language Lingala) clashes against the ADF in January 2014 and November 2018.[464]

From all the above, however, it should be noted that no text, up to the writing of this thesis, mentions the possibility for the Brigade Forces to be captured as well. This thesis considers, in fact, that armed groups, although they are not being signatories of the Geneva Conventions and their additional protocols, are bound to respect the general conditions of detention in armed conflict as part of the rules of *jus cogens.* Therefore, UN peacekeepers detainees will benefit from the protection under IHL. However, a strong recommendation is made to the UN and all states to take up this element of detention of peacekeepers, not as a crime under IHL, as they are protected, but rather as a "prisoner of war" or "detainee" as the case may be. This research argues that the implementation of Resolution 2098, even today with the resurgence of rebel groups in the eastern part of the DRC, will be a basis for redefining the application of IHL by UN forces as a party to the conflict. Thus, an analysis of the application of IHL by the brigade forces is necessary in order to identify plausible violations of rights and principles applicable in armed conflict.

3. International Humanitarian Law violations during the implementation of R2P in DR Congo

Dealing with violations of IHL during the implementation of Resolution 2098 brings us back to the analysis of compliance with all IHL rules appli-

---

462 *Draft of Arrangement on the Treatment of Persons Handed Over by the United Nations Organization Stabilization Mission in the Democratic Republic of the Congo (MONUSCO) to the DRC authorities,* available at https://digitallibrary.un.org/record/3978485?ln=en, accessed on 20th Jun 2020.

463 Captured Maimai by the Brigade ,Olivier Darren, "One SANDF soldier killed and two wounded in dawn DRC attack", *African Defence Review,* published 19 December 2016, Retrieved 23 December 2016.

464 *FARDC and MONUSCO launch joint operations against ADF,* 16.11.2018 available at https://monusco.unmissions.org/en, accessed on 20th Jun 2020.

cable during an armed operation in a conflict. The Intervention Brigade intervened either directly or indirectly in the conflicts against the M23, APCLS, MAI-MAI, FDLR and ADF. Although it is up to a judge to qualify facts as violations of IHL, several situations during the implementation of the Resolution 2098 that could lead to such a classification can be envisaged. In the very first offensive against the M23, in August 2013, the Brigade launched operations against M23 in the territory of Rutshuru. These offensives led to the defeat of the M23 rebel group, which was entrenched in the Virunga mountains.

The main question here would be the examination of compliance with IHL before, during and after these operations. Two principles will be analyzed: distinction and precaution.

Considered as 'cardinal' and 'intransgressible' principle that forms part of the 'fabric' of IHL,[465]the principle of distinction prohibits directing attacks against civilians and civilian objects.[466] Thus, this principle should be respected before and during any attack in war. The Additional Protocol I provides for the definition of a civilian objective (Art. 52 (2) AP I) and adds a list of examples (cf. Art. 52 (3) AP I). A military objective, by contrast, is an objective which is not civilian and must be targeted. Two criteria must be met: firstly, the object must make an effective contribution to the enemy's military action. This involves analyzing the use, purpose, nature and location of the object in question. Secondly, the capture or destruction of the object would offer a definite military advantage to the other party.

To the question of whether the principle of distinction in determining a military objective was respected in the Brigade's first official offensive, we are tempted to agree with the States' interpretation of the nature of a military objective. Indeed, several States have specified that a specific part of the territory may be considered as a military objective if its total or partial destruction would offer a military advantage.[467] Therefore, Rutshuru territory was lawfully a military objective because it was occupied by the M23 rebels. Moreover, the military operation in this territory was most welcomed by all as it led to the defeat of M23. However, the question that remains is whether all the loss of life in the Ruthsuru territory in order to capture the M23

465 ICJ, *Legality of the Threat or Use of nuclear weapons, Advisory Opinion,* 1996, paras 78–79.

466 *Additional Protocol I (1977),* Articles 48, 51 and 52; *ICRC, Study on Customary International Humanitarian Law, 2005,* Rules 1 and 7.

467 Marco Sassòli, "Legitimate targets of attacks under international humanitarian law." *HPCR Policy Brief,* 2003.

HQs at Chanzu and Rumagambo can be considered as "collateral damage" and not as a specific violation of IHL. Indeed, there are additional rules to confirm that this specific military objective can be attacked. However, this attack can indeed become unlawful if it results in excessive collateral damage. It would therefore be appropriate to consider that the dropping of bombs on the villages of Rugari and Kisimba, which caused the death and injury of civilians, would be considered as violation of IHL. Thus, even where the attack is legal, precautionary measures to minimize the consequences of war on civilians must be considered. Furthermore, in order to substantiate this violation, an analysis of the precautionary principle in these attacks would enlighten the judge as to whether or not there was a violation of IHL.

The precautionary principle, in addition to the principle of distinction[468], requires that, in an IAC or INAC, all feasible precautions must be taken to avoid and, in any event, to minimize, loss of civilian life, injury to civilians and damage to civilian objects. Although this principle must be examined before and during operations, the question remains as to whether the precautionary principle contains an obligation of means or an obligation of results.

The present thesis would lean towards the binary tendency of considering both. That is, the obligation of means and the obligation of results. There is an obligation of means, because the parties to the conflict must take measures before and during an operation, to reduce harm to civilians. This analysis is in line with Articles 57(1) and 58(c) of AP I in the case of an IAC and Article 13(1) of AP II in the case of an NIAC. These two contexts must be added rules 15 and 23 of international customary law.

There is an obligation of result, moreover, because the effectiveness of the precautionary measures taken before and during the launch of military operations will only be proven by the results of operations on the ground. Only the effects of a military operation on civilians will prove whether the precautionary principle has been respected. Respect for this principle will only be tangible when a military operation has avoided or reduced to a minimum the loss of human life and damage to the civilian population.

This is further enriched by the fact that international criminal liability for failure to respect the precautionary principle will be established based on the facts on the ground. Returning to the joint military operations of

---

468 The link between the principle of distinction and that of precaution was analysed by the ICTY judge. ICTY, *Kupreškić case, Judgment* (ibid., §§ 49 and 132).

the Brigade together with FARDC, the precautionary principle should be considered with a view to avoiding the loss of human life in the villages of Rugari and Kisimba, which was done and praised, on the other hand, during the military operations in Rumangabo. A member of civil society said that messages asking civilians to leave the combat zones were relayed and passed on to the population.[469] To name but few, the principle of precaution was respected in the military operation of the Brigade-FARDC against ADF/Nalu of 11.02.2020 in Mbau in Beni territory.[470]

The same analysis could also be envisaged, with a view to establishing whether precautionary measures were respected in the Brigade-FARDC's operations that led to the capture of the armed groups' bases. These include the attacks of 10.12.2013 against the FDLR in Kalembe,[471] those against the Mayi-Mayi NDC (Nduma Defense of Congo) which led to the liberation of Pinga and that of Mpofi-Bunyampuli[472] in November 2014. Furthermore, the offensive operations against the ADF in Beni require another analysis of the principle of distinction in times of conflict. The FARDC Brigade's offensives against the ADF in Beni territory from 2014 to 2022 included the dropping of bombs against ADF strongholds. These operations led to the destruction of several ADF strongholds and their capture. Although the Brigade has not been directly involved in the current operations, it intervened directly in the very first operations. A former mayor of the town of Beni, speaking on condition of anonymity, confirms that he is in possession of videos showing Brigade forces behind a bomber, information that has not been denied by either the MONUSCO Force Commander or the FARDC.

Unlike other rebel groups such as the M23, the ADF are still in the forest with their women and children, as well as kidnapped civilians. This is proof enough of the difficulty of strict compliance with IHL in operations against the ADF, but also of the choice of method of warfare to be used. This was confirmed by MONUSCO's Chief Commander, who said that "after the

469 Interview with a member of civil society of Rutshuru, interview held in Goma, 12.07.2023.

470 Focus group with the population of Mbau, held at Mbau on 12th June 2023, available at https://peacekeeping.un.org/fr, accessed on 22th Jun 2020.

471 *"Sokola2" To Disarm the FDLR rwandan rebels*, 30.01.2015 available at https://monusco.unmissions.org/en.

472 *Recent population displacements following military operations in bunyampuli*, 12.078.2014 available at https://monusco.unmissions.org/en, accessed on 22th Jun 2020.

defeat of the M23, we reduced our weaponry and made changes to our forces, because fighting the ADF requires a different approach to warfare. We are calling on forces with hand-to-hand combat capacities and those capable of fighting in the jungle. But the location of their strongholds is still a problem, because they are set up in inaccessible places".[473]

Moreover, International Custom stipulates that indiscriminate attacks are prohibited. This statement, taken up by rule 11 of the International Customary Law and in the practice of States, has already acquired a customary character and must be strictly applied in situations of IAC and NIAC. This has been taken up in the case law of the ICJ[474] and the ICTY[475].

In accordance with rule 12 (b), the term "indiscriminate attacks" means "attacks in which methods or means of combat are used which cannot be directed against a specific military objective".

This was the case with the attacks (offensive or defensive)[476] by the FARDC and the Brigade against the ADF which, to put it mildly, could not clearly identify the military objectives of the ADF in order to spare those hors de combat and their property from the bombardments launched.

Thus, this Thesis aligns itself with those who believe that the reality on the ground in the clashes against the ADF would prove the major challenge linked to a strict application of the principle of distinction. This would lead many to conclude that the principle of distinction has been violated in almost all operations against the ADF. This was confirmed by the Brigade's attitude a little later, when it suspended its collaboration with the FARDC and denounced the warlike approach taken by the joint operations between the FARDC and the UPDF, which it said, "did not respect IHL by failing to distinguish between civilians, women and children and armed forces in their operations". The Beni Brigade Commander, quoted from Mavivi, states that FARDC-UPDF operations carry out attacks without discrimination and in violation of IHL.[477]

In fact, IHL protects women and children during both CAI and CANI periods. Although this protection derives mainly from the general protec-

473 Interview with LTG Marcos Affonso da Costa.

474 ICY, *Procutor v. Strugar, case No IT-01-42-A,* judgement 17 jully 2008, par. 178.

475 ICTY, *Prosecutor v. Dario Kordić and Mario C^ erkez, Decision on the Joint Defence Motion* (ibid., para. 136) and *Prosecutor v. Zoran Kupreškić et al, Judgment (ibid., para. 137)* and *Prosecutor v. Duško Tadić, Judgment on the Defence Appeal on the Preliminary Objection to Jurisdiction (ibid., para. 134).*

476 The term "attacks" means "acts of violence against the adversary, whether such acts are offensive or defensive",

477 Interview with the Brigade commander in Beni, held in Beni/Mavivi 22.06.2023.

tion of civilians or persons not taking part in conflicts, there is also special protection for women and children under international law. An analysis of the Geneva Conventions and their Additional Protocols clarifies the status of children and women as protected persons. Articles 14, 17, 23, 24(2) and 24(3) of the Fourth Geneva Convention and many others specify the special treatment reserved for children during armed conflict. Articles 12 of the GCI and GCIII, Article 14 of the GCIIII, Article 27(2) of the GCI IV and Articles 75 and 76 of the IAP refer to the protection reserved for women. Whilst it should be noted that certain articles deal specifically with the protection of women in childbirth, it should be pointed out that women in general benefit from special protection under International Humanitarian Law. In practice and in accordance with Article 14 of GC III, parties to conflicts can even create safety zones to protect women and children. This was the case with the Safety Zone created in Bosnia-Herzegovina in 1993 by Resolution 19 of 16 April 1993 (S/res. 819). The concept of the Safety Zone was also used in the situations in Tuzla, Bihac, Zelpa, Sarajevo and Gorazde (S/res. 824).

The situation on the ground in Beni, according to several sources, stresses that children and women are involved in the massacres. This was confirmed by an FARDC authority, an ANR agent and survivors interviewed on the spot.[478]

This situation gives rise to an important debate about the loss of "protected" status under IHL for women and children taking part in the massacres. Protected status ceases when a person takes a direct or active part in hostilities. Direct participation in hostilities refers to specific acts committed by individuals as part of the conduct of hostilities between parties to an armed conflict.

The following cumulative criteria must be met in order to speak of direct participation in hostilities: the nuisance threshold, direct causation and the belligerency link.[479]

The harm threshold is explained by the fact that the act must be likely to impair the military operations or military capability of a party to an armed conflict, or the act must be such as to cause loss of life, injury or destruction to persons or property protected against direct attack. The direct causation

478 Focus group with survivors of ADF massacres in Eringeti, held in Eringeti 20.06.2023.

479 Christine Byron, "Direct participation in hostilities", *International Conflict and Security Law: A Research Handbook*, The Hague, TMC Asser Press, 2022, p.297.

criterion, for its part, simply specifies that there must be a direct causal relationship between the act and the harmful effects likely to result from that act or from a coordinated military operation of which that act forms an integral part. The belligerent link criterion, moreover, emphasizes that the act must be specifically intended directly to cause harmful effects reaching the requisite threshold, to the advantage of one party to the conflict and to the detriment of another. We could discuss here the example of the direct or active participation of civilians when they help in the construction or renovation of a road in the conflict zone. This brings to mind the distinction between the direct and indirect participation of a person in hostilities by distinguishing, on the one hand, the conduct of hostilities and other activities forming part of the general war effort or which may be described as activities in support of the war, on the other. The construction of a road can be considered as a general war effort and therefore in one way or another can contribute to the development and maintenance of the capacity to cause harmful effects to the other party to the conflict.[480]

This was the case with 30 civilians who were engaged by the Brigade in the renovation of the Kasinga-Kididiwe road in Beni territory. However, if these civilians are not to be considered as having participated directly in the conflict, the direct impact of this rehabilitation on the ADF will have to be analyzed. According to the MONUSCO press release of 20.05.2020, the difficulties of access to this stretch of road have facilitated the movements of the ADF, who have repeatedly attacked civilians in this region.[481] As this rehabilitation has a direct impact and has produced an advantage for one of the belligerents (Brigade and FARDC), these civilians will ipso facto lose their protection under IHL and will be vulnerable to attack. This is because the notion of direct participation in hostilities refers more to a person's involvement in specific hostile acts and not to their status or function.[482]

In the case of the participation of women and children in the massacres in Beni, some would confirm that the harm link criteria were met by the fact that these acts have caused and continue to cause loss of life, injury and destruction of innocent civilians and their property.

480 Claude Pilloud, Yves Sandoz, Christophe Swinarski and Bruno Zimmermann, (Eds.) *Commentary on the additional protocols: of 8 June 1977 to the Geneva Conventions of 12 August 1949*, Martinus Nijhoff Publishers, 1987.

481 *MONUSCO rehabilitates major road in Beni to facilitate troops and local populations' mobility*, 25.02.2020 available at https://peacekeeping.un.org/en, accessed on 22th Jun 2020.

482 *Background Doc. DPH 2004*, p. 30; *Report DPH 2004*, pp. 15-17; *Report DPH 2005*, p. 13.

The criterion of direct causation, for its part, would be proven by the fact that these massacres are always committed during attacks on villages by the ADF. The challenge would be to confirm that the massacres of civilians in the Beni and Lubero territories were committed with the aim of giving the ADF an advantage over the FARDC. The present thesis considers that these acts, i.e., the massacres, are part of the hostilities, even if they are not likely direct to harm military operations or the military capacity of the FARDC. The fact that women and children are directly involved in the hostilities in Beni and Lubero is clear from their strategies and their modus operandi before and after the massacres. Even when the massacres take place in villages far from ADF strongholds, in most cases, the ADF attacks the population in retaliation for attacks on their positions by the FARDC or by joint operations with the Brigade.[483] This is sufficient proof of the belligerent link between these acts of massacre, arson and looting and the aim of harming the FARDC, here representing the Congolese government. The example of the massacres in Oicha in retaliation for attacks on ADF strongholds on the Mwalika axis and around the triangle of death in February 2019, bears witness to this.

It should be added, however, that the loss of protection for civilians linked to their direct participation in hostilities is only valid for the duration of that participation. According to the commentary on the Additional Protocol, outside this period of participation, civilians must not be attacked because they do not present a danger to the adversary. This analysis has also been taken up by the ICTY in describing direct participation in hostilities as potentially "intermittent and discontinuous". Thus, these women will not forfeit their protection on an ongoing basis unless and until they join the ADF armed group. Where this possibility exists for adult women who become members of the rebel group, the situation is not easy for children, who cannot be members of either the regular armed forces of a State or the rebel groups. As this aspect is not analyzed in the present thesis, it is simply necessary to point out that the panoply of articles protecting children under IHL and customary law does not clearly take this aspect into consideration.

In view of the foregoing, the bombing of ADF strongholds where there are women and children, in short civilians, amounts to a violation of the

483 *Report on abuses and violations of human rights and international humanitarian law by ADF combatants and members of the defence and security forces in the territories of Beni in North Kivu and Irumu and Mambasa in Ituri, between 1 January 2019 and 31 January 2020* (translated) para. 21 and 25 available at https://www.ohchr.org/sites/default/files/Documents/Countries/CD/ADF_FR.pdf, accessed on 25th Jun 2020.

principle of distinction under IHL. These attacks would be justified and legal if they took place while these civilians were taking part in the massacres. All this raises the question of how to reconcile peace with strict respect for IHL in the context of the ADF. Several members of civil society in the Beni and Lubero territories are wondering what is more important now: respecting IHL by not destroying ADF strongholds containing women and children who participate or have participated in massacres or destroying them without taking these "protected persons" into account, with a view to restoring peace to both territories. This assessment was echoed by an anonymous FARDC officer, who wondered: "How can the lives and protection of these women and children be reconciled with the lives of an entire population that is being exterminated? Another FADRC officer expressed the view that the loss of human life in the context of the ADF would be considered collateral damage because the bombing of ADF strongholds was the only way to neutralize the enemy. This represented a major military advantage and was the only way to restore peace in this part of the DRC.

However, the principle of proportionality means that the concrete and direct military advantage expected from the attack in question must be greater than the loss of civilian life and civilian damage that can reasonably be expected from the operation. Nevertheless, this principle also implies the need to take every precaution in the choice of means and methods of attack with a view to avoiding or at least minimizing loss of civilian life and damage to civilian objects.

Although this question is not deeply addressed in this analysis, the research considers that to think of destroying everything without taking into account the principle of distinction would be to take a step backwards and ignore the very meaning of IHL, which is, first and foremost, to protect those "hors de combat".

By considering other methods of warfare to neutralize the enemy, such as capture, cutting off sources of weapons supply; it will be possible to achieve effective protection for these women and children, as well as for the entire population of Beni and Lubero and thus restore peace.

In joint Brigade-FARDC operations as part of the implementation of Resolution 2098, the FARDC are often asked to assess the effects of military operations on the ground. However, cases of torture and mutilation of corpses have been recorded. This has been the case with the torture of captured Mai-Mai and ADF, as well as the mutilation of the bodies of people presumed to be ADF.

International humanitarian law and customary law are unanimous on the protection of prisoners of war and captured persons. As the protection of prisoners of war is applicable in the context of an IAC, the protection of captured persons is of interest to this analysis because the conflict between the FARDC-Brigade and the ADF, Mai-Mai is an IAC. Thus, the protection of captured members of the ADF or any other member of a rebel group comes under Article 3 common to the four Geneva Conventions of 12 August 1949 and Additional Protocol II to the Geneva Conventions relating to the Protection of Victims of Non-International Armed Conflicts of 8 June 1977. These persons, although having taken a direct part in hostilities, must be treated humanely in all circumstances. In particular, they must be protected against murder, torture and cruel, humiliating or degrading treatment. Any action contrary to these provisions will be considered a violation of IHL.

In *Prosecutor v. Naletilic and Martinovic* case, the ICTY judge affirmed that torture, cruel treatment and acts intentionally causing great suffering constitute war crimes.[484]

Nicknamed the "mini-Geneva Convention", Article 3 common to the 4 Geneva Conventions is a compendium of humanity. Thus, while the protection of a prisoner of war is well detailed in the third Geneva Convention, that of the detainee or captured person is summed up by the principle of "humanity", which has not been well defined. Thus, for example, a POW is protected against any act of violence or intimidation, as well as insults and public curiosity. Although he has already fallen into the hands of the opponent, publishing his identity would be in breach of article 13 paragraph 2 of the 3rd GC. This raises the question of the publication of the identity of captured members of the ADF rebel groups, published and relayed by the DRC's national television channel and also by social networks. The present thesis considers that as these members are not POWs but rather detainees, their presentation to the public would not be considered a violation of the rules of IHL as long as it does not show any signs of inhuman or degrading treatment. That said, certain rules for the protection of POWs will be taken into account in the protection of detainees inasmuch as they prohibit inhuman and degrading treatment: let us cite here the example of reprisals set out in Article 13.1 of GC III.

Thus, the recording and publication of certain FARDC soldiers torturing and ill-treating captured members of the ADF after the joint operations of

484 *Prosecutor v. Naletilic and Martinovic, Case No. IT-98-34-T, judgment of 31 March 2003* (Trial Chamber I).

the Brigade and FARDC constitute violations of IHL and customary law because they violate the principle of humanity. The mutilation of corpses is prohibited under IHL. Although clearly taken up in the Geneva Conventions applying to international armed conflicts (articles 17 IGC, 120 III GC, etc.), the prohibition of mutilating corpses is taken up in customary law and also remains valid in the context of non-international armed conflicts. Rule 114 of international custom sets out the scope of application of this prohibition, which applies in all circumstances, i.e., during a CAI or CANI. This prohibition has been taken up by several national texts, such as that of the DRC, which makes the mutilation of corpses a war crime. That being the case, the mutilation of the corpses of members of the ADF and CODECO in the Beni and Ituri territories constitutes a war crime.

IHL authorizes attacks on military objectives. However, a crime is committed when an attack fails to take account of the principles of distinction, proportionality, necessity and precautions. In addition to these principles, the principle of humanity must also be respected. From the foregoing discussion, it can be deduced that violations of IHL in the implementation of R2P in Resolution 2098 are due to a failure to respect one or other of these principles.

It is therefore appropriate to analyze the responsibilities in the event of such violations of IHL in the lines that follow. As some of these operations were joint and others individual, the discussion will also turn to the possibility of sharing responsibility between the Brigade, the force mandated to implement Resolution 2098, on the one hand and the armed forces of the DRC on the other.

Chapter II: Responsibility for Violations of IHL in the Implementation of R2P under the Resolution 2098

International Humanitarian Law classifies failure to comply with its rules during conflicts as a violation. These violations can be attributed either to corporate bodies or to individuals.

A violation may trigger the application of two liability regimes simultaneously. The first is aimed at States and IOs for non-compliance with their international obligations and is based primarily on Public International Law. The second is for those who have committed crimes in the context of armed conflict. Different in nature, the two regimes of responsibility obey distinct rules. The responsibility of corporate bodies (States and International Organizations) is based exclusively on the principle of reparation. It is a "civil" responsibility, whereas individual responsibility is criminal in nature. Moreover, the distinction between the rules applicable to these two regimes of liability has a consequence on their establishment. In practice, the international liability of the State or an IO may be established or rejected without having any impact on individual liability and vice versa. Thus, for each violation, when established, international responsibility for an internationally wrongful act or criminal responsibility can be envisaged.

This applies to the implementation of R2P measures in the Congolese context. Indeed, in the implementation of R2P under Resolution 2098, a number of violations of the rules of IHL have occurred. As the Brigade is a UN mission, the UN would be held responsible for violations of IHL committed by the Brigade. Furthermore, as the UN does not have its own army and relies solely on its member countries, it will be necessary to analyze the responsibility of troop-contributing countries for the actions of their nationals. The reality on the ground having shown a not inconsiderable intervention of the armed forces of the DRC, the responsibility of the DRC for the acts committed by its armed forces will have to be cleared. Therefore, the legal framework of the responsibility of the Brigade for IHL violations will be analyzed (1). In addition, an analysis of the sharing of responsibility between the UN, the Troop-Contributing Countries (TCCs) and the DRC will be carried out (2). To close this chapter, individual responsibility (commanders and soldiers in the field) will also be examined (3).

1. Legal framework of the responsibility of the Brigade for IHL violations during R2P implementation in DRC

Responsibility is seen as an obligation to make reparation for a breach of a legal obligation. In international law, responsibility can be understood as "the institution whereby a subject of international law to whom an act or omission contrary to its legal obligations is attributable is required to make reparation to the subject of law who has been the victim". Thus, international responsibility is not broad but targeted and is based on the concept of an internationally wrongful act. Two questions will be elaborated in this section: the basis of the Brigade's responsibility for violations of IHL and the attribution of the Brigade's act to the United Nations.

A. Basis of International Responsibility for violations of IHL

International responsibility is based on the commission of an internationally wrongful act. The international responsibility of an IO will then be based on Article 3 of the Draft Articles on the Responsibility of International Organizations (DARIO), which provides: "Any internationally wrongful act of an international organization entails its international responsibility". Article 4 DARIO goes further by specifying two situations in which there is an internationally wrongful act: firstly, when conduct (action or omission) is attributable to the Organization under international law. An IO may incur liability in cases where an act constituting a breach of international law is directly or indirectly attributable to it. Direct imputation consists in attributing the acts of the organs and personnel of an IO to the latter.

Indirect imputation, on the other hand, refers to the fact that the IO is imputed with acts normally attributable to one of its member States participating in a peacekeeping operation. The question of whether, in this case, these States are completely absolved of their responsibility will be examined in the next section. Secondly, the conduct must constitute a breach of an international obligation of that organization. Although the international IHL obligations contained in the Geneva Conventions and their Additional Protocols are not directly binding on IOs, the obligation to respect and ensure respect for IHL in all circumstances contained in Article 1 common to the Geneva Conventions and their Additional Protocols reveals the erga omnes nature of humanitarian law obligations.[485] This obligation is incumbent on IOs and States alike. Although it is well known that the UN is not a party to the Geneva Conventions on IHL, its legal personality implies that customary rules and norms must be respected. Since most of the rules of IHL have already acquired customary status, the UN, its organs, agents and operational forces are obliged to respect them and any violations would require reparation. The responsibility of UN and associated personnel for non-compliance with IHL during PKOs can also be inferred from their duty to respect IHL as set out in the UN Secretary-General's Bulletin of 1999 and the 1994 Convention on the Safety of United Nations and Associated Personnel.

As the United Nations forces are bound to respect IHL, failure to do so will constitute an internationally wrongful act because it is contrary to the obligations laid down by international law in general and IHL in particular. The violation of IHL, being considered as the commission of an internationally wrongful act, would give rise to the responsibility of its author. This, in principle, refers to the responsibility of peace mission operations for violations of IHL. However, the violation of international law can only be established if it can be considered as having been committed by a subject of this order and acting as such. This being the case, as PKOs are not subjects of international law and do not have legal personality, responsibility cannot be envisaged in their hands, but rather in the hands of the international organizations to which they belong. The international responsibility of PKOs is therefore indirect and not a direct responsibility. The law of international responsibility stipulates that IOs[486] and States[487] being subjects of international law, will be held responsible for the acts of their agents and/or their organs. A PKO is considered a subsidiary organ of the UN if it is established by the General Assembly or the Security Council and is placed under the UN chain of command.[488]

Article 29 of the United Nations Charter states that the Security Council may establish such subsidiary organs as it deems necessary for the performance of its functions. This article, among many others, justifies the estab-

485 Maya Brehm, "The Arms Trade and States' Duty to Ensure Respect for Humanitarian and Human Rights Law", *Journal of Conflict and Security Law 12,* no. 3, 2007, p. 379.

486 Article 6 *DARIO.*

487 Article 4 *ASR.*

488 Certain Expenses of the United Nations (Article 17, Paragraph 2, of the Charter) (Advisory Opinion) [1962] ICJ Rep.151, at 165.

lishment of peace missions as subsidiary organs of the UN. With regard to the ONUC, for example, the Regulations of the United Nations Force in the Congo of 15 July 1963 stipulate that: "The United Nations Operation in the Congo (ONUC) is the subsidiary organ of the United Nations created by virtue of Security Council Resolution 143 of 14 July 1960, of which the United Nations Force in the Congo forms an integral part".[489]

In its observations to the International Law Commission, the United Nations confirms that a peacekeeping force is a subsidiary organ of the United Nations when it has been established by the Security Council or the General Assembly.[490]

This assertion was reiterated in its statement to the European Court of Human Rights (ECHR) when it stated that "UNMIK was a subsidiary organ of the United Nations and was headed by a Special Representative of the Secretary-General and reported directly to the United Nations Security Council through the Secretary-General".[491]

Returning to the legal nature of the Rapid Intervention Brigade (the Brigade) in the context of the DRC, it should be noted that the Brigade is a mission created by the UN Security Council as part of a peacekeeping mission, MONUSCO. Created by resolution 1925 (2010) adopted under Chapter VII of the Security Council Charter on 28 May 2010, MONUSCO is placed under the control of the SG.[492] The Brigade, which was created within MONUSCO, is under the command of the Force Commander who exercises operational authority under the executive and operational authority of the United Nations Secretary-General (UNSG).[493]

That being the case, the acts committed by the Brigade will be attributed by right to the United Nations. This responsibility is deduced from that of

---

489 *ST/SGB/ONUC/* 1 (mimeo) chap. I, para. 5, b).

490 *Statement by the United Nations Legal Counsel,* Mr. Hans Corell in A/CN.4/541, 2004, p. 18, para. 36. See also the *Report of the Secretary-General, 'Summary Study of the Experience derived from the establishment and operation of the force' (9 October 1958) UN Doc. A/3943,* para. 127.

491 *Application no. 71412/01 by Agim Behrami and Bekir Behrami against France and Application no. 78166/01 by Ruzhidi Saramati against France, Germany and Norway, European Court of Human Rights, Grand Chamber Decision as to the Admissibility,* 4 May 2007, 45 EHRR SE10, para. 118.

492 See *resolution 2348,* 2017, para. 52 and the *Special Report of the Secretary-General on the strategic review of MONUSCO (S/2017/826).*

493 Christopher Leck, "International responsibility in United Nations peacekeeping operations: command and control arrangements and the attribution of conduct", *Melbourne Journal of International Law 10,* no. 1, 2009, p.354.

the Security Council which authorized the use of force in accordance with articles 24 and 39 of the United Nations Charter.

Nevertheless, although the United Nations can be held responsible for the acts of its subsidiary bodies, another condition is necessary for it to engage this responsibility. The analysis in the following section will focus on the condition that must be met for the United Nations to incur responsibility for violations of IHL committed by the Brigade during its interventions in the DRC.

B. Attribution of an IHL violation committed by the Brigade to the United Nations.

In order to elaborate the condition of attribution of the international responsibility of an IO for the acts of its organs and agents, the concepts imputability and attribution or imputation must be analyzed. While imputability refers to "characteristics of conduct of individuals or groups that can or must be attributed to a State or an international organization",[494] imputation refers to the action of linking the conduct of a person or group of persons to a subject of international law.[495] Both concepts are important in the theory of international responsibility. According to this thesis, the first, imputability, refers to the notion of an internationally wrongful act, discussed in the first section. The second, imputation, relates to the attribution of an internationally wrongful act to an IO or a State. At the outset, it should be noted that the attribution of ultra vires conduct to the IO will not depend on the nature of the organ or its agent but rather on the mission it carries out according to "the rules of the organization".[496]

In its advisory opinion on the Dispute relating to immunity from legal process of a special rapporteur of the Commission on Human Rights, the Court stated that in the case of "damage suffered as a result of acts performed by the United Nations or by its agents in the exercise of their

494 Svitlana Andreichenko, "Imputability, the International Responsibility Law", *Ukr. J. Int'l L.* 2014, p. 234.

495 Marko Milanovic, "Special Rules of Attribution of Conduct in International Law", *international Law Studies*, Vol. 96, 2020, p. 295 available at SSRN: https://ssrn.com/abstract=3623309, accessed on 28th Jun 2020.

496 Article 6 *DARIO*. See also , Ahlborn, Christiane. "The rules of international organizations and the law of international responsibility." *international Organizations Law Review 8*, no. 2, 2011, pp. 397-482.

official functions [...] the Organization may certainly be required to bear the harmful consequences of such acts".[497]

According to the Court, in addition to the conduct of its principal organs and subsidiary organs, the United Nations will be held responsible for the acts and omissions of its agents. This was reinforced by the statement of the Swiss Federal Council in a decision of 30 October 1996: "As a general rule, the acts or omissions of an international organization's organs of any rank and nature and of its agents in the exercise of their competence are imputable to the organization".[498]

In addition, the expression "rules of the organization" provided for by Article 6 paragraph 2 of the DARIO, makes clear the legality of the tasks of these bodies or persons. In fact, the tasks may be derived from the constituent instruments, the decisions and resolutions and the acts of the organization adopted in accordance with these instruments.[499] Article 8 makes it clear that the responsibility of IOs for the ultra vires acts of their organs/agents will be established if they are acting within the framework of the general functions of the IO. In this case, it will be understood that the conduct of peace missions and their agents will be attributed to the UN, whenever the establishment of these missions is in conformity with UN "rules". This statement was repeated in the Report of the Secretary-General, Model status-of-forces agreement for peace-keeping operations.[500]

On the basis of the foregoing, it would be tempting to assert that any behavior by the Brigade and its members committed in accordance with their mandate under resolution 2098 can be attributed to the UN in the light of article 6, paragraph 2 of the DARIO. Indeed, by reading the preamble to resolution 2098, one can understand its conformity with the United Nations Charter. However, even if the organization's responsibility generally depends on the attribution of conduct, this does not necessarily occur in all circumstances. Indeed, it seems that in the event of a violation of humanitarian law, the organization's responsibility is not automatically

497 I.C.J. *Reports 1999*, p. 88, para. 66.

498 *Document VPB 61.75*, published on the website of the Swiss Federal Council.

499 Francesco Messineo, "Attribution of conduct" *Principles of shared responsibility in international law: an appraisal of the state of the art, Cambridge University Press, Cambridge,* 2014, p.70.

500 *Report of the Secretary-General, Model status-of-forces agreement for peace-keeping operations, A/45/594, 9* October 1990, ("Model SOFA"), para.15.

engaged.[501] Peacekeeping and peace enforcement forces can be of several kinds. One may be authorized and placed under the authority of the UN; the other, on the other hand, may be authorized but placed under the control of the UN. A case in point is the presence of Belgian troops in Somalia in 1993, which were part of the Unified Force (UNITAF) created by Resolution 794 (1992) and not of the United Nations Operation in Somalia (UNOSOM).[502]

This nuance brings all its weight when attributing ultra vires behavior to the UN in a peace mission. In practical terms, the difference between these two missions can be seen in the chain of command. For example, the conduct of a peacekeeping mission that is not under UN command cannot be attributed to the UN. Although created by virtue of and in accordance with the acts of the UN, the conduct of this mission and its members on the ground will be attributable to the Member States. This was confirmed during the Korean War, when US forces bombed targets in the Soviet Union and China. The US government undertook to pay for the damage inflicted on Soviet and Chinese property.[503]

The condition of effective control as a criterion for attributing conduct to an international organization is provided for in article 7 of the ILC's 2011 draft article on responsibility of international organizations, which states: "The conduct of an organ or agent of an international organization placed at the disposal of another organization shall be considered an act of the latter organization under international law to the extent that it exercises effective control over that conduct".[504]

Since effective control is factual, this argument is in line with the reasoning of the Higher Court of the Province of Vienna in the N.K. v. Austria case of 26 February 1979. The Court rightly considers that the important thing is not to determine to which body the person who caused the damage

501 Remy Jorritsma, "International responsibility and attribution of conduct: an analysis of Case Law on Human Rights and Humanitarian Law", *International and European Law Maastricht Centre for Human Rights,* 2021.

502 Letter from the Director of the Mission Administration and Logistics Division of the UN Department of Peacekeeping Operations (unpublished letter of 25 June 1998) quoted by https://legal.un.org/ilc/documentation/french/a_cn4_541.pdf, note 50. Accessed on 5th April 2024.

503 Letter addressed to the Secretary-General on 19 October 1950 by the Deputy Representative of the United States of America concerning the aerial bombardment of Chinese territory (S/813).

504 Article 7 *DARIO.*

belongs, but rather in whose name and on whose behalf the person acted at the time the act was committed.[505]

The duality of the institutional links between PKOs and the United Nations and troop-contributing countries raises the challenge of attributing their ultra vires acts to one entity or the other. The main question in attributing a given conduct remains that of who actually exercised control over the conduct in question. The condition of effective control remains a sine qua non requirement for establishing the responsibility of the UN for the acts of this PKO. This was also taken up by the UN Secretary-General, who stated that the international responsibility of the UN for activities carried out by UN forces during combat is based on the assumption that the operation is under the sole command and control of the organization.[506]

It would be difficult, for example, in the circumstances of UNAMIR[507] in Rwanda, UNOSOM II in Somalia or MONUC in DRC, to assert that the Force Commander exercised exclusive control over the national forces in the mission. In these missions, each contingent also had its commander to whom it reported.[508] In the context of MONUC, for example, there have been several incidents relating to the implementation of the command mandate in the east-western part of the DRC.

The MONUSCO situation deserves particular attention. A distinction must be drawn here between MONUSCO's regular forces and those of the Brigade, which are the subject of this thesis. Practically speaking, the former encounter the same difficulty of exclusive control by the Force Commander as the former forces. Each contingent has its own commander, and the largest contingent is chosen to appoint the Force commander. A number of operational problems were highlighted, such as the difficulty of pooling combat doctrine and mistrust of the Force Commander. Several incidents were reported.[509]

Although since 2019 the solution has been to find a force commander who is neutral, i.e. who does not belong to any of the member forces of the mission, it has emerged that MONUSCO keeps its sectors according

505 *Österreichische Zeitschrift für öffentliches Recht und Völkerrecht,* vol.31, n3 et 4, 1980, P.310.

506 *Report of the Secretary-General (A/51/389),* p. 7, paras. 17 and 18.

507 *Mukeshimana- Ngulinzira and Others v. Belgium and Others, RG Nos. 04/4807/A and 07/15547/A, Judgment of 8 December 2010,* Court of First Instance of Brussels.

508 *S/1994/653,* paras. 243-244. See also Berenice Boutin, "Attribution of conduct in international military operations: a causal analysis of effective control", *Melbourne Journal of International Law 18,* no. 2, 2017, p. 174.

509 Interview with LTG Marcos Affonso.

to the nationality of the contingents. The northern sector is controlled by Bangladesh, the center by India and the south by Pakistan. However, the Brigade is under the exclusive control of the MONUSCO Force Commander. In view of the discussion up to now, where the attribution of the conduct of a member of MONUSCO's regular forces to the UN would require an in-depth analysis with regards to the exclusive control that MONUSCO would have over his actions, that of a member of the Brigade would not pose any additional problem.

In view of the foregoing, would it be wise to think that only the UN would be held responsible for violations of IHL committed by members of the Brigade?

Indeed, in the following discussion, the present thesis analyzes this question based on the possibility of shared responsibility between the UN and States by virtue of the obligations of subjects of international law to comply with IHL.

2. Shared responsibility between the UN, the Troops Contributing Countries and the host Country

Responsibility for violations of IHL committed by the Brigade during the implementation of resolution 2098 may be attributable to the UN and/or to States. This sharing of responsibility is justified by the fact that the UN, having transferred its competence through the mandate or the authorization to intervene, may or may not have control over the actions of the troops on the ground.

As far as violations of IHL are concerned, several sources state that responsibility is shared, without being precise about the criteria for this sharing. The UN Secretary-General has referred to the concept of "concurrent responsibility" of the Organization and the State that provided the contingent. Furthermore, in the context of the implementation of Resolution 2098, the intervention of the DRC Forces cannot be ignored and violations of IHL committed during this period of their intervention may be attributable to them. In this section the shared responsibility between the UN and the contributing States and the DRC as host State will be analyzed (A). In a slightly more practical way, the criteria for sharing this responsibility (B) in order to identify the specific responsibilities of each actor will be analyzed (C).

A. Basis of concurrent responsibility between the United Nations, Troops Contributing Countries and the host country for violations of IHL

The Circular of 1999 containing recommendations and instructions to troops engaged in an operation under the command and control of the UN does not mention "concurrent responsibility". In order to establish shared responsibility, it will be necessary to analyze the concepts of agents or organs in relation to effective control in accordance with the articles of the DARIO and those of the ASR. The combined analysis of Article 6 of the DARIO and Article 8 of the ASR can be invoked in the situation in which an agent or organ of the IO acts under the control of the State. In the opposite situation, i.e. where a state body is acting under the effective control of the IO, Articles 4 of the ASR and 7 of the DARIO may be invoked. Indeed, in the commentaries on DARIO, the possibility of concurrent attribution of international responsibility was raised.[510] Thus, the attribution of conduct to a State does not exclude the possibility of attributing the same conduct to an IO and vice versa, or to both at the same time in case of joint command and control. In the context of peace missions, this responsibility can in fact be deduced from the nature of the peacekeeping and peace enforcement forces.

Firstly, these forces are subsidiary organs of the United Nations and are placed under the effective control of the organization. This has the legal consequence that the conduct of these forces is attributable to the Organization. Secondly, these forces originate from States. As the IO is responsible for the acts of its organs and agents, so is the State in accordance with Article 3 of the ASR. In practice, States have not denied their responsibility for the acts of their nationals who are members of a peace mission.[511]Furthermore, the contingent is not always placed fully at the disposal of the UN. This raises the question of who actually controls these forces on the ground. In practice, States and the IO may have this control.

This being the case, these two entities assume joint legal responsibility for the unlawful act committed by this body. However, the attribution of a breach of IHL will not depend on the status of the person (agent or

510 Amerasinghe Chittharanjan Felix, "Comments on the ILC's Draft Articles on the Responsibility of International Organizations", *International Organizations Law Review* 9, no. 1, 2012, p. 30. Available at https://doi.org/10.1163/15723747-00901002, accessed on 5th April 2024.

511 Gaja Giorgio. "Articles on the Responsibility of International Organizations." *United Nations Audiovisual Library of International Law*, 2014, p. 8.

official), but rather on the authority of his mission. As discussed above, this is determined by the authority that controls the mission. It is therefore judicious for the present thesis to admit, as do several other authors, that although peace missions are authorized by the United Nations, they can escape their control in their operationalization. Hence, in a peace mission, behavior can be attributed either to the UN, or to the State, or to both at the same time, depending on the reality on the ground.

The possibility of concurrent responsibility was taken up by the SG in one of his reports.[512] It should be noted, however, that the SG did not specify the basis for this liability.

In United Nations practice, a form of shared responsibility has been most experimented with in areas of human rights. Model Agreement between the United Nations and Member States Contributing Personnel and Equipment to United Nations Peace-Keeping Operation and the amended UN Model Memorandum of Understanding (MOU) seem to be an example of this. In cases of sexual exploitation or sexual violence committed by members of peacekeeping forces, the United Nations has dealt with civil liability, i.e. it has paid damages to the victims, while the States of origin of each accused contingent has dealt with the criminal aspect.[513] The conclusion is that in these agreements between States and the UN, only reparation was dealt with and not the attribution of conduct.

Returning to the breach of IHL, some would be tempted to base the concepts of concurrent liability on the general theory of international responsibility, which is based on an internationally wrongful act. The latter denotes conduct (act or omission) contrary to international law. It is, therefore, essential to analyze the concept of conduct. Without going into the dogma of the concept itself, two aspects are retained: commission and omission.

One point of interest here would be to know whether the UN and contributing States can assume simultaneous responsibility for the conduct of the same agent/organization. One can read in more than one report of the Secretary General that the responsibility of an IO does not exclude the

512 Marko Milanovic, "Special rules of attribution of conduct in international law", *International Law Studies 96*, 2020, p.295.

513 Zsuzsanna Deen-Racsmány, "The amended UN model memorandum of understanding: a new incentive for states to discipline and prosecute military members of national peacekeeping contingents?" *Journal of Conflict & Security Law 16*, no. 2, 2011, p. 331.

separate or concurrent responsibility of a State having participated in the execution of a wrongful act.[514]

This concurrent attribution of responsibility would be based on the general theory of commission or omission of an act. This refers to participation in the commission of a wrongful act or failure to comply with international obligations to prevent that act. Thus, in the case of peace missions, it would be possible for the UN or the State to incur liability either for omission or for commission.

Although the commission aspect has already been elaborated in the theory of effective control, this thesis asks whether it is possible for the UN or the State to be held responsible for the acts of its agents or organs by omission, by failing to stop the commission of violations of IHL. Some would be tempted to say that in order to stop the commission of a vicious act, it is necessary to have effective control over the operations.[515] This research, however, considers that in the specific context of peace missions, the UN and the troop-contributing States always have a certain amount of control over the troops. Thus, when they fail to stop the commission of a breach of IHL, they would be held responsible for omission for failing to fulfil their international obligations.

Consider the example of MONUSCO, which has conducted several military operations against rebel groups in the DRC. The national contingent in charge of operations always needs support in terms of weapons and equipment authorized by the Force Commander, who is based in Goma. In the event of a legitimate suspicion that a violation of IHL was committed through the use of these military materials, the Force Commander would be obliged to stop the supply of materials. In the opinion of the present research, by ignoring this, the mission could incur liability for failing to ensure compliance with IHL. Thus, the UN would be liable for omission and the State for acting. Double liability would then apply. This can be understood in the same logic as that evoked by the ICJ judge in the Corfu Channel case. In that case, the ICJ held Albania responsible for not having prevented the damage caused by the explosions of mines laid by Yugoslavia, of which it was aware or should have been aware.[516]

---

514 Deen-Racsmány, *The amended UN model memorandum of understanding*, p.340.

515 Charuka Ekanayake and Susan Harris Rimmer, "Applying effective control to the conduct of UN forces: connecting factual complexities with legal responsibility", *international organizations law review 15*, no. 1, 2018, p. 29.

516 Corfu Channel, *Merits, ICJ Reports 1949*, p. 4, 52.

Another argument relating to concurrent liability would be the deduction made by Article 48 of the DARIO and Article 47 of the ASR. Article 48 of DARIO, which deals with situations covered by articles 14 to 18 and 58 to 62, includes joint liability for aiding and assisting, coordinating, controlling and directing an entity in the commission of an unlawful act. Although its analogue, Article 47 of the ASR, applies only to States, it provides for the concurrent liability of States for the conduct of the body when States act jointly or through it. This would be permissible for troop-contributing States where they act jointly in the commission of a wrongful act.

Another example is MONUC's assistance to the FARDC during operations against rebel groups, where several violations of IHL were reported.[517] In addition to the above, the present thesis considers that there are grounds for establishing concurrent responsibility on the part of the UN for the actions of MONUC and on the part of the DRC for the actions of the FARDC. It must also be considered that MONUC's responsibility is not linked to its complicity but rather to its participation.

Furthermore, in the same vein, double imputation may also be admissible by committing an act in breach of IHL. This responsibility can be deduced from the memorandum of the Office of Legal Affairs concerning an accident involving a helicopter of the United Nations Peacekeeping Force in Cyprus (UNFICYP). In this memorandum, the United Nations confirms that it hears that the helicopter "could and normally should, be held liable" for damage caused to third parties by its aircraft.[518] In view of the foregoing, the UN cannot be absolved of its responsibility for violations of IHL committed by these aircraft.

This is also the case in military operations under Resolution 2098. Although this does not directly concern the troops-contributing countries to the Brigade, the Brigade has stopped its air support to the FARDC because of legitimate suspicions that the principle of distinction is being violated in the bombardments of ADF strongholds. An anonymous member of the Brigade said that if the Brigade continued to collaborate with the FARDC in these clashes, it risked being held responsible for these violations too.[519]

---

517 Peter F. Chapman, "Ensuring respect: United Nations compliance with international humanitarian law", *Human Rights Brief 17,* no. 1, 2009, p. 1.

518 Nations Unies, *Annuaire juridique,* 1980, numéro de vente F.83 V.1, p. 204 ; see also Novosseloff, Alexandra, *Assessing the effectiveness of the United Nations peacekeeping force in cyprus (UNFICYP) and the office of the special adviser to the secretary-general on cyprus (OSASG),* 2021.

519 *Interview with an "anonymous" FIB member held in Beni, Mavivi 20th June 2023.*

This is where the competing responsibilities of the UN, troop-contributing countries and the host country come into play. Without diminishing the basis of concurrent responsibility between the UN and the troop-contributing countries, the host country also has obligations under IHL, for which it would be held responsible in the case of violations. It follows from this analysis that the DRC must engage its international responsibility for the actions of the FARDC. The violations of IHL cited in the previous sections would also be attributable to the DRC as a party to the operations. There is no need to return here to the nature of the FARDC as an organ of the Congolese State. Under Article 3 of the ASR, the State is responsible for its agent or organ. This had already been recognized in 1923 by the ICJ, which stated that "States can act only by means of and through the persons of their agents and representatives" in its advisory opinion on "German Settlers in Poland".[520] On the basis of the above analysis, many will agree with this research that the theory of imputation of a violation of IHL and attribution of responsibility in the context of a specific peace mission applies at three levels: the international organization in whose name and on whose behalf the forces are acting, the States whose forces are nationals and, finally, the host State, i.e., the State in which the operations are carried out. This analysis would apply mutatis mutandis to the context of the Brigade in operations to implement Resolution 2098. Indeed, the Security Council has been clear in specifying that in the implementation of the mandate of resolution 2098 the Brigade must intervene with the FARDC. Thus, a relevant analysis would be to know to whom would the acts contrary to IHL during these operations be attributed.

The research clearly states that, in the context of operations to implement Resolution 2098, the UN, the DRC and the contributing countries may be jointly or concurrently responsible. However, beyond this shared responsibility, there are facts according to which one or another would incur responsibility separately from the others. In what follows, this research analyzes the criteria for distributing this responsibility.

520 *ICJ Reports*, 1923, p. 22.

B. Mechanisms for sharing responsibility between entities for IHL violations committed during the implementation of resolution 2098

Attributing wrongful conduct of agents and organs to subjects of international law is still not an easy task. The attribution of responsibility for conduct contrary to international law remains subject to one condition: "effective control". Although provided for in the ARS and DARIO, the definition of effective control is not clear. As demonstrated by the different interpretations and applications of the effective control test by several jurisdictions and certain States in their allegations.[521]

In the attribution of international responsibility, several tests have been developed: effective control, global control, test of ultimate authority and control. In all these tests, the main approach was to determine whether responsibility for a wrongful act could be attributed either to the State or to the international organization, or to both jointly.

Thus, as concurrent responsibility is generally accepted, this section focuses on the elements serving as criteria for the distribution of responsibility for internationally wrongful acts committed during the implementation of R2P.

The test of effective control, first mentioned by the ICJ in the Nicaragua case, should be applied to determine whether the USA had control over the Contras. This test determines the attribution of an act to a State if the agent or body acts on the instructions, under the direction or control of the State in the performance of the internationally wrongful act. The unclear content of this test and the difficulty of proving it on the ground led the Court to consider that the USA did not have effective control over the contras.[522] It is in this sense that Article 8 of the ASR provides that in order to establish effective control, the State must have directed or controlled the specific operations that led to the commission of a wrongful act. In the case of international organizations, the test of effective control was included

521 See cases : ICJ, *Nicaragua v. United States of America,Military and paramilitary activities in and against Nicaragua,* Merits Judgement , ICJ Reports 1986, pp. 64-65 paras 109 ; ICJ, *Bosnia and Herzegovins V. Serbia and Montenegro, Case concerning the Application of the Convention on the prevention and punishment of the crime of Genocide, judgement ,* ICJ reports 2007, P. 43, para 413 ; *Agim Behrami and Bekir Behrami v. France* (App. No. 71412/01*) Ruzhdi Saramati v. France, Germany and Norway* (App.no. 78166/01) ECtHR (2007); *Al-Jedda v. the United Kingdom* (App. No. 27021/08) ECtHR (2011).

522 ICJ, *Nicaragua v. United States if America, Military and paramilitary activities in and against Nicaragua Merits Jugement , ICJ Repports,* 1986, Para 110.

in article 7 of the DARIO. Thus, the responsibility of an IO cannot be considered if the agent or body acted within the scope of its functions although this does not directly concern the attribution of the acts of an agent or body to the IO. The fact that an agent acts in his official capacity is linked to the organization. This analysis was taken up by the ICJ judge in the Dispute relating to immunity from jurisdiction of a special rapporteur of the Commission on Human Rights, who declared that an agent, in his official capacity, acts in the name and on behalf of the UN and must therefore benefit from the immunities recognized by the organization.[523] This would mean admitting that the agent represents the organization and it could therefore be inferred that the UN would be held responsible for the agent's actions.

For this research, the understanding of the concept would even be in the sense that in peace missions, the attribution of responsibility to the UN will depend on the involvement of its subsidiary bodies (peace missions) in the operations, its direction or its control. This analysis was taken up again in the Srebrenica case, in which the UN considered that it did not have effective control over all the operations, but rather that the contributing countries were responsible for these events. Although the notion of global control remains predominant in the qualification of conflicts, it would not be out of place to take a look at it to complement effective control in the context of attributing responsibility. Raised in the Tadic case, global control and the attribution of responsibility to the State for the actions of military organizations. Thus, the ICTY judge considers that, in addition to funding, training and equipment, the State must play an important role in the organization and coordination of operations in the field.[524]

This thesis considers that the test of overall control cannot really be rejected out of hand, as it would be the easiest way to determine on the ground who had control of the troops between the Organization and the State. The notions of organization and coordination are therefore important in assigning and sharing responsibility between the IO and the State. Therefore, the European Court combined effective control and overall control in giving its opinion in the Behrami and Saramati cases. Indeed, France's allegation in the Behrami case that it was UNMIK that was respon-

523 ICJ., *Diference Relating to Immunity from Legal Process of a Special Rapporteur of the Commission on Human Rights, Advisory Opinion, ICJ Reports,*1999, p. 62.

524 *Prosecutor v. Tadic, ICTY-94-1-A,* 1999, 38 ILM.

sible for the demining operation,[525] it will be held responsible for the death of this boy and the injuries to the other, in violation of Article 2 of the ECHR. It is clear that the organization and coordination aspect comes under what France would understand by "responsible". In the Saramati case, moreover, France and Norway claimed that the fact that the UN had authority over the forces commanding KFOR made it responsible for the detention of this Kosovar in violation of Article 5 of the ECHR.[526]The ECtHR returned to the nature of the mission as a subsidiary force but also the delegation of power to another military organization. It is in this logic that the UN was held responsible for the facts in application of the test of authority and control.

Over and above all the above, however, it is clear that in practice, it is not always easy to differentiate between effective control and that of direction (authority) control. It was in this context that, in the Nuhanović case, the Supreme Court held the UN and the Dutch both responsible for human rights violations[527],one for having effective control and the other for not having prevented the commission of these acts. This reversed the decision of the district judge, who had held that the UN alone would be held responsible because it had operational control.[528]

This concept becomes more interesting in the context of the implementation of Resolution 2098 because several actors are involved. In this context, it should be pointed out that in joint operations, the Congolese army (the FARDC) is in command. Does this mean that the UN and the contributing countries will be absolved of their responsibility in the event of a violation of IHL on the ground? It is in this context that the judge's analysis in the Nuhanović and Mustafić cases will be useful in this specific case. Indeed, although the DRC is in command of operations on the ground, the Brigade assists in the planning of joint operations and intervenes. This is even the meaning of the expression joint operation. The Brigade is involved in all air operations, helps identify enemy strongholds, transports munitions to

525 CEtHR, *Agim Behrami and Bekir Behrami v. France* (App. No. 71412/01) CEtHR (2007) Para 43.

526 CEtHR, *Ruzhdi Saramati v. France, Germany and Norway* (App.no. 78166/01) ECtHR (2007) para 61.

527 *The State of Netherlands v. Hasan Nuhanovic, 12/03324,* Supreme Court, 06 Septembre 2013.

528 ILDC, *Nuhanović v. State of the Netherlands (Ministry of Defense of Foreign Affairs),* First Instance Judgement, Decision no. LJN: BFO181, case No. 265615, ILDC 1092, NL 2008, 10 September 2008, Netherlands, The Hague, District Court, para. 4.12.3, 4.8.

the field and supplies fuel and refreshments to FARDC and warring forces. This being the case, all parties will be held responsible for violations of IHL, each in accordance with their degree of involvement.

The present thesis proposes a combination of effective control and operational control, i.e. direction and control, to separate responsibilities. To do this, for each operation, it will be necessary to analyze the facts at two levels, which must be cumulative. Firstly, the degree of control between the parties (the UN and the contributing countries) must be analyzed. In the specific context of Resolution 2098, check, for example, in the operations against the ADF, FDL, APCLS, etc., who had effective control between the UN and Tanzania, Malawi and South Africa, on the one hand and the DRC on the other. Secondly, we need to analyze the degree of involvement in the operation. The question here would be whether the State or UN body or agent acted directly or indirectly, i.e. through assistance and how to assess the causal link between its assistance and the unlawful act in question.

The answers to this range of questions would be a criterion to help the judge determine who is responsible for this or that violation. Thus, in the following section, the present thesis will attempt to apply this exercise to the violations of IHL referred to in the previous sections in order to identify the specific responsibilities of each intervening entity.

C. The specific responsibility of entities involved in the implementation of resolution 2098.

Violations of IHL committed during the implementation of Resolution 2098 are attributable either jointly or separately to the UN and States. As information relating to the military organization of operations was not accessible, this section will attempt to analyze the facts relating to certain specific operations found either online or in the analysis of data collection in the field. This analysis will focus on three areas. Operations carried out directly by the Brigade, joint operations with the FARDC- Brigade and FARDC operations assisted by the Brigade. It should be pointed out here that this analysis is limited to the Brigade's unilateral operations and not to joint operations with MONUSCO's regular forces. Furthermore, this categorization also relies on the involvement of one or the other in each specific operation. It is in this sense, according to this research, that one could attempt to attribute a violation either separately or specifically to the parties involved.

The Brigade's very first operation was against the M23 rebel group. According to several sources, this was a unilateral operation by the Brigade. The FARDC at the time were not in good shape after the capture of the town of Goma. From these initial operations, as indicated above, it is possible to identify a number of violations of IHL, such as the bombing of villages in the territories of Nyiragongo and Rutshuru. In this specific case, the UN can be held internationally responsible for the actions of its organ, the Brigade.

One can also read the unilateral intervention of the Brigade in the operations against the FDLR and Mayi-Mayi NDC (Nduma Defense of Congo). In an interview with Radio Okapi, Force Commander Carlos Alberto dos Santos Crus acknowledged that on 10/12/2013, the Brigade launched the first offensive operation against the FDLR at Kalembe in the north of Goma. He also acknowledged that the brigade had also launched another offensive operation against the NDC in Pinga and welcomed the results of the operations.[529] In this context, any violation of IHL arising from these operations would be attributable to the UN. Regarding joint operations, there is collaboration between UN Forces and FARDC manifested in the technical memorandum signed between MONUSCO and the Congolese Defense Ministry. It has been shown that several operations have been recognized as joint operations between the Brigade and the FARDC.

In some reports, for example, the phrase "the FARDC in collaboration with MONUSCO through its Brigade Intervention Force launched an operation (...)." appears. We can cite here the joint operations of the Brigade and the FARDC against the ADF on 13 November 2018. It should be pointed out that these operations were planned together and carried out together on the ground, leading to the capture of ADF positions and the killing of FARDC and Brigade members, with 7 contingents killed, six Malawians and one Tanzanian, not counting the wounded.[530] The deaths of women and children, civilians present in the ADF strongholds at the time, can be attributed to the DRC and the UN, depending on who had effective control of the operations. According to an anonymous source, this operation was

529 *MONUSCO to track down FDLR after M23,* 11.12.2013 available at https://monusco.unmissions.org/en/monusco-track-down-fdlr-after-m23, accessed on 19th jun 2024. See also Pete Jones, *U.N. troops start military action against Congo's Rwandan rebels* available at https://www.reuters.com/article/congo-democratic-un-idINDEE9B90C I20131210, accessed on 19th jun 2024.

530 *FARDC and MONUSCO launch joint operations against ADF,* 16.11.2018 available at https://monusco.unmissions.org/en, accessed on 19th jun 2024.

the healthiest of all, because there was frank collaboration between the parties involved and both the Brigade and the FARDC had control of their troops. This operation, among many others, is sufficient proof, once again, of the difficulty in the field of applying the test of effective control or that of operational direction and control. In the Rwenzori II operation against the ADF, for example, where the Brigade was responsible for air operations and the FARDC for ground operations, the UN would be responsible for acts contrary to the law resulting from the tan bombing, while the FARDC would be responsible for those resulting from their hand-to-hand operations. In the implementation of Resolution 2098, there are also operations initiated by the FARDC and assisted by the Brigade. Indeed, the Brigade justifies its assistance in relation to Article 12 of Resolution 2098 specifying that it may "use all necessary measures to neutralize rebel groups". On 2 July 2014, for example, it was reported that the DRC, supported by MONUSCO via the Force Intervention Brigade, launched a military operation against the Sheka, Mayi-May-NDC militia in Bunyampuli, which led to the restoration of state authority in Mpofi-Bunyampuli.[531]

To these operations, we can also add the one against the ADF in January 2014, "SOKOLA 1" (clean up in the local language Lingala) and the one against the FDLR, "Sokola 2", in which an agreement was signed between the FARDC and MONUSCO to carry out regular joint tactical, operational and strategic assessments.[532]

In these and other operations, especially those launched against the ADF, there have been several violations of IHL, including failure to respect the principle of distinction and necessity, mistreatment of the "captured", failure to respect their privacy and even mutilation of corpses.

It is clear from all that has been mentioned in the previous sections that the DRC would be held responsible for these acts by the FARDC. Although these operations are a matter of national sovereignty and were never the object of joint planning, as General Thierry LION[533] pointed out, it appears that the FARDC received assistance in two forms: intelligence and reconnaissance support in areas inaccessible to the FARDC and evacuation of the wounded. That said, the UN would also be responsible for some of

531 *Recent population displacements following military operations in bunyampuli, 12.078.2014 at https://monusco.unmissions.org/en*, accessed on 19th jun 2024.

532 *"sokola2" to disarm the fdlr rwandan rebels,* 30.01.2015 available at https://monusco.unmissions.org/en, accessed on 19th jun 2024.

533 General Thierry Lion in beni: *"we are amidst sovereign and unilateral operations, prepared by the FARDC"* (interview), 18.11.2019 available at https://monusco.unmissions.org/en, on 20.11.2019.

these violations, perhaps because it failed to identify the ADF strongholds in which the women and children were present, thereby missing the lead of the FARDC, or because it was aware of the presence of these women and children in these strongholds and knew that the FARDC would fire without taking this into account, thus violating IHL. In the latter case, the UN would be held responsible for failing to act to stop the commission of an internationally wrongful act. Although the UN always reports on and monitors compliance with IHL on the ground in operations, whether joint or unilateral and this has an impact on the promotion of human rights and IHL on the ground, upstream intervention would be more to its benefit and would absolve it of its international responsibility. It should also be noted that the Brigade's decision to freeze its collaboration with the FARDC on the grounds of an IHL violation is to be committed but would not absolve it of the responsibility it has already committed.

However, one would think that the SADC was responsible for the violations of IHL committed in the context of Resolution 2098. Indeed, it was through the SADC that the UN set up the Brigade forces. This scenario may have its legal justification in the analysis of articles 7 and 19 of ARIO in relation to the attribution of international responsibility to the UN and/or the organization made available to it. To equate this context with that of NATO via the KFOR mission, to which the UN delegated the power to intervene, would be biased, since the SADC has neither effective control nor direction of the troops. In the humble opinion of the present research, there is no cooperation agreement between the UN and SADC for the deployment of troops, as was the case with NATO.

Rather, there is a cooperation agreement between the troop-contributing countries and the UN directly. That said, SADC can never be held responsible for the actions of troops on the ground. This point was echoed by the President of Tanzania, Ms. Samia, who felt that the Brigade was not a SADC operation under the cover of the UN, but that SADC had simply acted as a bridge to facilitate contact between the UN and the member countries. She added: "If we (SADC) had control and direction of the troops, things would be different, because the situation in the east of the DRC is also affecting the development of Tanzania(...)".[534] Another

534 *Statement of Ms Samia , South Africa-Tanzania Relations, President Ramaphosa hosts Tanzanian president Samia Suluhu Hassan,* 16.03.2023 available at #SABC-News and https://dailynews.co.tz/president-samia-attends-sadc-extra-ordinary-meeting/, accessed on 19th jun 2024.

argument is that the UN reorganized the operations and troops without involving SADC and DRC as well.[535]

However, another question that will not be analyzed in this paper is whether SADC would be completely absolved of its responsibility for the actions of troops provided to the UN to carry out a Chapter 7 mandate. The idea here is to find out whether a distinction can be made between the attribution of responsibility for a peacekeeping mission and for a peace enforcement mission. The difference here is the role played by the Security Council in each mission. The present thesis considers that, given the difference in the constitutions and mandates of these two missions, it would also be wise to consider a difference in the attribution of responsibility. Peace enforcement missions do not meet the conditions set out in the cap stone principle in terms of neutrality, impartiality and non-use of force and are therefore of a different nature. The present thesis supports the view that peace enforcement missions and even more so R2P missions, fall under the full direction and control of the Security Council. It is therefore difficult to believe that the contributing countries have any control over their troops. An argument in favor of this would be the chain of command, where they report directly to the Force Commander, who does not belong to any of the nationalities making up the troops.

Although the doctrine on peacekeeping missions' states that the fact that States hold criminal and disciplinary jurisdiction over their agents placed at the disposal of the UN would justify the basis of their responsibility for internationally wrongful acts committed during operations, would it not be time to specify this when it comes to peace enforcement missions? Because, by virtue of universal jurisdiction and the nature of the crimes covered by R2P, all states in the world have criminal jurisdiction in this respect. The disciplinary aspect, in fact, has been taken over, in our view, by the UN itself. Other large-scale training in IHL, HR and discipline is offered to contingents. Some would be tempted to say that the same training is also offered to peacekeeping missions. However, for the implementation of Resolution 2098, the training offered was not routine, as it included specialists in jungle warfare, hand-to-hand combat methods.[536] As the

535 *SADC takes dispute over DRC force reconfiguration to UNGA*, available at https://www.sardc.net/en/southern-african-news-features/sadc-takes-dispute-over-drc-force-reconfiguration-to-unga/,_accessed on 19th jun 2024.

536 Monusco, *Colonel Felicia Maganwe, chief of staff of the force intervention brigade (fib) of monusco calls for professionalism to achieve the expected results , beni: MONUSCO's malawian contingent trained in the jungle combat techniques,*

Brigade Commander in Beni, Mavivi, has argued, this Brigade force is a special force, which has a plus in its mandate that is not that of the ordinary MONUSCO force.[537]

This being the case, the present thesis considers that for the violations committed during the implementation of R2P under resolution 2098 only the UN and the DRC would be held responsible. The UN either through its actions and omissions in the commission of these acts contrary to international law and the DRC for its direct involvement. Tanzania, Malawi and South Africa, which are contributing countries, would not be held responsible because they have no control over operations in the east of the DRC. However, with a few exceptions, their responsibilities would only be considered on a case-by-case basis with an in-depth analysis of their implications. One example is the shooting at the Kasindi border, committed by forces from the brigade who were crossing the border to replace other forces on military leave.[538]

The question would be whether these forces received any orders from their countries. Moreover, even if this was not the case, their countries were in a position to stop this shooting. Another aspect that draws the attention of the present research is that no contributing country has said anything about this, only the UN has spoken out, expressing its regret and promising an investigation or even disciplinary action against these contingents. Although these acts were committed in the implementation of Resolution 2098, a question that unfortunately will not be analyzed here is whether these acts constitute war crimes or crimes against humanity, as the case may be. On the other hand, the responsibility of the contributing countries would be analyzed in the case of joint operations between MONUSCO's regular forces and the Brigade. Here, the contributing countries are only responsible for MONUSCO's forces, not those of the Brigade, the former being a peacekeeping mission and the latter a peace enforcement brigade. The present thesis considers that this is also one of the challenges posed by the creation of the Brigade within MONUSCO. These are challenges

---

07.04.2022 available at https://monusco.unmissions.org/en read also Tadziwana Kapeni, *the brazilian jungle warfare mobile training team (jwmtt) wrapped up, on april 1, a training in the jungle warfare mobile techniques for the malawian contingent (malbatt) troops deployed within monusco force intervention brigade,* available at https://monusco.unmissions.org/en, accessed on 19th jun 2024.

537 Interview with an "anonymous' FIB member held in Beni, Mavivi 20th June 2023.

538 *MONUSCO recognizes a serious incident at the border between the DRC and Uganda, in Kasindi* available at https://monusco.unmissions.org/en/monusco-recognizes-serious-incident-border-bet, accessed on 19th jun 2024.

that the UN and doctrinarians should add to the long list relating to the challenge of application of IHL to the Brigade; in order to provide a clear answer or understanding of attribution of responsibility for IHL violations in future Security Council peace enforcement missions.

Thus, although their home states would not be held responsible, individual responsibility would be envisaged.

3. *Individual international criminal responsibility for IHL violations during the R2P implementation*

As mentioned above, there are two types of responsibility for violations of IHL committed during the implementation of R2P via Resolution 2098. The first is "civil" liability, which applies to entities and the second is criminal liability, which applies to individuals who have committed or participated in the commission of acts contrary to international law.

It is true that in the history of the development of international law, the place of the individual on the international scene has evolved with it. The individual, who in the past could only appear on the international scene through the representation of his State, is now considered to be a subject of international law.

Indeed, the current state of international law confers on individuals rights and obligations and thus, it can be said, legal personality. Thus, failure by an individual to comply with an international obligation may give rise to criminal liability. Contingents of United Nations peacekeeping missions thus have an obligation to respect IHL. Failure to comply with this obligation gives rise to the contingent's international criminal liability for the act for which the act occurred. Article 4 of the Secretary-General's Bulletin on compliance with international humanitarian law expressly states that "in the event of a violation of international humanitarian law, members of the military personnel of a United Nations force shall be liable to prosecution".[539]

This proves from the outset that no violation of IHL can go unpunished, regardless of the nature of the person who committed it. Article 6 of the Circular reinforces the obligation to respect domestic law during operations. Contingents are also bound by the law of their country of origin. In fact, they will be bound by IHL either through their States when the latter

539 Article 4 *Bulletin.*

are contracting parties to the Geneva Conventions and their additional protocols, or by the very nature of the rules of IHL which, in most cases, have acquired a customary character. As part of the implementation of R2P under Resolution 2098, the FARDC are also required to respect IHL. Respect for IHL is also an obligation in the DRC. As the DRC is a contracting party to the Vienna Conventions and their additional protocols, these texts apply in the DRC. In addition, the code pénal militaire and the code de procédure pénal militaire refer to this. Thus, failure to comply with IHL in military operations in the DRC would not only be a violation of IHL at international level, but also a violation of Congolese domestic law. Any violation of IHL entails the international and domestic criminal responsibility of the perpetrator. As this personality is in principle individual, no person would incur liability without having participated in one way or another in the commission of the act. This is known as the '*nulla poena sine culpa*' principle.[540]

This principle was taken up by the ICTY judge. In the Tadić case, the judge stated that "nobody may be held criminally responsible for acts or transactions in which he has not personally engaged or in some other way participated".[541]

The exception to this principle comes in the case of mass crimes. For these crimes covered by R2P, the hierarchical superior is also responsible. The responsibility of the hierarchical superior is, by its very nature, a crime of omission rather than a direct attack emanating from a commander. This is how the notion of bystander came into being, for example in the fight against genocide and can be understood as follows: "bystanders [as] those who did not participate in crimes but nonetheless did not intervene to stop the carnage. They may have been silent supporters or opponents of the political and military forces that waged the war, but their role in the events is defined by their inaction and passivity."[542]

Thus, the inaction of a hierarchical superior will engage his responsibility for the conduct of one of the soldiers under his command. The case of General Hadžihasanović before the ICTY is significant. Under Article 7(3) of the ICTY Statute, for the first time charges were brought against a

540 Alexandru Matache, "The Inapplicability of the Nulla Poena Sine Culpa Principle in the EU Criminal Law: The Tendency towards Strict Liability Endorsement", *CDP*, 2017, p. 106.

541 *Prosecutor v Tadić (Appeal Judgment) IT-94-1-A*, 27 February 2001, para 186.

542 Laurel E. Fletcher, "From indifference to engagement: Bystanders and international criminal justice", *Mich. J. Int'l L. 26*, 2004, p. 101.

superior commander for having failed to prevent violations of international humanitarian law from being committed by his subordinates or to punish them if he knew or had reason to know that they had committed such violations.[543]

Article 28 of the Rome Statute sets out 5 conditions under which a superior may incur international criminal responsibility:

The existence of a superior, the possession of effective control, the link between the crime committed and the superior's failure to exercise control, knowledge of the commission of the crimes and, finally, the failure to take the necessary and reasonable measures to prevent or repress the commission of these crimes. The Rome Statute also specifies the possibility of military superior (28.a) and non-military superior (28.b). Without going back over the comments in favor and those against this legal provision, it should be pointed out that the Rome Statute was not clear about the boundary between the responsibility of the military superior and that of the non-military superior. In fact, it does not specify any criteria for distinguishing between them. This question should not be left to the ICC judge alone, as the nature of the accused would have an impact on the regime to be applied to him or her.[544]

In the light of the foregoing, some will consider the application of the doctrine of hierarchical superior in peace missions. The present thesis will therefore analyze the responsibility of the superior commander of the peace mission in relation to acts committed in violation of IHL and not what would be his responsibility in the scale of the protection of civilians in the general understanding of peace missions. This latter is an obligation of means and applicable during and after the conflict. Indeed, the protection of civilians here does not mean the same thing as the protection of civilians during armed conflict, it is in fact summed up by protection strategies. The protection of civilians refers to respect for the principles of IHL in relation to people who are not, or are no longer, taking part in combat. This being the case, for the Force Commander to engage his responsibility as a hierarchical superior, the analysis of the chain of command in peace missions

543 Christopher Greenwood, "Command responsibility and the Hadzihasanovic Decision", *J. Int'l Crim. Just. 2*, 2004, p. 598.

544 Nora Karsten, "Distinguishing Military and Non-military Superiors: Reflections on the Bemba Case at the ICC", *Journal of International Criminal Justice 7*, no. 5, 2009, p. 987.

must be an important element.[545] The present research shall return to this analysis a little later in the following chapter in relation to the jurisdiction of the International Court of Justice.

Thus, the Force Commander of MONUSCO, being also the Force Commander of the Brigade, could be held criminally responsible for the actions of the members of the Brigade if the five elements are met. In fact, not only the Force Commander but also the base commanders of the Brigade contingents could be held responsible, for example the one in Mavivi/Beni for the actions of the contingents during operations against the ADF. In fact, according to the general rules of IHL, the CGIV specifies that all the contracting State parties have jurisdiction to hear cases involving violations of IHL. Some may therefore understand that in matters of violations of IHL, the host state of peace missions and many other states may exercise their jurisdiction. The jurisdiction of a State includes legislative jurisdiction, which is the power to enact laws; declaratory jurisdiction, which is the power to interpret or apply laws; and enforcement jurisdiction, which consists of taking measures to ensure compliance.[546]

Although for these powers to be exercised there must be a direct link with the national territory, in certain circumstances, as recognized by International Law, a State may extend its jurisdiction to events that have no link with its territory. This is known as extraterritorial jurisdiction.[547] All these jurisdictions may justify the intervention of one or other State to repress crimes committed in the DRC. However, as far as peace missions are concerned, the State of Agreement (SOFA) grants jurisdictional immunities to contingents. The SOFA is a bilateral agreement signed between the UN and the host State that defines the privileges and immunities enjoyed by the UN mission and its personnel. These include immunity from arrest, detention and seizure, immunity from legal process in respect of words spoken or written and official acts. It should be noted, however, that the UN may waive these privileges and immunities without prejudice, as they are granted to staff members in the interests of the Organization and not for their personal benefit.

545 Lenneke Sprik, "Command responsibility in peacekeeping missions: Normative obligations of protection in a criminal law environment", *Journal of Conflict and Security Law 22*, no. 3, 2017, p. 500.

546 Chandra Lekha Sriram, *Globalizing justice for mass atrocities: a revolution in accountability*, Routledge, 2013.

547 Sriram, *Globalizing justice for mass atrocities*, p. 56.

It should be added that the immunities of the peacekeepers are not linked to those of the UN under Article 105 of the 1946 Convention on Privileges and Immunities. This is because they are not UN officials. Only the SOFA is applicable in their camps. This does not mean that they will not be held responsible for acts contrary to IHL. As Serge Bambara has pointed out, "The existence of immunities does not prevent the existence of individual criminal responsibility. The latter survives independently of immunities, which do not call into question the existence of responsibilities per se, but their implementation".[548]

The host states of peace missions have no jurisdiction over crimes committed by their contingents. Host States can neither try nor extradite contingents that have committed crimes during operations. Paragraphs 42b, 43 and 46 of the SOFA specify that even when another State requests the extradition of a Peacekeeper, the host State must not execute this request, as it is bound by the SOFA in the sense that only the transfer to its State is admissible. The SOFA attributes jurisdiction primarily to the States of origin. This is not the case with EU and NATO SOFAs. In the latter, all troop-contributing States and Host States have jurisdiction to judge crimes against national security, such as sabotage, espionage, etc. committed by military personnel. However, the condition is that these crimes must not be provided for in the laws of the countries of origin of these soldiers.[549]

However, although the SOFA assigns primary jurisdiction to the States of origin to judge its contingent nationals, this jurisdiction is not exclusive. Indeed, nothing would prevent other contributing or non-contributing States from trying the contingent that committed serious crimes. The SOFA's silence on this point would mean that this exception is limited to the host country. As the SOFA is a bilateral agreement between the host country and the UN, it will have no effect, in principle, on other states when it comes to their jurisdiction over serious crimes. That said, they retain their jurisdiction to judge and when they are unable or unwilling, they may proceed with extradition. Thus, the DRC will not have jurisdiction over crimes committed by contingents of the Brigade during the implementation of R2P by Resolution 2098, but it will retain jurisdiction as a natural judge over crimes committed by the FARDC during operations.

548 Serge Théophile Bambara, *"La justiciabilité des infractions des forces armées dans les opérations de paix"*, *Revue québécoise de droit international* 29, no. 1, 2016, p. 10. https://doi.org/10.7202/1045108ar, accessed on 19th jun 2024.

549 EU, *SOFA* art 7 para 3 and 4, *NATO, SOFA* article VII para a and b.

By contrast, another contributing state, for example Tanzania, would have jurisdiction over crimes committed by its own nationals or any other contingents during operations. Another argument to justify the jurisdiction of other States to judge the perpetrators of crimes would be linked to the very nature of these crimes. Being qualified as atrocious and having disturbed international public order, crimes committed in violation of IHL are imprescriptible and likely to bring into play the extraterritorial jurisdiction of States. One of the bases of this extraterritorial jurisdiction is universal jurisdiction. Universal jurisdiction over war crimes is based on both treaty law and customary international law.

Consider as an example in treaty law, articles 49, 50, 129 and 146 of the Geneva Conventions, the Convention against Torture adopted in 1984, the 2006 International Convention for the Protection of All Persons from Enforced Disappearance and many others. Customary international humanitarian law also establishes that States have the right to confer universal jurisdiction over war crimes on their national courts, in accordance with rule 175. The analysis of universal jurisdiction will be developed in the following section as one of the mechanisms to facilitate reparation for IHL crimes committed during R2P operations in the DRC.

Chapter III: Victims Reparation Remedies for Violations of IHL in the Implementation of R2P

Recognition of the victim's right to obtain reparation for violations of IHL is self-evident. Indeed, the idea of international responsibility is not only to make the person who has committed a crime face up to these acts, but also to repair the damage caused by these acts. The concepts of responsibility always refer to two subjects: the "executioner" and the "victim". The concept of reparation is set out in article 31 of the draft article on responsibility of States for internationally wrongful acts, which states that "the responsible State is under an obligation to make full reparation for the injury caused by the internationally wrongful act". The idea of reparation has also been modelled on the obligation of the IO, for any material or moral violation.[550]

Responsibility for violations of IHL is no exception to this approach. Indeed, Rule 150 of the ICRC Study on Customary IHL provides that a State responsible for violations of IHL must make full reparation for the loss or injury caused, for any type of armed conflict. The UN system provides reparation of violations of IHL in the UN Basic Principles and Guidelines on the Right to a Remedy and Reparation for Victims of Gross Violations of Human Rights and Serious Violations of International Humanitarian Law. Reparation for acts committed during peace operations is also somehow provided in the MOU and SOFA.

In addition, the obligation to make reparation is provided for in the articles common to the four Geneva Conventions dealing with the responsibility of the contracting parties. The State remains responsible and is required to pay compensation in the event of violations of the Geneva Conventions. Although IOs, in this case the UN, are not contracting parties to the Geneva Conventions, the nature of their obligations will be analyzed within the customary framework. Thus, from the moment it recognizes the possibility that it may incur responsibility, reparation will be a natural consequence. That was recognized by the PCIJ in the *Chorzów* case in 1928. The Court stated that: 'It is a principle of international law and even a general conception of the law, that any breach of an engagement involves an obligation to make reparation ... Reparation is the indispensable com-

550 Article 31 *DARIO.*

plement of a failure to apply a convention and there is no necessity for this to be stated in the convention itself".[551]

The analysis of article 3 of the Hague convention (1907) and article 91 API also deal with reparation by providing for total reparation. It can therefore be accepted that reparation is provided for in all types of conflict, international and internal. In the practice of international courts, reparation has also been provided for. Paragraph 7 of Resolution 827 on the creation of the ICTY provides that: " that the task of the Tribunal shall be accomplished without prejudice to the right of victims to seek reparation through appropriate means for damage resulting from violations of international humanitarian law".[552] Reparation is also provided for in the Rules of the Criminal Tribunal for the former Yugoslavia[553] and the Rules of the Criminal Tribunal for Rwanda.[554] Article 75 of the Rome Statute and the Rules of the ICC allow the victim to intervene and participate in order to obtain reparation.[555]

Although reparation is provided for in all these texts, the nature of the beneficiaries of this reparation has been the subject of debate in the past. While some considered that only States could be beneficiaries,[556] in accordance with the *ratio legis* of IHL, others also considered that individuals could also be beneficiaries of reparation. However, this debate is no longer topical, because as many have pointed out, it is important to focus on an obiter on the state of the law and not on the scope of application of Article 91 IP. This can be seen in the report of the United Nations International Commission of Inquiry on Darfur in 2005. On the basis of articles 3CIY

---

551 *Chorzów Factory Case (Jurisdiction),* 1927, Series A no 22, p.102.

552 *Resolution 827 of 25 May 1993 for the trial of persons presumed responsible for serious violations of international humanitarian law committed in the territory of the former Socialist Federal Republic of Yugoslavia since 1991, Res. CS 827 (1993) Off. Off. CS, 3217" sess, UN Doc. S/RES/827* (1993) *[Resolution 827 of 25 May 1993,* TPIYJ.

553 Criminal Tribunal for the former Yugoslavia, *Rules of Procedure and Evidence,* IT/32/Rev. 37, 2006, online: Criminal Tribunal for the former Yugoslavia, http://www.un.org/icty/legaldoc-ffindex-f.htm, accessed on 19th jun 2024 (page visited on 1 August 2007) [TPlY Rules].

554 Criminal Tribunal for Rwanda, *Rules of Procedure and Evidence, online: Criminal Tribunal for Rwanda,* available at http://v,,ww.un.org/ictr/l1Jlcs f.html, accessed on 19th jun 2024. [ICTR Rules].

555 *Regulations of the Court, ICC-BD/O 1-0 1-04/Rev.0 1-05, adopted on 26 May 2004 and amended on 9 March 2005, regulations 86 et seq.* [ICC Regulations].

556 Oscar M. Uhler and Henri Coursier, *Commentary IV: Geneva Convention Relative to the Protection of Civilian Persons in Time of War,* Geneva, ICRC, 1958, pp.645-646.

(1907) and 91PAI, the commission affirmed that: "serious violations of humanitarian law and human rights law entail not only criminal responsibility for the perpetrators, but also responsibility for the State (or State-like party to the conflict) in whose name the act was committed". Thus, for the purposes of the present thesis, the term victims here refer to the State, the DRC and to individuals (people who have been victims of these violations). The term individual refers to the human person and/or his or her community.

That being the case and in accordance with the previous chapters, institutions and individuals can be held responsible for IHL violations committed during the implementation of Resolution 2098. Having analyzed accountability for violations committed during the implementation of R2P, this chapter will now analyze the second aspect, which is reparation. This can take place in different forms: restitution, compensation, rehabilitation, satisfaction and guarantees of non-repetition. As stated in the proceedings of the 1949 Geneva Diplomatic Conference: "It is not enough to grant rights to individuals and to impose responsibilities on States; protected persons must also be provided with the support they need to assert their rights, without which they would be legally helpless [...]".[557]

Although remedies for reparation might differ according to whether they are sought by the UN, States or individuals, this chapter will analyze these remedies in two main points: Jurisdictional mechanisms (1) and non-jurisdictional mechanisms (2).

1. Judicial remedies for violations of International Humanitarian Law

Victims of violations of IHL committed in the implementation of resolution 2098 may have recourse to jurisdictional mechanisms to obtain reparation. Whether at the international, regional or national level, victims of violations of IHL can intervene either directly, i.e. by participating in the proceedings, or indirectly, i.e. by virtue of the diplomatic protection of the DRC or any other State whose national was the victim of violations during R2P operations. This section will analyze the mechanisms at the international and regional level (A) and those at the national level (B).

557 *Acts of the Geneva Diplomatic Conference of 1949*, vol.II-A at p. 805 as cited in *ICRC Commentary CGIV*, p. 230, art. 30.

A. Mechanisms provided for at International and Regional level

Although the Geneva Conventions and their Additional Protocols contain many provisions for the punishment of individuals who have committed grave breaches, they do not provide for any remedy for the victims of these crimes. The only procedure provided for by the Geneva system would be that set out in Article 90 of the API, which provides for the creation of an International Fact-Finding Commission for parties to conflicts. However, it must be admitted that at the international level, there is recognition of the international mechanisms provided for reparation for violations of IHL. These mechanisms are accessible to both legal persons and individuals. This was taken up by the ICJ in the wall case, where the court stated that Israel was obliged under international law to afford reparation to all natural and legal persons injured by the construction of the wall. The UN Principles on the Right to a Remedy have taken a giant step forward in the recognition of international reparation mechanisms for individuals. Principle 12 states that the right to an adequate remedy against a violation of IHL includes "all available international processes in which an individual may have legal standing".[558]

Although reparation for violations of IHL is provided for internationally, there is no general mechanism enabling victims to seek reparation. This being the case, this section will analyze the mechanisms provided for under public international law and those provided for under international criminal law.

i. Mechanisms provided for under Public International Law

For the context of the implementation of Resolution 2098, it should be noted, as already mentioned in the introduction to this thesis, that only violations committed by members of the Brigade Force and the FARDC in implementing this resolution have been analyzed. Violations committed by internal and international rebel groups, which raise questions about the characterization of the conflict, will be the subject of a different analysis.

558 Cherif M. Bassiouni, "The right to restitution, compensation and rehabilitation for victims of gross violations of human rights and fundamental freedoms", *Commission on Human Rights Resolution 2002/44, 23 April 2002. Read the final Report of the Special Rapporteur,* Mr. M. Cherif Bassiouni, submitted in accordance with Commission Resolution 1999/33, *Post-Conflict Justice,* Brill Nijhoff, 2002, pp. 243-252.

The reparation mechanisms provided for by international law are mainly based on the theory of responsibility for internationally wrongful acts and the institution of diplomatic protection. These two theories, in principle, have reparation as the other side of the coin. The theory of responsibility for internationally wrongful acts directly implicates the State as the victim of the violations and therefore liable to claim reparation. Thus, the DRC is entitled to reparation for all violations committed during the implementation of Resolution 2098. Although it is a party to the operations, it will be necessary to identify the crimes that are attributable solely to the UN according to the criteria set out in the previous chapter.

The present thesis considers that, in principle, only the UN can be held responsible and not the countries contributing to the Brigade Force, nor SADC. The States would only be liable if there was tangible evidence implicating their nationals in the commission of violations of IHL outside the command of the Brigade. The case of Kasindi involving members of the Tanzanian Brigade would be an example. Although we will not go into the classification of the facts as war crimes or crimes against humanity, it is clear that these contingents had never received orders from the Force Commander to fire on the population and police officers at the Kasindi border. In this case, Tanzania would be required to make reparations for the actions of its contingents.

It should be noted, however, that the Kasindi incident was described by the Congolese magistrate of the Beni Auditorat Militaire as a murder, attempted murder and vicious destruction, while specifying that the 50 Tanzanian contingents have already been repatriated.[559] Another question would be whether the Kasindi incident was an operational imperative with the legal consequence that it could not be repaired. This idea will be elaborated in the second section. In addition, other countries contributing to MONUSCO's regular forces for joint operations carried out in application of Resolution 2098 could also be considered responsible for making reparation for acts committed by their troops. This being the case and considering the nature of the "persons" who allegedly committed the violations of IHL, the ICJ would be competent to hear the case. Indeed, in the practice of the ICJ, it has been mentioned that violations of IHL are fundamental and give rise to obligations *erga omnes*[560] and thus founded the obligation to make reparation under international custom. In the Wall Opinion case, the

559 *Affaire MONUSCO KASINDI, RI no 129/IOP/AMG/Bni/022 registered le 04/08/2022*

560 *Wall Opinion (n94) [154-159].*

Court identified violations of articles 46 and 52 of the Hague Regulations of 1907, as well as articles 49 and 53 of the Fourth Geneva Convention of 1949. This case, among many others, proves that the ICJ would have jurisdiction to hear cases seeking redress for violations of IHL. Even when the ICJ would be the most appropriate mechanism for the DRC to obtain reparation, it has always faced challenges related to the acceptance of its jurisdiction and also to the enforcement of its decisions. The ICJ has two jurisdictions: contentious and advisory. Contentious jurisdiction is only admitted in a dispute between States and is subject to acceptance of the Court's jurisdiction. The DRC, which has already had one "unfortunate" and one "semi-unfortunate" experience in connection with a claim for reparations before the ICJ, is a living example of this. These two experiences are all linked to the military activities in Kisangani, the so-called Six-Day War.

In the DRC v Rwanda case, the question of acceptance of the Court's jurisdiction was raised. The Court affirmed that it did not have the prima facie jurisdiction necessary to indicate the provisional measures requested by the Congo since Rwanda had not recognized the Court's jurisdiction in this case. While declaring itself incompetent, the Court recalled that States remain responsible for acts contrary to international law in general and to IHL in the event of conflict, including GC IV[561], as recalled by the Security Council in its resolutions[562] concerning the situation in the DRC and the Great Lakes region. In addition, the Court recalled the obligation of States to prevent violations of human rights and IHL.

Although in its decision the Court recognized the responsibility of States and indirectly that of Rwanda, for non-compliance with international law, it did not address the question of reparation, as this is a substantive issue. The Court recalled that: "there is a fundamental distinction between the question of the acceptance by a State of the jurisdiction of the Court and the compatibility of certain acts with international law; jurisdiction requires consent; compatibility can only be assessed when the Court exam-

561 *International court of justice reports of judgments, advisory opinions and orders case concerning armed activities on the territory of the congo (new application : 2002) (democratic republic of the congo v. Rwanda) request for the indication of provisional measures*, Order of 10 july 2002, Para 92 available at https://www.icj-cij.org/fr/decisions?type=3&from=2002&to=2002&sort_bef_combine=order_DESC, accessed on 17 august 2024.

562 *UNSC resolutions 1234 (1999), 1291 (2000), 1304 (2000), 1316 (2000), 1323 (2000), 1332 (2000), 1341 (2001), 1355 (2001), 1376 (2001), 1399 (2002) et 1417 (2002)*; as quoted in the Order of 10 July 2002.

ines the merits, after having established its jurisdiction and heard both parties fully argue their case in law".[563]

Given that it is a matter of State sovereignty to accept or refuse the Court's jurisdiction, this example, among many others, raises questions about the ICJ as an effective mechanism for reparations for violations of IHL. Given the principle of adversarial adjudication, it would be difficult to assert a system of judgement by default before the ICJ. Even if, by chance, judgement by default were to be admitted, voluntarism/state sovereignty would always be a brake on the execution of such a decision. The "semi-unfortunate" experience would be that of the DRC v Uganda case, known as Armed Activities on the Territory of the Congo of 19 December 2005. The court attributed to Uganda violations of IHL committed by UPDF (Uganda People's Forces) troops. It should be noted that this case, which would be considered by many as a landmark case in relation to the obligations of the occupying power, took up the State's responsibility with regards to IHL.

The Court condemned Uganda, as the occupying power, for having failed to take all possible measures to restore and ensure public order and security under Article 43 of the 1907 Hague Regulations. The ICJ ordered Uganda to pay damages. The judgment provided that the DRC and Uganda would have to agree on the total amount of damages as well as the terms of payment and that the court could only intervene when a compromise was not possible. As the DRC and Uganda were unable to reach a compromise, the DRC again referred the matter to the Court for compensation on 13 May 2015.

The Court delivered its judgment on 9 February 2022, awarding USD 225,000,000 for damages to persons, USD 40,000,000 for damages to property and USD 60,000,000 for damages to natural resources. The Court also set the method of payment in five annual instalments of USD 65,000,000 and default interest at an annual rate of 6%. This experience could be described as semi-unfortunate, given Uganda's attitude to reparation for acts committed in the DRC. Time has had an impact on the identification of the direct victims of these activities. Another impact that should not

563 ICJ, *International court of justice reports of judgments, advisory opinions and orders case concerning armed activities on the territory of the congo (new application : 2002) (democratic republic of the congo v. Rwanda) request for the indication of provisional measures* ,Order of 10 july 2002, Para 93 available at https://www.icj-cij.org/fr/decisions?type=3&from=2002&to=2002&sort_bef_combine=order_DESC, accessed on 17 august 2024.

be overlooked is the financial aspect. The DRC was obliged to commit financial resources to this action.

It is easy to deduce from this 2022 judgment that States can obtain reparation for damage caused to individuals in violation of IHL and this in one way or another answers the question raised by Marxsen, who considered that: "States on the other hand could claim losses in regard to State infrastructure, but it is unclear to which extent States could also claim violations suffered by its citizens".[564]

Moreover, the question that arises is whether individual victims have direct access to these funds. In the case under consideration, Uganda paid the sum of USD 65 million in September 2022 as agreed.[565]However, the Fonds Spécial de Réparation de l'Indemnisation aux Victimes des activités illicites de l'Ouganda en République Démocratique du Congo ou à leurs ayants droits (FRIVAO) was not established until May 2023.[566]

Without being pessimistic, this analysis considers that preparations should have been made beforehand since the first judgment in 2005. This would enable the correct identification of individual victims and the form of reparation that would respond effectively to victims' needs.

Another analysis, which will not be developed here, would be the reasons why Uganda decided to pay in 2022 and not in 2005, without going back on the fact that a compromise on the calculation of damages was not even possible. There are two possible explanations for Uganda's attitude: the first is purely political and refers to the state of diplomatic relations between Uganda and the regimes in place in the DRC at the time and the second is linked to the sacrosanct principle of international law, namely sovereignty. It is clear that the same sovereignty that poses a barrier to the jurisdiction of the ICJ can also pose barriers to the enforcement of the latter's decisions,

564 Marxsen, Christian. "Unpacking the International Law on Reparation for Victims of Armed Conflict." *Reparation for Victims of Armed Conflict, Max Planck Institute for Comparative Public Law and International Law (MPIL),* Research Paper 2018-19, 2018, p.538.

565 *Uganda says paid first instalment in Congo war reparations,* available at https://www.reuters.com/world/africa/uganda-says-paid-first-instalment-congo-war-reparations-2022-09-12/, accessed on 17 august 2024.

566 *RDC:le gouvernement informé de l'opérationnalisation du Fonds spécial de réparation et de l'indemnisation des victimes des activités armées de l'Ouganda,* available at https://actualite.cd/2023/08/20/ 3.

even though it has declared itself competent. The *La Grande*[567] case and several others are proof of this.

In its advisory jurisdiction, the ICJ would be competent to give its opinion on the DRC's claim for reparation against the UN for violations of IHL committed by the Brigade's forces during the implementation of Resolution 2098. As long as the UN has legal personality, it is entitled to reparations for any damage it suffers, and also to reparation for any damage it may have caused. The ICJ judge confirmed the UN's legal personality in the case reparation for Injuries Suffered in the Service of the United Nations.[568]

It appears, however, that this mechanism would not be the most appropriate for the DRC to obtain reparation given the nature of an advisory opinion. An advisory opinion does not have the force of res judicata. As its name suggests, it remains an "opinion". When even the Court's judgments in contentious matters are subject to State sovereignty, what could be more normal than an advisory opinion?

Moreover, by virtue of the institution of diplomatic protection, which requires a State to represent its nationals before international courts in order to seek redress, the ICJ may have jurisdiction. The theory of diplomatic protection, which is accepted by many as an individual mechanism for reparations of violations of IHL, has however shown a certain uncertainty as to its effectiveness due to the conditions under which it is exercised. Indeed, three conditions are necessary to trigger diplomatic protection. These are nationality, exhaustion of domestic remedies and, last but not least, its discretionary nature. Exhaustion of domestic remedies is easy to prove because there are exceptions, such as the impossibility of meeting this condition or being expelled and perhaps not having the material means to do so, whereas the discretionary nature poses more of a problem. This is because by virtue of its discretion the State can decide to represent the one case and not the other without giving detailed reasons for its choice.

Another challenge, which has been raised by many, is that of ensuring that the victim actually receives the sums allocated to him by his State. In addition, the individual victim must also be able to pay a certain sum to his or her State so that the latter can represent him or her before an

567 *LaGrand (Germany v United States of America), Provisional Measures, Order of 3 March 1999,* 1999, ICJ Rep 466. See also *Vienna Convention on Consular Relations (Paraguay v United States of America), Provisional Measures,* Order of Posted: 1998-04-09.

568 ICJ, *Reparation for injuries suffered in the service of the Nations, Advisory Opinion,* [1949] ICJ Rep 174, ICGJ 232, 1949, 11th April 1949.

international body. This was in line with the idea that, "*whether the action concerned the State directly or its national through diplomatic protection, the action remained the action of the State*"[569], which remained in control of it and determined its fate. Although the idea has been developed in the discussion concerning the place of the individual victim in the preparation of damage suffered in violation of IHL, it emerges that even in the enforcement of judgments in which individuals have benefited from diplomatic protection, States have proved that they were the only ones to decide the fate of the individual.

An example of this is the 2012 case *Ahmadou Sadio Diallo, Republique de Guiné v. RDC*. After the DRC had been condemned to pay 95,000 US dollars in damages on behalf of the Guinean citizen, Mr. Diallo, he died 8 years later, without obtaining compensation and the Republic of Guinea seems not to be interested in summoning the DRC to pay. Without going back over the whole litany behind the *res judicata* effect of the ICJ's decisions, whether in a case within its advisory or contentious jurisdiction, it appears that this mechanism, although accessible, still presents many challenges. It would not, therefore, be the most appropriate mechanism for the DRC or its victim population to obtain reparation for violations committed by members of the Brigade.

Although there is no direct system of reparation for violations of IHL in the African human rights system, the combination of IHL and human rights may be a solution. As is well known, although IHL is considered a *lex specialis*, it has been proven in practice and by virtue of reparation that the rules of international human rights law can also be applied during armed conflicts. Indeed, almost all human rights systems have recognized this possibility. For the Inter-American Court of Human Rights, even if it is incompetent to declare a State internationally responsible for violations of treaties that do not fall within its jurisdiction, it may find that certain acts or omissions in treaties over which it has jurisdiction are directly related to the content of the Geneva Conventions and in particular Article 3 common to those conventions. In the Las Palmeras Case (2000), the court states that the relevant provisions of the Geneva Conventions may be

---

569 Annemarieke Vermeer-Künzli, "A matter of interest: Diplomatic protection and state responsibility Erga Omnes", *international & Comparative Law Quarterly 56,* no. 3, 2007, p. 560.

taken into consideration as elements for the interpretation of the American Convention."[570]

Even though the European Court of Human Rights, for its part, has not been very clear about its competence in relation to IHL, it is clear that the latter has been used as an instrument of interpretation before the Court.[571] The relevant practice may be categorized under the following headings: detention and treatment of detainees, destruction of property and displacement of the civilian population, conduct of military operations and unlawful killings. Moreover, the African human rights system would also be a mechanism for reparation for violations of IHL committed by the implementation of R2P under resolution 2098. Unlike other human rights systems, the African Commission on Human and Peoples' Rights (here the Commission) has been clear about the link between IHL and human rights. In its mission, as set out in Article 45 of the Charter, which is to interpret the African Charter on Human and Peoples' Rights (here the African Charter) and promote human rights, the Commission states that violations of IHL can be interpreted in relation to human rights. Indeed, in its Resolution on the Promotion and the Respect of International Humanitarian Law and Human and Peoples' Rights, the Commission returns to the main objective of international humanitarian law and IHL, which is the protection of the individual.[572]

Furthermore, in its comments, the Commission interpreted its competence in relation to the right to life and the scope of prohibition on the arbitrary deprivation of life. This explains why the Commission is able to examine cases relating to human rights violations in both peacetime and wartime.[573]

Although there are not yet any cases before this Commission relating directly to IHL, victims of violations of IHL in the implementation of

570 *Case Las Palmers, Preliminaries Exceptions, Judgement of 04 de February 2000,* Serie C, No. 66 Paras. 205-210.

571 Humanitarian law has been applied in the context of the following ECHR rights: Article 2 (right to life), Article 3 (prohibition of torture/inhuman treatment), Article 8 (right to family life) and Article 1 of Protocol 1 (right to property).

572 *Annual Activity Report of the African Commission on Human and Peoples' Rights,* 1993, p.94, ACHPR/RPTl7th at Annex XI.

573 *General Comment No.3 on the African Charter on Human and Peoples' Rights: The Right to Life (Article 4), Adopted During the 57th Ordinary Session of the African Commission on Human and Peoples' Rights Held From 4 to 18 November 2015 in Banjul,* available at: http://www.achpr.org/files/instruments/general-comments-rig ht-to-life/general_comment_no_3_english.pdf, accessed on 17 august 2024.

Resolution 2098 may refer their case to the African Commission on Human and Peoples' Rights. In accordance with articles 46 and 51 of the African Charter, the Commission has the right to receive and examine state or individual communications relating to violations. It should be pointed out here that individual communications, also known as "other communications", are acceptable under seven conditions, including the following: domestic remedies must have been exhausted; the complaint must not be anonymous, insulting or incompatible with the African Charter on Human and Peoples' Rights; it must be submitted within a reasonable period of time and must not be limited to news reports disseminated by mass media. Finally, the application of the ne bis in idem principle in the sense that the case must not have already been settled in accordance with the principles of the UN Charter or the African Charter on Human and Peoples' Rights.[574]

In view of the foregoing, the Congolese State may refer to the Commission on Human Rights or the African Court of Justice on Human Rights any matter relating to human rights for which another Member State of the African Union is responsible. By ricochet, the DRC would refer to the Commission violations of IHL committed on its territory and against its citizens by AU member states involved in the intervention brigade. In the same vein, individual Victims, subject to the conditions set out above, may also bring a case before the Commission against the DRC and other African States for violations of IHL in relation to human rights committed by the FARDC or their forces as members of the Brigade. However, this mechanism before the Commission would be more diplomatic than legal. One noteworthy fact is the Commission's reluctance to recognize outright the violations of IHL in the six-day war in the DRC. On the other hand, the Commission generally considered the actions of the DRC's neighbors, in this case Rwanda and Uganda, as a violation of the peoples' right to peace and security, to cultural development and to self-determination.[575]

The commission does not pass judgement but seeks an amicable solution to the situation. In the event of failure, the Commission will simply transmit its report and recommendations confidentially to the States concerned and to the Conference of Heads of State.[576] Once again, it is important to rely on the good faith of States to take account of the Commission's recommendations, as these are not binding (Article 52). In addition to the

574 Art 56, *African Charter on Human and Peoples' Rights*

575 *Democratic Republic of Congo v. Burundi, Rwanda and Uganda, African Commission on Human and Peoples' Rights,* Communication No. 227/99, 2006.

576 Arts 58-59, *the African Charter on Human and Peoples' Rights.*

Commission, The African Court on Human and Peoples' Rights (ACHPR Court) is also a mechanism, not the least of the possibilities which victims can use to obtain reparation. The ACHPR Court, established by the Protocol to the African Charter on Human and Peoples' Rights (1998 Protocol), may have jurisdiction in human rights matters. However, the Protocol on the African Court of Justice and Human Rights, which proposes combining the ACHPR and the African Court of Justice (ACJ), could be more comprehensive in its jurisdiction over violations of international humanitarian law. Unfortunately, this court is not yet operational and the ACHPR remains operational with its initial mandate. This mandate, which, according to the present thesis, appears to be strict, would pose challenges in terms of referral to it by individuals and NGOs, but also in terms of its competence to hear cases of violations of IHL, since the ACHPR's mandate would be limited to human rights issues as envisaged in 1998. The African Court of Justice and Human Rights (hereinafter referred to as the African Court), which is the judicial organ of the African Union, shall have jurisdiction over all disputes and differences relating to the interpretation and application of the African Charter on Human and Peoples' Rights and all protocols to the Charter and all other human rights conventions ratified by the States concerned, as well as all matters of international law.

Indeed, many would understand that the Court's jurisdiction is broad and not limited to violations of human rights in the strict sense. Moreover, in the light of Article 28 of the Protocol on the Statute of the African Court of Justice and Human Rights, the African Court has jurisdiction in matters of reparation if it is established that an act constitutes a breach of an obligation owed to another State party to the Union. It follows from this article that the African Court may have jurisdiction in respect of claims for reparation for violations of IHL as breach of customary law and therefore, for all violations committed during the implementation of resolution 2098. The Court can rule on the forms of reparation and compensation[577]or urgent provisional measures.[578]

This would be justified by the very desire of the AU to create a criminal chamber within the meaning of this court.[579] In fact, since February 2009, the draft Protocol for the establishment of the Criminal Chamber within the African Court has made it clear that the Court's competence to deal

577 Art. 45, *Protocol on the Statute of the African Court of Justice and Human Rights.*

578 Art. 35, *ibid.*

579 *Assembly/AU/Dec. 292 (XV).*

with violations of IHL is to be included. According to art 28 of this draft protocol , the International Criminal Law Section of the Court shall have power to try persons for the following crimes: Genocide, Crimes against Humanity, War Crimes, The Crime of Unconstitutional Change of Government, Piracy, Terrorism, Mercenaryism, Corruption, Money Laundering, Trafficking in Persons, Trafficking in Drugs, Trafficking in Hazardous Wastes, Illicit Exploitation of Natural Resources and the Crime of Aggression.[580] Although it will not be the subject of analysis in the present work, the question that many would ask is whether a protocol that is not enforced can serve as an object of amendment. Indeed, if we limit ourselves to international law in general, it would not be admissible to envisage an amendment to a treaty which, unofficially, does not exist, because it is not in force. On the other hand, the practice of States in treaty law proves that a treaty can always be amended before it enters into force in order to clarify its ratio legis. Another question would be the attitude of States that have already ratified the amended text before it enters into force.

To return to the African Court of Justice on Human Rights, this mechanism would have a significant impact because the Court's judgments are binding on States.[581]Thus, the DRC, the Commission and all authorized institutions[582] may refer to the Court acts committed in the DRC. However, individuals and NGOs may only refer cases to the Court if they have observer status with the Commission and the State that has ratified the Protocol has made a special declaration accepting the Court's jurisdiction to receive this type of application.[583]

At the African level, moreover, as all the contributing States are members of the SADC and the EAC, the courts of these organizations are also mechanisms to which victims of violations of IHL can have recourse. It should be pointed out that, in fact, this possibility could only be envisaged within the same logic as the repression of IHL violations by the human rights protection system. The present research considers that this will not be an easy task for the judge of the East African Court of Justice, which has acknowledged that it has no jurisdiction over human rights, let alone over international humanitarian law. However, while basing itself on its interpretation mission as provided for by Articles 6, d), 7, paragraphs 1 and 2, 8,

580 *Draft Protocol on the African Court of Justice and Human and Peoples' Rights,* (n 14), art 28A.).
581 Art. 46, *ibid.*
582 Arts. 29 and 30, *ibid.*
583 Arts 8.3 and 30.f, *ibid.*

paragraph 1, c) of the treaty, in the *James Katabazi and 21 others*, the Court held that "while this Court does not assume jurisdiction to rule on disputes relating to human rights, it will not shirk the exercise of its interpretative jurisdiction under Article 27 (1) merely because the application contains a reference to alleged violations of human rights".[584]

This analysis has been repeated in a number of the Court's other cases, taking up the States' human rights objections. It follows from the above that individual victims of IHL violations committed during the implementation of R2P in the DRC may have recourse to the East African Court of Justice for reparation. The Tribunal of the Southern African Development Community (SADC), in accordance with its jurisdiction, may also be seized by countries as well as by individuals, in order to seek reparation. It should also be pointed out that this tribunal would be more appropriate because, as raised in the first parts of this thesis, the adoption of Resolution 2098 is one of the merits of SADC. Moreover, the constitution of the members of the Brigade force was done under the SADC. However, as in the case of other African human rights mechanisms, it should be noted that the jurisdiction of this tribunal will only be derived from its human rights jurisdiction, a jurisdiction that has not been clearly provided for in the constitutive texts. Furthermore, the good faith of States in implementing the Tribunal's decisions is an important factor in its effectiveness, as demonstrated by the Zimbabwean government's refusal to implement a Tribunal decision on land reform. This refusal led to the suspension of the Tribunal and the reform of the texts on the Court's jurisdiction.[585]

This being the case, when it is established that violations of IHL were committed during the implementation of R2P in the DRC, the victims have the possibility of resorting to the mechanisms provided for by international law in order to obtain reparation. Without wishing to be pessimistic about these mechanisms, it must be stressed that their effectiveness will depend not solely on the will of States and their commitment to respect international humanitarian law, but also on compliance with the obligation to restore the rights of victims of violations of IHL.

---

584 *James Katabazi and 21 Others v. Secretary General of the East African Community and the Attorney General of the Republic of Uganda,* Reference n° 1 of 2007, 1st November 2007, para 16.

585 *Case of Mike Campbell (Pvt) Ltd and others v Republic of Zimbabwe,SADC (T)* (case no. 2/2007, 28- 11-2008).

ii. Mechanisms under International Criminal Law

One of the most significant contributions to the promotion of IHL is the notion of individual international responsibility in international criminal law. This criminal responsibility goes hand in hand with reparation, which contains not only the obligations of the perpetrator of the violation but also the rights of the victims of these violations. This concept has evolved from responsibility for acts to responsibility for omissions. This is evident in the history of ad hoc international criminal tribunals such as Nuremberg, Tokyo, the former Yugoslavia, the ICTR and the International Criminal Court. For example, the concept of joint criminal enterprise (JCE) at the Nuremberg trials was developed in the case law of the ad hoc international criminal tribunals of the 1990s. Thus, it is inadmissible to invoke the defense of a principal who claims that he was only responding to orders or that he was only doing his job and to hold hierarchical superiors liable where they aided or abetted the planning, preparation or execution of an international crime.[586]As many confirm, these mechanisms remain, at least in the current state of IHL, the most appropriate for establishing the responsibilities of each party and determining reparation.

As regards the implementation of R2P and violations of IHL in the DRC, the International Criminal Court has jurisdiction over these crimes. The jurisdiction of the ICC is *ratione loci*, *ratione materiae* and ratione temporis. The ICC's temporal jurisdiction over crimes committed in the DRC has been justified since 2002. When the DRC deposited its instrument of ratification of the Rome Statute, it became a party to the treaty with all its consequences. Consequently, crimes committed between 2013 and 2023, the years of implementation of Resolution 2098 and the research period of this thesis, can be tried by the ICC. Ratification of the Rome Statute by the DRC has produced another consequence, namely territorial jurisdiction. The ICC therefore has jurisdiction over crimes committed on the territory of the DRC. This means that the Rome Statute is an integral part of the nomenclature of Congolese laws. Article 215 of the DRC constitution stipulates that treaties and agreements that have been duly ratified are superior

586 Articles 86 and 87 of the *Additional Protocol for the Protection of Victims of International Armed Conflicts*, 8 June 1977, 1125 U.N.T.S. 3, [PI].

to domestic laws. Although it is a monist country, the DRC has adopted a law implementing the Rome Statute in the DRC.[587]

Passed in 2015, the law implementing the Rome Statute in the DRC amends the Military Penal Code and recognizes the jurisdiction of common courts to deal with crimes affecting peace and human security in the DRC. Another innovation is the consideration of superior responsibility for mass crimes. These two legal instruments, i.e. the Rome Statute and the 2015 implementing law, provide sufficient justification for the Court's territorial jurisdiction over crimes committed in the DRC. The history of the relationship between the ICC and the DRC is one proof of this jurisdiction. Indeed, several cases have already been transferred to the ICC in relation to violations of IHL committed on the territory of the DRC.[588]

As regards the ICC's subject-matter jurisdiction over violations of IHL committed during the implementation of R2P, the nature of the crimes themselves provides the basis for this. Articles 5 to 9 of the Rome Statute set out the crimes over which the ICC has jurisdiction. These are war crimes, crimes against humanity, genocide and aggression. In fact, if we go back to the "qualification" of the facts constituting violations of IHL during the implementation of Resolution 2098, the Court would in one way or another end up with the crimes of its jurisdiction, in this case war crimes. Article 8 defines war crimes as grave breaches of the Geneva Conventions of 1949 and other serious violations of the laws and customs applicable in international armed conflict within the established framework of international law.

In this specific context, the Court would have jurisdiction by virtue of Article 8 b(i)(ii) (iv) and (v), which prohibit attacks on civilians and their property. The attacks on ADF strongholds, which did not take into account the presence of kidnapped civilians, women and children, are a violation of the customs of war. This can be compared to the analysis taken up by the ICC in the case of *The Prosecutor v. Ali Muhammad Ali Abd-AlRahman ('Ali Kushayb')*. The ICC then affirmed the attack on Four civilians who were

587 Loi n° 15/023 du 31 décembre 2015 modifiant la Loi n° 024-2002 du 18 novembre 2002 portant Code pénal militaire, *JO de la RDC*, numéro spécial du 18 novembre 2002.

588 There are many cases before the ICC concerning DRC and Congolese. The Bemba, Mathieu Ngunjolo, Thomas Luaka , Thomas Lubanga, Bosco Ntaganda, etc. and warrant of arrest .

hors de combat even when they were in the same localities as the insurgents as a war crime under Article 8 (v) of the Rome Statute.[589]

Even when it could be confirmed that when the military advantage of the attack is weighed against the lives of civilians and the protection of their property, precautionary measures must be insisted upon. It was with this in mind that pretrial Chamber II of the ICC confirmed the war crimes charges against Ali Kushayb. Another element on which the ICC could base its prosecution of war crimes would be the fact that these strongholds were also bombed when the ADF, their women, children and all the civilians kidnapped were performing the obligatory evening prayer.[590]

The exercise of the ICC's jurisdiction will not be an exception and must therefore be possible in the following situations: The situation in the DRC is referred to the ICC, when the Prosecutor himself has reason to believe that crimes within the jurisdiction of the Court have been committed. This reinforces the idea that international criminal law links the Prosecutor with an individual who has committed a crime affecting the entire international community. In addition, under Chapter VII of the United Nations Charter, the Security Council may also refer a case to the Court. The situation in the DRC, particularly in the context of Resolution 2098, has already been declared by the Security Council to be a threat to international peace and security. Thus, even if the DRC does not refer the situation to the ICC or the Prosecutor does not take up the case proprio motu, the Security Council could itself refer the situation.

It should be noted that this work is limited to violations committed by those involved in the operations under Resolution 2098 and not those against whom the operations were carried out. Attacks by rebel groups, limited to the ADF, APCLS and M23, constitute either war crimes or crimes against humanity, depending on the case. (In fact, there is quite a lot of case law on the ADF, APCLS and M23 in terms of war crimes and crimes against humanity. The Beni mobile court, the *Tcheka* trial in Goma, etc. are proof of this). The question here is whether the ICC has jurisdiction to try members of a UN force mandated to implement R2P. What about their immunities?

As noted in the previous pages, the prohibition on prosecution is based on the SOFA agreements and binds only the host state and the United

589 *Situation in Darfur, Sudan in the case of the prosecutor v. Ali Muhammad Ali Abdalrahman 'Ali kushayb'*, para 30, p 54, No. ICC-02/05-01/20, 9 July 2021.

590 *Testimony of one of the survivors of the ADF kidnappings, interviewed in Oicha, June 2023.*

Nations. The consequence of this is that all other jurisdictions, including the ICC, that have the material jurisdiction to judge crimes committed in the DRC are competent. The only limitation on the ICC's jurisdiction in this context would be the *ne bis in idem* principle, which is a fundamental principle of procedural criminal law and the ICC is no exception. Therefore, if the members of the Brigade have been tried or their cases are pending before a national court, the ICC will not have jurisdiction. As the ICC is a complementary court, it cannot intervene if the State is unable or unwilling to hear the case. Parody of justice is also one of the exceptions to the Court's complementarity. Another analysis, which unfortunately will not be developed here, is that of the cases of sexual violations committed by members of the Brigade in the middle of a conflict zone and during the conflict. When would the ICC be competent in one way or another to deal with sexual offences committed during conflicts and the implementation of R2P? Indeed, the offences of rape and sexual violence committed by members of the Brigade in Beni do not meet the elements of war crimes or crimes against humanity provided for in Articles 8(2) and 7(1) respectively of the Rome Statute. This being the case, it would not be foolish to consider the influence that an act of sexual violence committed by a member of a United Nations force during the conflict would have. While congratulating the administrative measures taken against the eight peacekeepers who were members of the Brigade in Beni, the present thesis considers that the UN should reassure itself of the repression of these acts and consider the nature of the force's mandate as an aggravating circumstance in the case of its agents. It is in this context that the encouragement of the creation of courts martial in Situ within the United Nations could also constitute a very important step in the repression of offences by peacekeeping forces.

B. Domestic remedies

The element that always comes to mind in connection with mechanisms for redressing violations of IHL at the domestic level is the self-executing nature of IHL. A number of discussions have taken place in Japanese and American courts in the *"comfort women"* case and several US cases such as *Hamdi v. Rumsfeld and Leo Handel et al v. Andrija Artukovic* in relation to the rejection of the immediate execution of the 1907 Hague Convention and the Geneva Convention on Prisoners of War. However, even where the Geneva Conventions are not immediately enforceable, individuals may bring claims before the courts for violations of IHL under other laws or treaties that are already enforceable.

This is the case in the US, for example in *Filartiga v. Pena Irala*, relatives of a victim of State torture and murder in Paraguay sued the alleged perpetrator for damages in a federal district court in New York. The district court dismissed for lack of jurisdiction, but on appeal, the Second Circuit found federal court jurisdiction under the ATCA, allowing US courts to provide foreigners with a remedy for violations of international law wherever they took place.

In addition, in accordance with Principle 2 of the UN Principles, domestic legislation must incorporate IHL and thus accept individual action by victims before national courts.

Principle 2, which states: "States shall ensure that domestic law is consistent with international legal obligations by (...) incorporating norms of international human rights and humanitarian law into their domestic law, or otherwise implementing them in their domestic legal system", has been superseded by principle 8 in relation to the obligation of States and the right to reparation. [591]

What follows is an analysis of the implementation of the Geneva Conventions in countries that have jurisdiction for IHL violations committed in DRC during the implementation of R2P.

i. Jurisdiction of the Troops Contributing States and the DRC

The natural judge for crimes committed by members of peace missions is a court of their country of origin. This jurisdiction covers violations of both national and international law.[592] As stated in the State of agreements (SOFA), peacekeeping forces enjoy immunity from jurisdiction in the host country. However, this immunity does not mean impunity, as contributing countries are obliged to prosecute their nationals for violations committed in the host country.[593]

591 Principles 8(d) and 10(a), *UN Principles on the Right to a Remedy.*

592 *Model Agreement,* supra note 77, art 47(b).

593 "Letter to the Acting Chair of Special Committee on Peacekeeping Operations, United Nations, regarding immunities of civilian police and military personnel" *United Nations Juridical Yearbook 2004,* New York, UN, 2007 at 323 (UN Doc ST/LEG/SER.C/42).

Although a kind of impunity would be virtually visible where dual criminality is lacking, i.e. acts committed in the host country are an offence in the home country but not in the host country. This remains a major challenge in terms of impunity for ordinary offences during peace operations. As stated in the 2008 resolution, prosecution is conditional on dual criminality.[594] For instance, the cases of sexual violence committed by peacekeepers in the DRC, Goma, in 2009 raised the challenge of the age of consent in sexual matters. In the DRC, consent is only required at the age of 18, so any sexual act with a person under the age of 18 is rape of a minor. However, this is not the case in other legislation, such as that of contributing countries, where 16-year-olds can have sexual relations. Despite the existence of the preparatory measures provided for by the United Nations in this case, it is still difficult for victims to obtain compensation. Zaire's proposal at the time would be one of the solutions for reform and thus avoid impunity for lack of dual criminality. Indeed, the Zairean rapporteur had envisaged that the host State would be competent to prosecute, but in agreement with the country of origin of the peacekeeper presumed to have committed the offence.[595]

However, the model provided by NATO would be the most appropriate, leaving jurisdiction to national courts in the event of failure to establish double criminality.[596]

This being the case and with regards to violations of IHL specifically, one cannot imagine this possibility of impunity at the textual level. In accordance with the very nature of the rules of IHL that have acquired a customary character and with the nature of the obligations of States contributing to United Nations forces, impunity cannot be envisaged. Indeed, the application of IHL in the domestic law of contributing countries is a condition for the acceptance of troops into a peacekeeping force. In the case under consideration, the countries contributing to the Force Intervention Brigade are competent to deal with violations of IHL committed during the implementation of R2P after having met the exception established in the previous chapter, which is acting outside the mandate.

594 *Res AG 63, Doc off AG UN, 2008, Doc UN A/RES/62/63* at para 3.

595 Dörenberg, A. J. T. "Opérations de maintien de la paix aspects juridiques", *The Military Law and the Law of War Review 28*, no. 3-4, 1989, p. 36, available at https://doi.org/10.4337/mllwr.1989.3-4.02.

596 *Agreement between the States Parties to the North Atlantic Treaty regarding the Status of their Forces*, supra note 80 art VII (2)(b).

When it is established that the commander of the force would also be held responsible as a hierarchical superior, the question of the difference between jurisdictional immunities and functional immunities arises. Indeed, in the context of the Brigade, the Force Commander does not come from the contributing countries but rather from another country and is an international civil servant. Unlike the members of the Brigade, who enjoy only jurisdictional immunities, the Force Commander enjoys both jurisdictional and functional immunities. Although jurisdictional immunity tends to be confused with functional immunity, functional immunity does not replace jurisdictional immunity. Functional immunity is total regarding prosecution for the sole fact of having taken part in an operation, of having acted in accordance with the mandates and according to the recommendations of the rules of engagement. This immunity is based on the absence of an offence and does not imply general impunity.[597] As official status does not apply to international criminal law[598], the Force Commander would be prosecuted before the courts of his country.

The problem arises when the contributing State does not prosecute or does not want to prosecute. As the commitment to prosecute remains subject to the discretion of the contributing State, the host country and the United Nations have no binding mechanism to compel the State to comply with its commitments.[599]

Only negotiation can facilitate the process. The example can be given here of the Tanzanian forces, members of the Brigade, who opened fire on civilians and police at the Kasindi barrier. They were repatriated to their homes, but no action was taken on their fate. It would also be important for the victims and their dependents to witness that all States are committed to prosecuting their nationals who are members of UN forces, as Uganda did

---

597 *Secretary-General's bulletin on compliance with international humanitarian law by United Nations forces,* UN Doc off CES, 1999, UN Doc ST/SGB/1999/13.

598 The non-consideration of immunity has been codified in: *the 1948 Convention on the Prevention and Punishment of the Crime of Genocide* (Art. 4); *the 1984 Convention against Torture and Other Cruel, Inhuman, or Degrading Treatment or Punishment* (Art. 1); *the 1949 Geneva Conventions (GCI* Art. 59, GCII Art. 50, GCIII Art. 29 and *GCIV* Art. 146*); the Statute of the International Military Tribunal of Nuremberg* (Art. 7); *the Statutes of the two International Criminal Tribunals* (Art. 7.2 of *ICTY Statute and* Art. 6.2 of *ICTR Statute); and the Statute of the International Criminal Court* (Art. 27).

599 Tarcisio Gazzini, *The changing rules on the use of force in international law,* Manchester University Press, Melland Schill Studies in International Law, 2022.

in a similar case and condemned three peacekeepers for having opened fire carelessly in Somalia.[600]

While the courts of the contributing countries would have jurisdiction over violations of IHL committed by their nationals who are members of the Brigade, the DRC would have jurisdiction over violations committed by members of the FARDC who took part in the implementation of Resolution 2098. The legal basis for the jurisdiction of Congolese courts can be found in the Rome Statute, the Constitution, the Military Penal Code, the Code of Judicial Organization and Jurisdiction, etc. Indeed, all this nomenclature provides for the implementation of the Geneva Conventions, in one way or another, in Congolese law. In the DRC, violations of IHL can be prosecuted before military courts and ordinary courts, depending on the status of the perpetrator. It should be pointed out that since 2013, the year in which the Brigade and the FARDC implemented R2P, a number of cases have been investigated and judgments handed down against certain members of the FARDC and also against members of rebel groups for war crimes and crimes against humanity.[601]

Is it possible for other States to have jurisdiction to prosecute members of the Brigade who may have committed war crimes under the principle of universality? This question will be analyzed below.

ii. The jurisdiction of other Courts: Universal Jurisdiction

Because of the seriousness of certain crimes, which the ICC judge calls international crimes, the entire international community has jurisdiction to punish them. This jurisdiction, described as universal, is provided for in both customary and treaty law. It may be either mandatory, in the sense that States are obliged to prosecute, or optional, in the sense that States have the right to prosecute.

For the repression of IHL crimes, in accordance with the Geneva Conventions (articles 49, 50, 129 and 146 respectively), States undertake to seek out the alleged perpetrators in order either to try them or to extradite them.

Compulsory universal jurisdiction would ensure that no serious crime goes unpunished. This jurisdiction would require the State to act regardless

600 Ray Murphy, *The Criminalisation of International Humanitarian Law and Human Rights Law Violations Committed by Peace Forces: What Happens in Practice?*, Collegium, afl. 42, 2011, p.137

601

of the place where the acts were committed or the nationality of the alleged perpetrator. According to principle 4 of the United Nations Basic Principles and Guidelines on the Right to a Remedy and Reparation for Victims of Gross Violations of International Human Rights Law and Serious Violations of International Humanitarian Law ("Principles and Guidelines"), States have an obligation to investigate, prosecute and punish. The Nuremberg military tribunals[602] was well received in considering the jurisdiction of States for breaches of humanitarian law irrespective of nationality. The ICJ has recalled in several of its cases that States do not have the possibility of avoiding this obligation "*aut dedere aut judicare*" unilaterally or by agreement.[603]

Customary international law, has in fact, provided for universal jurisdiction while extending this jurisdiction to all serious violations of the laws and customs of war during international and non-international armed conflicts. Rule 157 on customary international humanitarian law establishes that States have the right to confer universal jurisdiction on their national courts and that universal jurisdiction can be exercised either through national legislation or through the judgement of defendants.

In the United Nation system, Principle 5 of the "Principles and Guidelines" states that States are required to make appropriate provision for universal jurisdiction. To ensure the fight against impunity for IHL crimes, principles 6 and 7 provide for the nonprescription of statutes of limitations. Several States have already incorporated universal jurisdiction into their national law and some have already been judged by virtue of this same jurisdiction. In view of the above, all States in the world have jurisdiction over crimes committed during the implementation of Resolution 2098 in the DRC. Thus, the principle of universal jurisdiction would be one of the mechanisms that could enable victims to regain their rights.

For the other States to exercise their jurisdiction, they will have to consider conditions such as respect for the *ne bis in idem* principle and consideration of sentences already handed down by other jurisdictions. Although the answer to the question of whether members of the Brigade can be tried by other States is clear, the question that persists is whether some States have already had the courage to prosecute a member or former member

602 Kevin Jon Heller, *The Nuremberg military tribunals and the origins of international criminal law*, Oxford University Press, 2011.

603 *Reservation to the Convention on the Prevention and Punishment of Genocide, Advisory Opinion*, [1951] ICJ rec 15 at p 23; ICJ, *Armed Activities on the Territory of the Congo (Democratic Republic of the Congo v Rwanda)*, [2006] ICJ rec 1).

of the peace forces under universal jurisdiction. Indeed, the present thesis considers that the exercise of universal jurisdiction by other States would be a solution to the limits of the jurisdictional privileges enjoyed by the members of the Brigade in the DRC, but also to the limits of the exercise of jurisdiction by the ICC. Thus, for victims of crimes to obtain reparation, States must also work to reveal all the challenges regarding respect for the rights of the defence and the protection of witnesses and victims, without ignoring the challenges of gathering evidence. As in the case of mechanisms before international courts, the will of States and effective cooperation between States remain an important element in the fight against impunity and reparation for war crimes.

By virtue of universal jurisdiction, ad hoc criminal tribunals are another mechanism to which victims of violations of IHL can have recourse. Indeed, it was only at the end of the Second World War that the international community realized the importance of ad hoc criminal tribunals to bring the perpetrators of heinous crimes to justice. The example here is that of the Treaty of Versailles (article 297 e), which provides for a mixed arbitral tribunal with jurisdiction to deal with claims by Allied Nations for compensation against Germany. The ad hoc criminal tribunals were set up to combat impunity and respond to the limitations that existed in national and international law in the punishment of IHL crimes in general.

It was after the Nuremberg trials that the ad hoc criminal tribunals were created for a specific objective and situation. The International Criminal Tribunal for the former Yugoslavia (ICTY)[604] to try those allegedly responsible for war crimes committed in the Balkans during the conflicts of the 1990s, the International Criminal Tribunal for Rwanda (ICTR)[605] to try those allegedly responsible for the genocide committed in Rwanda in 1994. In addition to ad hoc criminal tribunals, mixed tribunals also have jurisdiction over IHL crimes. These include the Special Court for Sierra Leone (2002-2013)[606], which judged violations committed since 1996, the Extraordinary Chambers in the Courts of Cambodia (2003)[607] for the main crimes committed by the Khmer Rouge regime between 1975 and 1979 and

604 *UNSC Resolution 827, 25 May 1993.*

605 *UNSC Resolution 955. S/RES/955(1994) 8 November 1994.*

606 *Statute of the Special Court for Sierra Leone,* available at https://www.rscsl.org/Documents/scsl-statute.pdf, accessed on 14th 2020.

607 John D. Ciorciari and Anne Heindel, *Hybrid Justice: The Extraordinary Chambers in the Courts of Cambodia,* University of Michigan Press, 2014.

the Special Tribunal for Lebanon (2009)[608] for crimes committed during the attack on 14 February 2005 that cost the life of former Lebanese Prime Minister Rafić Hariri.

For a long time now, a number of authors and political players have been stressing the need to set up an ad hoc criminal tribunal with a mandate to judge the crimes committed in the east of the DRC.[609] According to most received wisdom and with the support of the European Union[610], this international criminal tribunal for the DRC would have jurisdiction to try crimes committed before 2002. While agreeing on the importance and urgent need for this ad hoc criminal tribunal, the present research insists on the "hybrid" model of this jurisdiction. Given the nature of the forces involved in the conflicts in the DRC, including those of international organizations (UN, SADC, EAC), national organizations (DRC, Uganda, Rwanda) and national and foreign rebel groups, it will be imperative for this court to be managed by national judges but also under the aegis of each organization, depending on the case brought before it. This approach will allow a certain "check and balance" and thus enable national and international judges to assess the realities as objectively as possible.

In addition, the present thesis proposes that the jurisdiction of this hybrid tribunal should not be limited to crimes committed before 2002. As mentioned in the previous chapters, the eastern part of the DRC has been facing conflicts that led to UN intervention for more than two decades now. It was as a result of this interminable cycle of conflicts that Resolution 2098 instituting R2P was adopted. Although this thesis is limited to events between 2013 and 2023, it will undoubtedly be necessary to consider events committed in the past that have a direct link with the current situation. The ad hoc mixed criminal tribunal will not only decide on crimes committed outside the scope of R2P, but also on those committed in the general context of the eastern DRC. Its jurisdiction will not be based solely on the nature or mandate of the forces involved in implementing R2P, but rather

608 Annex – *Agreement between the United Nations and the Lebanese Republic on the establishment of a Special Tribunal for Lebanon,* Preamble, 30 May 2007, United Nations Security Council Resolution 1757 (2007).

609 Pierre Claver Mupendana, "Necessity and Difficulties to establish a repressive system for International crimes committed in the DRC", *Actual Problems of International Relations 1,* no. 150, 2022, p. 39.

610 Sarah Williams, *Hybrid and Internationalized Criminal Tribunals: Jurisdictional Issues,* PhD diss., Durham University, 2009.

on the conflict situation in the DRC, as has been the case for the other ad hoc criminal tribunals.

A chamber of this court would be created to hear cases against peacekeeping forces in the DRC and those of other international organizations as soon as their responsibilities are established.

Some would agree with this analysis, firstly because the situation in the DRC is unique and requires specific measures to restore peace, punish the crimes committed and restore the rights of the victims. Secondly, although it has been recognized that human rights and IHL violations have been committed by peacekeeping forces in the DRC during their presence there starting over 60 years ago, reparations are still a problem. This jurisdiction could respond to the limitations of national and international courts such as the ICC in prosecuting members of MONUSCO in general and those of the Brigade in particular for the IHL and human rights crimes they are alleged to have committed in the DRC. Although this question is not developed in this research, there is a direct link between the non-reparation of crimes committed in the history of the DRC and the endless cycle of conflict. The violence and/or the intervention of some in the conflicts are provoked by the non-reparation or, better still, the dissatisfaction of the victims. Thus, yesterday's victims have become today's persecutors. For a lasting solution to this cycle of conflict, reparation should take into account all the aspects set out in the principles and guidelines, such as restitution, compensation, rehabilitation, satisfaction and guarantees of non-repetition. Provided for in principles 19, 20, 21, 22 and 23, it should also be pointed out that some of these forms of reparation are not judicial and may be included in transitional justice mechanisms. One approach in this struggle is to strengthen non-judicial remedies as measures of reparation for crimes committed in the DRC during the implementation of R2P.

2. Non-judicial Mechanisms for violations of International Humanitarian Law

The best form of reparation would not depend on the approach or method of reparation but rather on the satisfaction of the victim, or better still, the restoration of the victim's rights. For reparations for crimes of IHL or international crimes in general, general conflict resolution mechanisms and ad hoc reparations would also be appropriate in the DRC context. By General mechanisms in this context means measures such as transitional justice. The term "transitional justice" has come to be used to refer to the various processes accompanying political transition by societies emerging from a period of violence that aims to deal with the serious human rights violations committed during the conflict and to achieve national reconciliation.[611]

The link between transitional justice mechanisms and IHL would be found before and after the conflict. Before the conflict, because States have the obligation to ensure the implementation of IHL, and after, because States have the obligation to punish violations of IHL. It is the latter that will be of most interest to this analysis in the passage that follows. In this context, transitional justice mechanisms include both judicial and non-judicial mechanisms. This analysis focuses on non-judicial transitional justice mechanisms because jurisdictional ones have been analyzed in the previous section. Although the idea of the link between transitional justice and IHL has led many to reflect on the whole package that transitional justice brings, including truth, amnesty, reconciliation, etc., this thesis will limit itself to one of the modes of reparation provided for by transitional justice, which is the creation of compensation funds for victims of crimes committed during the conflict. In order to restore the rights of the victims of international crimes, the States and IOs 'responsible' for these acts can make reparation by creating compensation funds. In the context of reconciliation, reparation measures may be taken. For example, in 2000 Austria set up the Austrian Fund for Reconciliation, Peace and Cooperation to provide financial compensation to victims of Nazi labor camps,[612] forced labor and other injustices committed during the Nazi regime.

In the same context, the German Foundation Remembrance, Responsibility and the Future was founded to provide financial compensation to victims of forced labor and other injustices committed during the National Socialist regime. Other states, such as Canada, have since been in the midst of discussions about redress for the Japanese for measures taken against them under the War Measures Act during the Second World War.[613]

---

611 "The rule of law and transitional justice in conflict and post-conflict societies", *UN Security Council, S/2004/616,* 3 August 2004, p. 4.

612 *Austrian Fund for Reconciliation, Peace and Cooperation,* available at http://www.zukunftsfonds-austria.at/download/book_reconciliationfund_ForcedLaborInAustria.pdf, accessed on 14th 2020.

613 Canada, *Debates of Parliament, 38th Parliament, 1st Session,* Revised Hansard, No. 61, February 21, 2005.

In addition, an agreement between Ethiopia and Eritrea was signed in December 2001 for the creation of a claims commission. Under Article 5 of the agreement, individual victims may apply directly to the commission for compensation.[614]

Within the framework of the United Nations, similar initiatives have been undertaken to enable victims of armed conflicts to obtain reparation. One example is Security Council Resolution 687 (1991), which established the United Nations Compensation Commission (UNCC) for Iraq and Kuwait. For this Commission, the term victim was extended to individuals and States. Its competence was to receive claims for compensation from States and individuals who were victims of post-conflict violations of IHL.[615]

It should be noted that other institutions have been set up either under the authority of the UN or other organizations to deal with victims' claims. These include, for example, the Commission for Looted Art in Europe (CLAE) whose mandate is to represent the European Council of Jewish Communities (ECJC) and the Conference of European Rabbis (CER),[616] the Housing and Property Claims Commission in Kosovo,[617]etc.

There is a direct link between R2P and the cessation of hostilities. It is in this context that the obligations of prevention and reconstruction under R2P have a direct link with transitional justice mechanisms. Both concepts (R2P and transitional justice) have two main objectives: literally protection and non-repetition. This is most clearly reflected in the situation in the east of the DRC.

However, as mentioned above, the guarantees of cessation and non-repetition are complementary to the obligation of compensation. Even where financial compensation is not a guarantee of non-repetition, it has been found that collective compensatory arrangements have a positive impact in terms of victims' expectations. Satisfying victims through compensation may be a better way of putting an end to the conflict. Thus, a compensation fund for victims of crimes committed during the implementation of R2P

---

614 *Agreement between the Government of the Federal Democratic Republic of Ethiopia and the Government of the State of Eritrea,* Vol. 40, No. 2, March 2001, International Legal Materials, 2001, p. 260.

615 *Concerning the Restoration of Peace and Security in Iraq and Kuwait, Res. CS 687 (1991) Doc. UN S/RES/687,* 1991.

616 More details at https://www.lootedartcommission.com/, accessed on 14th 2020.

617 *Khaled Hassine, Housing and Property Directorate/Claims Commission in Kosovo (HPD/CC): eine Studie zur Modellwirkung von HPD/CC für den international en Eigentumsschutz Privater,* Neuer Wissenschaftlicher Verlag, 2009.

would at the same time be a form of reparation but also a guarantee of cessation or even non-repetition. In addition, the creation of a commission to receive claims from victims of crimes committed during the implementation of R2P would be most welcome with a view to restoring victims' rights.

The UN has long recognized the need to compensate victims of damage for which it is responsible, in accordance with international law in general. Although for the United Nations, paragraph 51 of the SOFA model agreement would only be considered for damages under private law and not those under international law, the present thesis would be in line with Rwanda's analysis, which has called for a commission to be set up to investigate UNAMIR's failings, in accordance with article 51 of the SOFA model.[618]

Paragraph 51 of the SOFA model was taken up by paragraph 55 of the Agreement between the United Nations Organisation and the Democratic Republic of Congo concerning the Status of the United Nations Organisation Mission in the Democratic Republic of Congo, which states: "(...) a standing claims commission established for this purpose shall adjudicate any dispute or claim arising under private law, not relating to damage attributable to the operational requirements of MONUC, to which MONUC or any of its members is a party and in respect of which the courts of the Democratic Republic of the Congo do not have jurisdiction by reason of any provision of this Agreement (...)".[619] The expressions "any dispute" and "any claim arising under private law" seem to be clear and are not limited solely to private law damages. This being the case, the commission would also be one of the mechanisms to which victims can have recourse in order to obtain compensation. This is because the Commission's procedural rules state that its jurisdiction is limited to individual victims and not to States. Thus, although the DRC cannot directly exercise diplomatic protection on behalf of its citizens before the Commission, nothing would prevent it from demanding that the Commission be set up to enable the people of North Kivu and Ituri (where the resolution was implemented) to benefit from reparation. Unfortunately, in practice, to the best of our knowledge, this commission has never been set up to deal with the accounts of victims of violations of IHL. It is clear that there are mechanisms for reparation of violations of IHL to which victims of violations committed in the DRC can

618 Eric David and Burgorgue-Larsen, L. "Des occasions manquées de mettre en cause la responsabilité de la communauté internationale", *La répression internationale du génocide rwandais,* 2003, p. 248.

619 SOFA, *DRC-United Nations,* para 51.

have recourse in order to obtain reparation. However, it is unfortunately clear that individual victims have no guarantee of reparation unless States and the United Nations are willing to help them.

Furthermore, with the exception of the Ethiopia-Eritrea Commission, there does not yet appear to be a single, clear mechanism for redressing acts of IHL violations committed by peacekeeping forces during armed conflict. After analyzing jurisdictional and non-jurisdictional mechanisms with their limitations, the present thesis believes that the establishment of *in situ* court-martials, as envisaged by the 2017 Report of the Secretary-General,[620] within the United Nations could also constitute a very important step in the repression of offences by peacekeeping forces. In this report, the aim is to put the victim first in order to guarantee impunity for human rights violations such as sexual abuse. A recommendation was made to the SG's representatives in peace missions where there was a high rate of sexual abuse and exploitation, such as MONUSCO, to "identify a position at the mid-to-senior level to perform the functions of the victims' rights advocate on the ground."[621]

It would be wise to consider *a fortiori* the possibility of also considering violations of international humanitarian law, given that the Brigade and MONUSCO are under the same command.

For this jurisdiction to be effective, it must not limit its jurisdiction to military offences. Disciplinary violations must not be separated from violations of IHL and other grave breaches, as is the case in Germany.[622] It adopted the Act on the Jurisdiction of Armed Forces Specially Deployed Abroad in 2013 and established service military tribunals to deal with criminal cases and has jurisdiction over disciplinary matters occurring abroad involving German forces.[623]

In addition, although there is no perfect and uncritical approach, this court martial must operate in compliance with the norms of international human rights law, guaranteeing the principle of independence, efficiency

620 *Special measures for protection from sexual exploitation and abuse: a new approach Report of the Secretary-General, UN Doc A/71/818,* 2017, para 59,Xii.

621 *Special measures for protection from sexual exploitation and abuse,* para 30.

622 In ordinary times, Germany has no military jurisdiction. Article 96 of the German Constitution authorizes the creation of military courts in specific circumstances, such as wartime.

623 *Information exchange on the Code of Conduct on politico-military aspects of security,* FSC.EMI/81/13, 15 April 2013 ENGLISH Original: GERMAN https://www.osce.org/files/f/documents/5/c/100750.pdf, accessed 20 september 2024.

and due process. As stipulated in articles 7 and 26 of the African Charter on Human Rights, fair trail must be respected before all courts. This was analyzed in the case on this issue is *Civil Liberties Organisation & Others v Nigeria*, in which the African Commission stressed that 'military tribunals must be subject to the same requirements of fairness, openness, justice, independence and due process as any other process'.[624]

Moreover, the Court-martial must also limit its *ratione personae* jurisdiction over military personnel and servicemen, as was a key recommendation of the UN Commission on Human Rights.[625]

As the task of investigating crimes falls to the commander of the forces, it will be the responsibility of MONUSCO's Force Commander. However, this thesis considers that the installation of a third-party commission of inquiry, i.e. one that has not taken part in R2P implementation operations in the DRC, would be more effective in establishing the criminal responsibility of both the contingents and the Force Commander when necessary. Only in this approach would it be easier for the court martial to prosecute the alleged perpetrator of IHL violations even after repatriation or when no State has initiated proceedings. Given the nature of the mandate of the Brigade's forces and the difficulty of establishing individual responsibility, these court-martials would be a step forward for the United Nations in the fight against impunity for serious crimes.

624 *Civil Liberties Organisation & Others v Nigeri (2001) AHRLR 75 (ACHPR 2001).*

625 Office of the United Nations High Commissioner for Human Rights. (1999). *Core document forming part of the reports of States Parties,* Poland. 16/04/99, HRI/CORE/1/Add.25/ Rev.1. [online] Available at: http://www.bayefsky.com/core/poland_hri_core_1_add.25_ rev.1_1999.php, accessed on 12 October 2024.

Conclusion

The analysis of Responsibility to Protect (R2P) and violations of International Humanitarian Law (IHL) in the DRC attracts the curiosity of many. While many will ask whether there is a link between the two concepts, i.e. R2P and IHL, a question to which the present thesis provides an answer, the analysis has focused more on the legal implications of applying IHL during R2P and the criteria for distributing responsibility for IHL violations committed during the implementation of R2P in the DRC.

To this end, the thesis is anchored in doctrinal legal analysis and recognizes that the interpretation of international humanitarian law (IHL) and the Responsibility to Protect (R2P) cannot be understood in abstraction from their practical application. By integrating a socio-legal dimension, the research connects legal doctrine with the realities on the ground in eastern DRC, where the implementation of R2P intersected with IHL principles amid complex political and military dynamics. Qualitative insights from interviews and documentary analysis reveal how norms designed to protect civilians were negotiated, adapted, and at times undermined in practice. A complementary philosophical-normative reflection further addresses questions of justice and accountability that extend beyond positive law, particularly regarding violations committed during R2P operations. Taken together, these approaches allow the study not only to assess how IHL informs R2P in theory, but also to highlight the persistent challenges of ensuring legal responsibility and civilian protection in contexts of protracted conflict.

Apart from the introduction and conclusion, this paper is divided into two main parts: R2P and IHL in the context of the DR Congo (Title I) and the legal implications of the applicability of IHL during the implementation of R2P (Title II). The first section sets out the legal understanding of the principle of R2P in relation to International Humanitarian Law and the analysis of R2P in the specific context of the DRC.

After its failure to protect populations from the killings in Srebrenica and the genocide in Rwanda, the international community considered a new approach which, while taking into account the existence of other principles, could promote the protection of populations from mass crimes. At the 2005 World Summit, States adopted the principle that it is the primary responsibility of a State to protect populations against four mass crimes (war crimes, crimes against humanity, genocide and ethnic cleansing). The States went further by specifying that all States of the world have the obligation to accompany and assist each State in fulfilling its obligation to protect. In addition, when a State is unable to protect its population, the international community has an obligation to intervene to ensure this protection. These three stages are referred to as the three pillars of R2P. In accordance with paragraphs 138 and 139 of the 2005 World Summit Document, States and the international community must take measures to prevent the commission of mass atrocity crimes.

And when these crimes are committed, they must react. The reaction can be either diplomatic or military. In such cases, the reaction does not always refer to the use of force because the use of force must be the last resort and coordinated under the aegis of the United Nations. Once intervention has taken place, states have an obligation to rebuild. This obligation, which, according to this research, has been on paper for a very long time, has the same value as the other two, because without it, the cycle would repeat itself and the R2P measure would not be effective. This was the case in Libya, where R2P was invoked and applied by Resolution 1973/2001 of the United Nations Security Council, but where there was no insistence on the obligation to rebuild.

However, R2P as a principle raises questions about its legal nature. In the literature on R2P, there are two main trends. The first is that of those who believe that R2P is a legal principle because it creates new obligations for states. The second is that R2P is not a legal principle because it was not specifically and clearly designed to be one. To understand the legal nature of this principle, the present thesis analyzes R2P as a source of law as international custom in accordance with Article 38 of the ICJ Statute. This analysis leads to the conclusion that R2P cannot be considered as an international custom or a general principle of law because it does not meet the two constituent elements of international custom, namely State practice and *opinio juris,* which are cumulative.

Although States recognize the principle, they have not yet considered it to be law. In addition, R2P does not create new obligations for States inasmuch as the older concept of sovereignty was already understood not only as a right but also as an obligation for States to protect not only its citizens but the entire population on its territory. Indeed, this notion of sovereignty-responsibility can be deduced from an analysis of Articles 1(3) and 55 of the United Nations Charter. Thus, in the view of the present thesis, R2P can be considered as a soft law because States have not specified what is meant by "responsibility" and what the legal consequences are when a State or the UN does not fulfil this obligation. However, as has been demonstrated throughout the development of this thesis, the implementation of R2P raises pertinent questions of law in relation to the applicability of IHL to peacekeeping forces with an R2P mandate and in relation to the implication of non-compliance with the rules of IHL during the operations of its involvement. It is from this perspective that the link between IHL and R2P is analyzed. R2P and IHL both have the same objective, which is to protect people. However, this protection has not been developed in the same way. Whereas IHL is applicable in the context of an armed conflict (international or non-international), R2P can be invoked whether there is an armed conflict or not, at any time when the four mass crimes within its scope are committed. However, R2P does not provide any rules of conduct when States or the United Nations intervene in a conflict. This is where IHL comes into play in the implementation of R2P. Indeed, collective responsibilities under R2P and IHL do not seem to be very different. It is in this sense that some authors consider that these two standards are complementary. While aligning itself with this perspective, the present thesis notes that this complementarity runs the risk of politicizing IHL. Another risk is the emergence of two parallel and competing regimes applicable to the protection of civilians in the context of armed conflict, which could lead to a situation where the rules for the protection of civilians in the context of armed conflict are fragmented and inconsistently applied.

To establish the link between R2P and IHL in the context of the DRC, it was first necessary to analyze the DRC context that led to the implementation of R2P. The first condition for invoking R2P is the existence of four mass atrocity crimes. For more than two decades, the DRC has faced a cycle of interminable conflicts. These conflicts, described in a number of reports by national and international human rights organizations and analyzed by UN experts, have been described as a threat to international peace and security through the commission of war crimes and crimes against humanity. To resolve conflicts and protect populations, several organizations have intervened, including the UN, SADC and, more recently, the EAC. In 2013, after the M23 rebel group had occupied the town of Goma and the Congolese government and MONUSCO forces had failed to protect the town and its inhabitants, the Security Council, in Resolution 2098, set up a Rapid Intervention Force called the Brigade, with a mandate to use all necessary measures to disable all rebel groups present in the eastern part of the DRC (paragraph 12 of resolution 2098).

Although some authors believe that Resolution 2098 simply reinforces the mandate of MONUSCO forces by giving it a robust mandate, the present study considers that this resolution is indeed the underpinning of R2P in all its three pillars in the DRC. Indeed, while the first and second pillars are clearly set out in the resolution, in the preamble and paragraph 10 respectively, the third pillar can only be demonstrated by reference to the Brigade's mandate. Thus, the idea that Resolution 2098 is not a resolution under R2P because it does not clearly use the language of Resolutions 1973 on Libya and 1975 on Côte d'Ivoire is not entirely well-founded. In fact, it has been recognized by several authors that a Security Council resolution can be covered by R2P without this being clearly stated. Recourse to this principle would rather be analyzed in relation to the context of its adoption, the preparatory work, the language of the resolution and also the mandate of the Force deployed. Resolution 2098 fulfils all these criteria and the Brigade formed by it cannot be considered to be a "normal" peacekeeping force but rather a force that has an obligation to stop violence by force. Although placed under the command of MONUSCO, this force has a special mandate. It should also be remembered that it was for operational reasons and to avoid precedents that the Brigade was placed under the command of MONUSCO.

Since the Brigade has engaged in offensive and defensive combat against rebel groups such as M23, APCLS, FDLR and Mai-Mai, the examination of the legal implications of the application of IHL during the implementation of R2P is relevant. Before the rules of IHL applicable to the situation or to the intervention of the Brigade can be identified, the qualification of the conflict is important. The Brigade intervened in a complex conflict context. As mentioned above, several armed forces and groups are operating in the east of the DRC. As long as the Brigade is fighting a foreign rebel group such as the FDLR or the ADF, the conflict remains a non-international armed conflict because no foreign state is involved. However, the situation becomes more complicated when the Brigade fights against the M23 rebel group. Several reports by human rights NGOs, including those of the United Nations, prove that the M23 rebel group is supported by other states in the region. The application of effective control and global control (as analyzed in the Nicaragua and Tadic cases) to the M23 context will differ depending on whether the first offensives took place in 2013 or the second in early December 2022.

For the former, the conflict remains a non-international armed conflict because nothing on the ground has proved that Rwanda had effective control over the M23. On the other hand, for the latter, it has been proven by many that the M23 is acting in the name and on behalf of Rwanda. The present thesis argues, however, that the nature of the Brigade Forces as an R2P implementation mission does not change the nature of the conflict. This force, at least in the context of the DRC, intervenes alongside the FARDC and its nature as an "international force" has no influence on the qualification of conflicts. That said, the application of IHL to the conflicts in which the Brigade's forces intervened has several legal implications. Firstly, there is no need to return to the question of whether IHL applies to peace-enforcement forces, as it seems to be clear from the outset that such forces take part in conflicts and their members may become prisoners of war or detainees in, as the case may be, an International armed conflict (IAC) or non-international armed conflict (NIAC). As a result, the Brigade will not be able to benefit from the protection afforded by the rules of IHL to UN and humanitarian personnel. They are therefore vulnerable to attack by the enemy. Unfortunately, this has had a negative impact on the general protection of other MONUSCO personnel, both civilian and military. On the ground, one rebel group said it was having difficulty distinguishing between combatants and non-combatants. This concern has been raised by some contributing states, which have proposed a protection mechanism for their forces involved in MONUSCO.

Secondly, this involves the Capstone principles that normally govern peace missions. Neutrality, impartiality and consent are at stake. The fact that the Brigade is placed under the same command as MONUSCO's regular forces confuses the application of these principles. This confusion has been noticed on the ground by repeated attacks on MONUSCO premises where civilian and military personnel have been injured and killed.

Unfortunately, although UN rules provide for the treatment of prisoners of war, no rules have been provided for the possibility that UN forces may also be held as POWs or detainees. The application of IHL in the context of the DRC by all parties to the conflict must be without exception. Some might wonder whether there would be an exception for the Brigade, whose mission is to neutralize rebel forces by all possible means in the implementation of R2P. In principle, no, as this would undermine the principle of neutrality in the application of IHL by parties to conflicts. It is with this in mind that violations of IHL during R2P operations have been analyzed.

During these operations and in order to neutralize rebel groups such as the ADF, bombings took place in the camps at night, with the result that women, civilians and children were on the spot. The principle of distinction, a sacrosanct principle of IHL, was violated. This situation raises the question of whether, with a view to peace and the protection of civilians, it was necessary to proceed by such forceful means to neutralize rebel groups. This question seems to have been answered a long time ago by legal practitioners in the sense that the principle of necessity and proportion must limit as far as possible the impact of operations on civilians and their property. However, the question remains as to when damage to civilians and their property during operations to implement R2P can be considered collateral damage. This question will have to be answered by the competent judge to establish the responsibility of each party during the operations. With this in mind, the establishment of international responsibility for violations of IHL committed during R2P operations was analyzed. These operations were carried out either by the Brigade alone or in collaboration with the FARDC.

The research presented here aligns itself with the ideas of those authors, who specify that in addition to the responsibility of States and the UN, individual criminal responsibility is applicable. Thus, the UN, contributing states and the DRC can be held responsible either separately or concurrently, depending on the context. The criterion for the distribution of responsibility would be based on the notions of organization and coordination as set out in the *Behrami* and *Saramati* cases. Although this may seem easy, the R2P context in the DRC is complex because there are autonomous Brigade operations and joint operations with the DRC. This being the case, the combination of command control and operations control will determine who is responsible for a specific action or in which context responsibility is shared. Even when the Brigade forces were formed under the SADC, the SADC could never be held responsible because it has no command or control over the forces on the ground.

Having determined who could be held responsible for the violations, it was appropriate to analyze the jurisdictional and non-jurisdictional mechanisms of reparation available to the victims to recover their rights. Although the question of the international responsibility of the UN no longer needs to be demonstrated, the question of the application of its responsibility remains topical. The analysis of the subject of this study has made it possible to envisage not only the advisory jurisdiction of the ICJ as a reparation mechanism for any action against the UN, the contributing States and the DRC respectively. However, before the ICJ, the DRC can bring a case either as a direct victim or through the representation of individual victims by virtue of the principle of diplomatic protection. It has also been demonstrated that individuals also have opportunities at regional court level to assert their rights. The affirmation of respect for national and international law by military operations is more than precise in the literature of international law and the Brigade Forces are no exception to this reality. However, the implementation of their responsibilities comes up against certain challenges, including jurisdictional immunities and the reluctance of States to prosecute members of peace missions and this in violation of the *aut dedere aut judicae* principle. Be that as it may, this study has demonstrated that, on the one hand, the ICC and state courts, in the name of universal jurisdiction, do indeed have jurisdiction to punish violations of IHL committed in the implementation of R2P.

In addition, for the specific context of the DRC and in order to somehow circumvent all the challenges related to the measures raised above, the creation of a hybrid ad hoc criminal tribunal for the DRC would also be appropriate to deal with violations of IHL. However, the effectiveness of criminal proceedings against the military contingent of peace operations can only be real if it is enshrined in the permissiveness and will of States and the UN. This will can be demonstrated through institutional and state assistance and cooperation. It is only by these means that States and organizations can make use of all the avenues of action and recourse that the law opens up, particularly at the domestic and international level. Thus, as Antonio Cassese observes, "most international rules cannot work without the constant help, cooperation and support of national legal systems."[626]

Pending the effective involvement of the UN and States in the fight against impunity for violations of IHL, regardless of the nature of the forces involved in the conflict, the UN's revolution would be to set up a *Court martial in situ* within the UN, which already offers a mechanism for dealing with human rights violations and sexual abuse committed by peacekeeping forces and to extend its jurisdiction to violations of IHL. It should be remembered, however, that there is no specific mechanism for obtaining reparation for crimes committed during the implementation of R2P. As the best method of reparation is not linked to its form but rather to the level of satisfaction of the victim, non-judicial mechanisms that have already proved their worth in the history of conflicts can also be envisaged in the context of the DRC. Thus, the creation of a compensation fund for victims of IHL violations committed in the DRC would be a means of reparation and would have a positive effect on the cycle of interminable conflict in

626 *Cassese, Antonio. International Law. 2nd edition, Oxford University Press, Oxford, 2005, p. 9*

the DRC. The direct link between reparation mechanisms and R2P in its obligations to prevent and rebuild is thus established and would require further research.

Bibliography

Books

Australian Red cross. International Humanitarian Law and the Responsibility to Protect: A handbook, Red cross 2011.

Badescu, Cristina. Humanitarian intervention and the responsibility to protect: Security and human rights. Routledge, 2010.

Bellamy, Alex J. Responsibility to protect. Cambridge: Polity Press, 2009.

. Responsibility to protect: A defense. OUP Oxford, 2014.

Bothe, Michael and Thomas, Doerschel (Eds.) UN Peacekeeping: A Documentary Introduction. BRILL, 2021.

Cammaert, Patrick and Fiona, Blyth. The UN intervention brigade in the Democratic Republic of the Congo. International Peace Institute, 2013.

Cassese, Antonio. International Law. 2nd edition, Oxford University Press, Oxford, 2005.

Ciorciari, John D. and Anne, Heindel. Hybrid Justice: The Extraordinary Chambers in the Courts of Cambodia. University of Michigan Press, 2014.

Copeland, Thomas F. Civilian protection in the Eastern DRC: Evaluation of the MONUSCO Peacekeeping Operation. Naval Postgraduate School Monterey ca dept of national security affairs, 2012.

Cornu, Gégard. Vocabulaire juridique, Paris : P.U.F., 7 Coll. Quadrige - Dicos Poche. 2005.

D'Aspremont, J., Samantha, Besson and Sévrine, Knuchel. (Eds). The Oxford handbook of the sources of international law. Oxford University Press, 2017.

Deng, Francis M., Sadikiel, Kimaro, Terrence, Lyons, Donald, Rothchild and William, Zartman. Sovereignty as responsibility: conflict management in Africa. Rowman & Littlefield, 2010.

Donnelly, Jack. International Human Rights. Boulder, Colorado: Westview Press, 2007.

Dörmann, Knut. Elements of war crimes under the Rome Statute of the International Criminal Court: sources and commentary. Cambridge University Press, 2003.

Doria, José, Hans-Peter, Gasser and Cherif, Bassiouni M., (eds). The legal regime of the International Criminal Court: essays in honour of Professor Igor Blishchenko. Vol. 19. Brill, 2009.

Engberg, Katarina. The EU and military operations: a comparative analysis. Routledge, 2013.

Evans, Gareth. The responsibility to protect: ending mass atrocity crimes once and for all. Rowman & Littlefield, 2009.

Gazzini, Tarcisio. The changing rules on the use of force in international law. Manchester University Press, Melland Schill Studies in International Law, 2022.

Hassine, Khaled. Housing and Property Directorate/Claims Commission in Kosovo (HPD/CC): eine Studie zur Modellwirkung von HPD/CC für den internationalen Eigentumsschutz Privater. Neuer Wissenschaftlicher Verlag, 2009.

Heller, Kevin J. The Nuremberg military tribunals and the origins of international criminal law. Oxford University Press, 2011.

Jenkins, Rob. The UN Peace-Building Commission and the Dissemination of International Norms. Crisis States Research Centre, 2008.

Knight, Andy W. and Frazer, Egerton, (Eds.) The Routledge handbook of the responsibility to protect. London: Routledge, 2012.

Louis and Nichols, Michelle. Exclusive: Rwanda, Uganda Arming Congo Rebels, Providing Troops—U.N. Panel, Reuters 2012.

Matheson, M. and Momtaz, D. (eds), Rules and Institutions of International Humanitarian Law Put to the Test of Recent Armed Conflicts, Brill/Nijhoff, 2011.

Melzer, Nils. Interpretive guidance on the notion of direct participation in hostilities under international humanitarian law. International Committee of the Red Cross, 2009.

NATO, Glossary of Terms and Definitions, AAP-06, Brussels, Belgium, 2013.

Nzongola-Ntalaja, G., The Congo: From Leopold to Kabila: A People's History, London: Zed Press, 2002.

Olivier, Corten. Méthodologie du droit international public. Bruxelles, Edition de l'Université de Bruxelles, 2009.

Orford, Anne. International authority and the responsibility to protect. Cambridge University Press, 2011.

Pilloud, Claude, Yves, Sandoz, Christophe, Swinarski and Bruno, Zimmermann, (Eds.) Commentary on the additional protocols: of 8 June 1977 to the Geneva Conventions of 12 August 1949. Martinus Nijhoff Publishers, 1987.

Reyntjens, Filip. The great African war: Congo and regional geopolitics, 1996-2006. Cambridg University Press, 2009.

Rodenhäuser, Tilman. Organizing rebellion: Non-state armed groups under international humanitarian law, human rights law and international criminal law. Oxford University Press, 2018.

Sheeran, Scott and Stephanie, Case. The Intervention Brigade: Legal issues for the UN in the Democratic Republic of the Congo. New York: International Peace Institute, 2014.

Tsagourias, Nicholas and Alasdair, Morrison. International humanitarian law: cases, materials and commentary. Cambridge University Press, 2018.

Uhler, Oscar M. and Henri, Coursier. Commentary IV: Geneva Convention Relative to the Protection of Civilian Persons in Time of War. Geneva: ICRC, 1958.

Zifcak, Spencer. United Nations reform: Heading north or south ?. Routledge, 2009.

Articles and Book Chapters

Abaya, Miriam. "No Place for Immunity: The Arguments against the African Criminal Court's Article 46BIS", in *Temp. Int'l & Comp. LJ* 30 (2016): 189.

Adams, Simon. "The Responsibility to Protect and the Fate of the Rohingya", in *Global Responsibility to Protect* 11, no. 4 (2019): 435-450.

Africa Center for Strategic Studies, "The Role of External Actors in the DRC Crisis," January 12, 2017, available at https://africacenter.org/spotlight/role-external-actors-drc-congo-crisis-sadc-au-icglr-un-eu/ accessed on 19 July 2022.

Aggestam, Lisbeth and Francesco, Anesi. "The Security Development Nexus", in *Stockholm: Swedish Institute for European Policy Studies* (2008).

Ahlborn, Christiane. "The rules of international organizations and the law of international responsibility", in *International Organizations Law Review* 8, no. 2 (2011): 397-482.

Ali, Khalil Mona. "Peace Forces at War" panel discussion at the annual general meeting of the American Society of International Law, April 7–12, (2014).

Allyn, Danielle N. "The Promise of Peace: UNSC 2098 and 2147 and the Protection of Congolese Civilians", in *Global Africana Review* Volume 1, Issue 1 Spring 2017 (2017).

Allyn, Danielle N. "The Promise of Peace: UNSC Resolutions 2098 and 2147 and the Protection of Congolese Civilians", Carolina Digital Repository. (2015) available at https://cdr.lib.unc.edu/, accessed on 11th January 2022.

Allyn, Danielle N. "The Promise of Peace: UNSC Resolutions 2098 and 2147 and the Protection of Congolese Civilians", *cdr.lib.unc.edu* (2015).

Amerasinghe, C. F. "Comments on the ILC's Draft Articles on the Responsibility of International Organizations", *International Organizations Law Review* 9, no. 1 (2012): 29-31.

Ambos, Kai. "What does 'intent to destroy'in genocide mean?", *International Review of the Red Cross* 91, no. 876 (2009): 833-858.

Andreichenko, Svitlana. "Imputability in the International Responsibility Law", *Ukr. J. Int'l L.* (2014): 234.

Anson, Rabinbach, "Raphael Lemkin et le concept de génocide", *Revue d'Histoire de la Shoah*, 2008/2 N° 189 (2008) :511-554

Arbour, Louise. "The responsibility to protect as a duty of care in international law and practice", *Review of International Studies 34*, no. 3 (2008): 445-458.

Arato, Andrew and Jean, Cohen. "Banishing the sovereign? Internal and external sovereignty in Arendt", *Constellations* 6, no. 2 (2009).

Arnold, Roberta and Noëlle, Quénivet. "International Humanitarian Law and Human Rights Law", *Towards a new merger in International Law. Leiden: Martinus Nijhoff Publishers* (2008).

Autesserre, Séverine. "The responsibility to protect in Congo 1: The failure of grassroots prevention", *Reassessing the Responsibility to Protect*, pp. 93-113. Routledge, 2015.

Bambara, Serge Théophile. "La justiciabilité des infractions des forces armées dans les opérations de paix", *Revue québécoise de droit international* 29, no. 1 (2016): 1-26, available at https://doi.org/10.7202/1045108ar, accessed on 23th January 2022.

Bannon, Alicia L. "The responsibility to protect: The UN world summit and the question of unilateralism", *Yale LJ* 115 (2005): 1157.

Bassiouni, Cherif M. "The right to restitution, compensation and rehabilitation for victims of gross violations of human rights and fundamental freedoms" Commission on Human Rights Resolution 2002/44 (23 April 2002).

Bellamy, Alex J. *The Three Pillars of the Responsibility to Protect, Pensamiento propio* 41, available at http://www.cries.org/wp-content/uploads/2015/09/006-bellamy.pdf accessed on 5th June 2022.

. "The responsibility to protect and the problem of military intervention", *International Affairs* 84, no. 4 (2008): 615-639.

. "The three pillars of the responsibility to protect", *Pensamiento propio* 41 (2015).

and Catherine, Drummond. "The responsibility to protect in Southeast Asia: between non-interference and sovereignty as responsibility", *The Pacific Review* 24, no. 2 (2011): 179-200.

Bennouna, Mohamed. "Prevention and International Law", *Collected Courses of the Xiamen Academy of International Law, Volume 4 (2011)*, pp. 157-209. Brill Nijhoff, 2013.

Benson, Jay. "The UN Intervention Brigade: Extinguishing Conflict or Adding Fuel to the Flames", *A One Earth Future Discussion Paper* 2 (2016): 1-12.

Berkowitz, Peter. "Leviathan Then and Now", *Policy Review* 151 (2008): 18.

Bohm, Alexandra and Garrett, Wallace Brown. "R2P and prevention: the international community and its role in the determinants of mass atrocity", *Global Responsibility to Protect* 13, no. 1 (2020): 60-95.

Jane, Boulden. Mandates Matter: An exploration of Impartiality in United Nations Operations, [2005] Global Governance 11, 147-160 available at http://www.atypon-lin k.com, accessed on 13th February 2019.

Berenice, Boutin. "Attribution of conduct in international military operations: a causal analysis of effective control", *Melbourne Journal of International Law* 18, no. 2 (2017): 154-179.

Breakey, Hugh and Angus, Francis. "Points of Convergence and Divergence: Normative, Institutional and Operational Relationships between R2P and PoC", *Security Challenges* 7, no. 4 (2011): 39–50. Available at http://www.jstor.org/stable/26467115, accessed on 11th January 2022.

Brehm, Maya. "The Arms Trade and States' Duty to Ensure Respect for Humanitarian and Human Rights Law", *Journal of Conflict and Security Law* 12, no. 3 (2007): 359-387.

Brig-Gen, James and Mwakibolwa, Aloizi. "NGOs Concerned about New DRC Intervention Brigade", *IRIN News*, May 31, 2013, available available at www.irinnews.org/report/98140/ngos-concerned-about-new-drc-intervention-brigade, accessed on 11th January 2022.

Bruce, Oswald. "The Security Council and the Intervention Brigade: Some Legal Issues," *American Society of International Law Insights* 17, No. 15 (June 6, 2013), available at www.asil.org/insights.

Brollowski, Hanna. "The Responsibility to Protect and Common Article 1 of the 1949 Geneva Conventions and Obligations of Third States'", *Responsibility to Protect: From Principleto Practice, Amsterdam* (2012): 93-110.

Burchard, Stephanie and Stephen, Burgess. "US training of African forces and military assistance, 1997–2017: Security versus human rights in principal–agent relations", *African Security* 11, no. 4 (2018): 339-369.

Byron, Christine. "Direct participation in hostilities", *International Conflict and Security Law: A Research Handbook*, pp. 277-300. The Hague: TMC Asser Press, 2022.

Calic, Marie-Janine. "Ethnic Cleansing and War Crimes, 1991–1995" *Comparative Southeast European Studies* 55, no. 1 (2007): 70-106.

Tatiana, Carayannis and Aaron, Pangburn. "AU and UN Cooperation in Peace Operations in the Democratic Republic of Congo". *African Politics, African Peace*, Paper n0 14, (JUNE 2016).

Chapman, Peter F. "Ensuring respect: United Nations compliance with international humanitarian law", *Human Rights Brief* 17, no. 1 (2009).

Charbonneau, Louis and Nichols, Michelle. "Exclusive: Rwanda, Uganda Arming Congo Rebels, Providing Troops—U.N. Panel", *REUTERS* (Oct. 17, 2012), https://perma.cc/Z5YYn, accessed on 11th January 2022.

Clark, Roger S. "History of efforts to codify crimes against humanity: From the Charter of Nuremberg to the Statute of Rome", *Forging a Convention for Crimes Against Humanity*, Cambridge University Press,(2011): 8-27.

Commentary on Rule 3, IHL Databases, available at https://ihl-databases.icrc.org/fr/customary-ihl/v1/rule3, accessed on 11th January 2022, Creegan, Erin. "Justified uses of force and the crime of aggression", *Journal of International Criminal Justice* 10, no. 1 (2012): 59-82.

Crush, Jay. "A Critical Analysis of the Status and Implementation of the Responsibility to Protect in International Law" in *e-international relations*, May 31 2013 on https://www.e-ir.info/2013/05/31/the-responsibility-to-protect-in-international-law/, accessed on 16th september 2022.

Daley, Patricia. "Challenges to peace: Conflict resolution in the Great Lakes region of Africa", *Third World Quarterly* 27, no. 2 (2006): 303-319.

Dan, Kuwali. The African Union and the Challenges of Implementing the "Responsibility to Protect," *Policy Notes 2009/4*, The Nordic Africa Institute, March 2009.

David, Eric and Burgorgue-Larsen, L. "Des occasions manquées de mettre en cause la responsabilité de la communauté internationale", *La répression internationale du génocide rwandais* (2003): 239-250.

Decaux, Emmanuel, Sébastien, Touzé and Jean-Paul, Costa. "La prévention des violations des droits de l'Homme: actes du colloque des 13 et 14 juin 2013", *Coll. Publications de l'Institut International des Droits de l'Homme, Sous-Coll. Institut René Cassin de Strasbourg.* Paris : Pedone (2015).

De Coning, Cedric, Julian, Detzel and Petter, Hojem. "UN Peacekeeping Operations Capstone Doctrine", in *Norwegian Institute of International Affairs,* (2008).

Deeks, Ashley. "How Does the UN Define 'Direct Participation in Hostilities'?" Lawfare (blog), October 21, 2013, available available at www.lawfareblog.com/2013/10/how-does-the-un-define-direct-participation-in-hostilities/, accessed on 16th september 2022.

Deen-Racsmány, Zsuzsanna. "The amended UN model memorandum of understanding: a new incentive for states to discipline and prosecute military members of national peacekeeping contingents?", *Journal of Conflict & Security Law* 16, no. 2 (2011): 321-355.

DeMeritt, Jacqueline HR. "International organizations and government killing: Does naming and shaming save lives?", *International Interactions* 38, no. 5 (2012): 597-621.

Dekker, I.F. "Accountability of international organizations: an evolving legal concept? ", Wouters, Jan, Eva, Brems, Stefaan, Smis and Pierre, Schmitt. (eds) *Accountability for human rights violations by international organisations.* Intersentia, 2010.

Dhammika, Herath. "Post-conflict Reconstruction and Reconciliation in Rwanda and Sri Lanka in Post-Conflict", *Social Cohesion* (31 May 2018) https://www.accord.org.za/conflict-trends/post-conflict-reconstruction-and-reconciliation-in-rwanda-and-sri-lanka/, accessed on 16th september 2022.

Dörenberg, A. J. T. "Opérations de maintien de la paix aspects juridiques", *The Military Law and the Law of War Review* 28, no. 3-4 (1989): 16-112.

Durham, Helen and Phoebe, Wynn-Pope. "The relationship between international humanitarian law and responsibility to protect: From solferino to srebrenica", *collections.unu.edu* (2013): 175-196.

Ekanayake, Charuka and Susan, Harris Rimmer. "Applying effective control to the conduct of UN forces: connecting factual complexities with legal responsibility", *International organizations law review* 15, no. 1 (2018): 9-38.

Fahey, Daniel. "Congo's "Mr. X" The Man who Fooled the UN", *World Policy Journal* 33, no. 2 (2016): 91-100.

Feil, Scott R. "Could 5,000 Peacekeepers Have Saved 500,000 Rwandans?: Early Intervention Reconsidered", *Institute for the Study of Diplomacy III* (1997): 1-5.

Feinstein, Lee. "Darfur and beyond: what is needed to prevent mass atrocities", (2007), available at http://www.cfr.org/sudan/darfur-beyond/p12444, Accessed 09th Jun 2022.

Fernández, Rosa Ana Alija and Jaume, Saura Estapà. "Towards a Single and Comprehensive Notion of 'Civilian Population'in Crimes against Humanity", *international criminal law review* 17, no. 1 (2017): 47-77.

Ferraro, Tristan. "The applicability and application of international humanitarian law to multinational forces", *International Review of the Red Cross* 95, no. 891-892 (2013): 561-612.

Ferraro, Tristan. "The ICRC's legal position on the notion of armed conflict involving foreign intervention and on determining the IHL applicable to this type of conflict", *International Review of the Red Cross* 97, no. 900 (2015): 1227-1252.

Fiott, Daniel. "The use of force and the third pillar", *The Responsibility to Protect and the Third Pillar: Legitimacy and Operationalization*, pp. 130-145. London: Palgrave Macmillan UK, 2015.

Fletcher, Laurel E. "From indifference to engagement: Bystanders and international criminal justice", *Mich. J. Int'l L.* 26 (2004): 1013.

Froitzheim, Meike and Fredrik, Söderbaum. "Building peace from the outside': the role of the EU in the Democratic Republic of Congo", *Globalization and Development,* Routledge (2013):193-214.

Gaeta, Paola. "On what conditions can a state be held responsible for genocide?", *European Journal of International Law* 18, no. 4 (2007): 631-648.

Gagro, Sandra Fabijanić. "The Responsibility to Protect (R2P) Doctrine", *International Journal of Social Sciences* 3, no. 1 (2014): 61-77.

Gaja, Giorgio. "Articles on the Responsibility of International Organizations", *United Nations Audiovisual Library of International Law* (2014): 1-10.

Gallagher, Adrian. "The promise of pillar II: analysing international assistance under the Responsibility to Protect", *International Affairs* 91, no. 6 (2015): 1259-1275.

Gareth, Evans. "The Responsibility to Protect: Revisiting Humanitarian Intervention", *Foreign Affairs* 81 (2002), available at https://www.crisisgroup.org/global/r esponsibility-protect. accessed on 19th september 2022.

Garwood-Gowers, Andrew. "China's "Responsible Protection" concept: Reinterpreting the Responsibility to Protect (R2P) and military intervention for humanitarian purposes", *Asian Journal of International Law* 6, no. 1 (2016): 89-118.

Genser, Jared. "The United Nations Security Council's Implementation of the Responsibility to Protect: A Review of Past Interventions and Recommendations for Improvement", *Chi. J. Int'l L.* 18 (2017): 420.

Gierycz, Dorota. "From humanitarian intervention (HI) to responsibility to protect (R2P)", *Criminal Justice Ethics* 29, no. 2 (2010): 110-128.

Greenwood, Christopher. "Command responsibility and the Hadzihasanovic Decision", *J. Int'l Crim. Just.* 2 (2004).

Greenwood, Christopher. "International Law and the NATO Intervention in Kosovo", *The International and Comparative Law Quarterly*, vol. 49, no. 4, (2000) pp. 926–34. *JSTOR*, http://www.jstor.org/stable/761769, accessed on 19th december 2022.

Gifkins, Jess. "*R2P in the UN Security Council: Darfur, Libya and beyond*", Cooperation and Conflict 51, no. 2 (2016): 148-165.

Harff, Barbara. "No lessons learned from the Holocaust? Assessing risks of genocide and political mass murder since 1955", In *Genocide and Human Rights*, Routledge (2017): 329-345.

Hathaway, Oona A., Paul Strauch K., Beatrice, Walton A. and Zoe, AY Weinberg. "What is a war crime", in *Yale J. Int'l L.* 44 (2019).

Hemdi, Bayolo, H. "L'Eglise profane" *chronique des violations des droits du clergé pen-dant la guerre d'agression* (1998–2000).

Henckaerts, V. J.-M. and Doswald-Beck, L. *Droit international humanitaire*, Bruylant, CICR, 2 vol. 2006. at https://www.icrc.org/fre/assets/files/other/ icrc_001_pcustom.pdf, accessed on 19th december 2022.

Howard, Lise Morjé and Anjali, Kaushlesh Dayal. "The use of force in UN peacekeeping", *International Organization* 72.1 (2018): 71-103.

Hrnjaz, Miloš and Janja, Simentić Popović. "Protracted Armed Violence as a Criterion for the Existence of Non-international Armed Conflict: International Humanitarian Law, International Criminal Law and Beyond", *Journal of Conflict and Security Law* 25.3 (2020): 473-500.

Hunt, Charles T. "The responsibility to protect and the protection of civilians in UN peace operations: interaction, feedback and co-evolution". *Constructing the Responsibility to Protect: Contestation and Consolidation.*Charles T. Hunt and Phil Orchard. Abingdon, Oxon, (eds) *Taylor and Francis.* (2020),89-112.https://doi.org/10.4324/9780429352430-5.

Jaclyn D. "The Responsibility to Protect: Can we prevent mass atrocities without making the same mistakes?", *Streitfeld-HalL, Global Centre for the Responsibility to Protect*, available at

https://www.civicus.org, accessed on 19th december 2022.

Jalloh, Charles Chernor. "What makes a crime against humanity a crime against humanity", *Am.U. Int'l L. Rev.* 28 (2012).

Jamestown Foundation. *Congolese Forces Take the Offensive Against Uganda's ADF-NALU Militants.* (20 March 2014) available at: https://www.refworld.org/docid/5333fc864.html, accessed on 19th december 2022.

Jay , Crush. "The Responsibility to Protect in International Law", *E-international relations* (May 31st 2013) https://www.e-ir.info/2013/05/31/the-responsibility-to-protect-in-international-law/ accessed on 12th January 2023.

Jorritsma, Remy. "International responsibility and attribution of conduct: an analysis of Case Law on Human Rights and Humanitarian Law", In International and European Law Maastricht Centre for Human Rights, (2021).

Judson, Anne-Marie. "Where is R2P grounded in International law?", Master diss., University of Otago, 2012.

Kajtar, Gabor. "An overall critique of the overall control test", *Gabor Kajtar: An overall critique of the overall control test. In: Zsuzsanna Csapó (Ed.): Emlékkötet Herczegh Géza születésének* 85 (2018): 82-98.

Kalandarishvili-Mueller, Natia. "Transforming a Prima Facie NIAC into an IAC: Finding the Answer in IHL", *Israel Law Review* 53.3 (2020): 334-354.

Kalere, Jean Migabo. "Genocide in the African Great Lakes States. Challenges for the International Criminal Court in the Case of the Democratic Republic of Congo", *International Criminal Law Review* 5, no. 3 (2005): 463-484.

Karsten, Nora. "Distinguishing Military and Non-military Superiors: Reflections on the Bemba Case at the ICC", *Journal of International Criminal Justice* 7, no. 5 (2009): 983-1004.

Kennes, Erick and Wilén, Ninah. Multi-Layered Violence in the DRC: *Is History Repeating Itself? 27.01.2023* at https://www.institutmontaigne.org accessed on *27.01.2023*

Kennedy, Robin. "The Prevalence of Sexual Violence in the Context of Armed Conflicts: the Case of the DRC", *History* (2020).

Keranen, Outi. "What Happened to the Responsibility to Rebuild?", *Global Governance: A Review of Multilateralism and International Organizations* 22, no. 3 (2016): 331-348.

Krain, Matthew. "The effect of economic sanctions on the severity of genocides or politicides", *Journal of genocide research* 19, no. 1 (2017): 88-111.

Kreß, Claus. "The Crime of Genocide and Contextual Elements: A Comment on the ICC Pre-Trial Chamber's Decision in the Al Bashir Case", *Journal of International Criminal Justice* 7, no. 2 (2009): 297-306.

Lansana, Gberie. "La brigade d'intervention : fin de la guerre en RDC ? Une dimension nouvelle des opérations de maintien de la paix", (August, 2023) available at https://www.un.org/africarenewal/fr/magazine/ao%C3%BBt-2013/la-brigade-d%E2%80%99intervention-fin-de-la-guerre-en-rdc, accessed on August, 2023

Lagrange, Marc-André, Les mécanismes de paix régionaux dans les Grands Lacs : des outils incapables de promouvoir la démocratie ?". *Revue Tiers Monde* 2016/4 (N° 228),Pp pages 143 à 161.

Lawrence, Daniel H. "A Government-Based Framework for Conflict Classification", *Texas Law Review* 101.1 (2022).

Leck, Christopher. "International responsibility in United Nations peacekeeping operations: command and control arrangements and the attribution of conduct", *Melbourne Journal of International Law* 10, no. 1 (2009): 346-364.

Luck, Edward. "Sovereignty, choice and the responsibility to protect", *Global Responsibility to Protect* 1, no. 1 (2009): 10-21.

Lurweg, Meike. "Coherent Actor or Institution Wrangler? The European Union as a Development and Security Actor in Eastern Democratic Republic of the Congo", *African Security* 4, no. 2 (2011): 100-126.

Lopez, George A. "Mobilizing Economic Sanctions for Preventing Mass Atrocities: From Targeting Dictators to Enablers", *Reconstructing Atrocity Prevention,* Rosenberg S., Galis T., and Zucker A. (Eds.) Cambridge: Cambridge University Press (2016): 379-392.

Lopez, George A. "Tools, tasks and tough thinking: Sanctions and R2P", *Global Center for Responsibility to Protect* (2013).

https://sanctionsandsecurity.nd.edu › assets ›, accessed on August, 2023.

Maedl, Anna. "Rape as Weapon of War in the Eastern DRC? The Victims' Perspective", *Human Rights Quarterly* 33, no. 1 (February 2011): 128-47.

Major, Claudia. EU-UN *cooperation in military crisis management: the experience of EUFOR RD Congo in 2006. European Union Institute for Security Studies* Vol. 72, (2008).

May, Larry. "Responsibility to rebuild and collective responsibility: legal and moral considerations", *Normative Pluralism and International Law: Exploring Global Governance,* Klabbers J. & Piiparinen T. (Eds.) Cambridge University Press. 2013: 323-339.

Martinelli, Marta. "Helping transition: the EU police mission in the Democratic Republic of Congo (EUPOL Kinshasa) in the framework of EU policies in the Great Lakes", *European Foreign Affairs Review* 11, no. 3 (2006).

Marxsen, Christian. "Unpacking the International Law on Reparation for Victims of Armed Conflict", *Reparation for Victims of Armed Conflict, Max Planck Institute for Comparative Public Law and International Law (MPIL) Research Paper* 2018-19 (2018).

Matache, Alexandru. "The Inapplicability of the Nulla Poena Sine Culpa Principle in the EU Criminal Law: The Tendency towards Strict Liability Endorsement", *CDP* (2017): 106.

Mayroz, Eyal. "The legal duty to 'prevent': After the onset of 'genocide'", *Journal of Genocide Research* 14, no. 1 (2012): 79-98.

Mbokani, Jacques. "La jurisprudence congolaise en matière de crimes de droit international", *une étude de l'Open society initiative for Southern Africa (Osisa)* (2016).

Messineo, Francesco. "Attribution of conduct", *Principles of shared responsibility in international law: an appraisal of the state of the art. Cambridge University Press, Cambridge* (2014): 60-97.

Milanovic, Marko. "Special Rules of Attribution of Conduct in International Law" *International Law Studies*, Vol. 96, p. 295 (2020) at SSRN: https://ssrn.com/abstract =3623309, accessed on August, 2023.

Milanovic Marko. What Exactly Internationalizes an Internal Armed Conflict? May 7, 2010, Blog of the European Journal of International Law at https://www.ejiltalk.org/, accessed on August, 2023.

Müller, Lars. "The Force Intervention Brigade—United Nations forces beyond the fine line between peacekeeping and peace enforcement", *Journal of Conflict and Security Law* 20, no. 3 (2015): 359-380.

Mooney, Erin. "The Guiding Principles and the Responsibility to Protect", *Forced Migration Review* 1 (2008): 11-12. https://www.fmreview.org/GuidingPrinciples10/mooney, accessed on 27th August, 2023.

Mupendana, Pierre Claver. "Necessity and Difficulties to establish a repressive system for International crimes committed in the DRC", *Actual Problems of International Relations* 1, no. 150 (2022): 31-46.

Murphy, Ray. "United National military operations and international humanitarian law: What rules apply to peacekeepers?" *Criminal Law Forum* vol. 14 (2003): 153-194.

. "The Criminalisation of International Humanitarian Law and Human Rights Law Violations Committed by Peace Forces: What Happens in Practice?", *Collegium* : afl. 42 (2011).

Murthy, Jaya. 'Mandating the protection cluster with the responsibility to protect: a policy recommendation based on the protection cluster's implementation in South Kivu, DRC', *Journal of Humanitarian Assistance* (5 Oct. 2007) https://sites.tufts.edu/jha/archives/55.

Mutisi, Martha. "SADC Interventions in the Democratic Republic of the Congo", *Conflict Trends* 2016, no. 3 (2016): 27-35.

Mvé Ella, Léandre. "La responsabilité du Conseil de sécurité en cas de manquement à la responsabilité de protéger", *Civitas Europa* 2 (2018): 111-127.

Pacifique, Mwambusa Makuta, Emmanuel, Kandate, Léon, Irenge, Pascal, Kaboy, Didier, Munguakonkwa and Justin, Matete. "Acteurs de la vie politique et violences identitaires à Beni, RDC", *Research Initiatives for Social Development (RISD)*, (2021).

N. KOK, "From the International Conference on the Great Lakes Region-led negotiation to the Intervention Brigade", *African Security Review*, vol. 22, issue 3, (2013) 175-180.

Nirmal, B. C. "Responsibility To Protect: A Political Doctrine Or An Emerging Norm (With Special Reference To The Libyan And Syrian Crises)", *Journal of the Indian Law Institute* (2015): 333-375.

Nkusi, Fred. "Legal Implications of Shifting Paradigm: Intervention Brigade – MONUSCO's Enforcement Action in the DRC", *Berkeley Journal of International Law* (BJIL), Vol. 2, No. 2 (2013) Available at SSRN: https://ssrn.com/abstract=2326376, accessed on 27th September, 2024.

Nlandu, Thierry Mayamba. "Mapping Police Services in the Democratic Republic of Congo: Institutional Interactions at Central, Provincial and Local Levels", *IDS Research Reports* 2012, no. 71 (2012): 1-103.

Novosseloff, Alexandra. "Assessing the effectiveness of the united nations peacekeeping force in cyprus (UNFICYP) and the office of the special adviser to the secretary-general on cyprus (OSASG)", (2021).

Ntanyoma, Rukumbuzi Delphin and Helen Hintjens. "Expressive Violence and the Slow Genocide of the Banyamulenge of South Kivu". *Ethnicities* 22, no. 3 (2022): 374-403.

O'Brien, Patricia. "Respecting IHL: Challenges and Responses," statement made at 36th Roundtable on Current Issues of International Humanitarian Law, San Remo, Italy, September 5, 2013, at http://legal.un.org/ola/media/info_from_lc/POB-San-Remo-36th-Roundtable-5-September-2013.pdf, accessed on 27th September 2024.

O'shea, Elizabeth. "Responsibility to Protect (R2P) in Libya: ghosts of the past haunting the future", *International Human Rights Law Review* 1, no. 1 (2012): 173-190.

Okimoto, Keiichiro. "The Legal Protection of Personnel of United Nations Peacekeeping Operations in Times of NIAC", *International Humanitarian Law and Non-State Actors: Debates, Law and Practice* (2020): 79-111.

Olivier, Darren. "One SANDF soldier killed and two wounded in dawn DRC attack". *African Defence Review (published 19 December 2016)*. Retrieved 23 December 2016

Oxford Analytica. "Congo's Beni crisis may become more complex", *Emerald Expert Briefings* oxan-db (2019).

Pacholska, Magdalena. "(Il) legality of killing peacekeepers: the crime of attacking peacekeepers in the jurisprudence of international criminal tribunals", *Journal of International Criminal Justice* 13, no. 1 (2015): 43-72.

Pak, Hui-Chol, Hye-Ryon Son and Son-Kyong Jong. "Analysis on the Legal Nature of 'Responsibility to Protect'", *International Studies* 57, no. 3 (2020): 279-295.

Pape, Robert A. "When duty calls: A pragmatic standard of humanitarian intervention", *International Security* 37, no. 1 (2012): 41-80.

Payandeh, Mehrdad. "With Great Power Comes Great Responsibility-The Concept of the Responsibility to Protect within the Process of International Lawmaking", in *Yale J. Int'l L.* 35 (2010): 469-516.

Patricia, O'Brien. statement by the under-secretary-general for Legal Affairs and UN legal counsel delivered to the International Law Commission, Geneva, May 23, 2013, available at http://legal.un.org/ilc/sessions/65/Statement%20byTheLegal%20Counsel.pdf, accessed on 28th September 2024.

Peters, Anne. "Humanity as the A and Ω of Sovereignty", *European Journal ofInternational Law* 20, no. 3 (2009): 513-544.

Pfanner, Toni. "Various mechanisms and approaches for implementing international humanitarian law and protecting and assisting war victims", *International Review of the Red Cross* 91, no. 874 (2009): 279-328.

Polgreen, Lydia. "A Massacre in Congo, Despite Nearby Support". *N.Y. TIMES* (Dec. 11, 2008), available at http://www.nytimes.com/2008/12/11/world/africa/11congo.html, accessed on 31 October 2022.

Pourtier, Roland. "Le Kivu dans la guerre: acteurs et enjeux", *EchoGéo* (2009).

Popovski, Vesselin. "The Concepts of Responsibility to Protect and Protection of Civilians: 'Sisters, but Not Twins", *Security Challenges* 7, no. 4 (2011): 1–12. available at http://www.jstor.org/stable/26467112, accessed on 28th September 2024.

Rafti, Marina. "South Kivu: a sanctuary for the rebellion of the democratic forces for the liberatin of Rwanda", (2006).

Reike, Ruben. "Conflict prevention and R2P", *The Oxford Handbook of the Responsibility to Protect.* Bellamy, Alex and Tim Dunne, (Eds.) Oxford University Press, 2016.

Reynaert, Julie. "NONUC/MONUSCO and civilian protection in the Kivus", *Interns andVolunteers series, IPIS* (2010).

Roberts, Hugh. "Who said Gaddafi had to go?", *London Review of Books* 33, no. 22 (2011): 8-11.

Robinson, Paul. "Is There an Obligation to Rebuild?", In *Justice, Responsibility and Reconciliation in the Wake of Conflict.* Dordrecht: Springer Netherlands (2012): 105-116

Robinson, Darryl. "Defining "crimes against humanity" at the Rome Conference", *American Journal of International Law* 93, no. 1 (1999): 43-57

Robinson, Nehemiah. "The genocide convention", *Case W. Res. J. Int'l L.* 40 (2007).

Rudolph, James P. "Gaza and Israel–A case for International Humanitarian Law, Not R2P", *Justice in Conflict* (2014).

Rusamira, Etienne. "La dynamique des conflits ethniques au Nord-Kivu: une réflexion prospective", *Afrique contemporaine* 207, no. 3 (2003): 147-163.

Sadat, Leila Nadya. "Crimes against humanity in the modern age", *American Journal of International Law* 107, no. 2 (2013): 334-377.

Salzman, Todd A. "Rape camps as a means of ethnic cleansing: Religious, cultural and ethical responses to rape victims in the former Yugoslavia", *Human Rights Quarterly* 20, no. 2 (1998): 348-378.

Sassòli, Marco. "Legitimate targets of attacks under international humanitarian law", *HPCR Policy Brief* (2003).

Sassoli, Marco. "Introducing a sliding-scale of obligations to address the fundamental inequality between armed groups and states?", *International Review of the Red Cross* 93, no. 882 (2011): 426-431.

Scheffer, David. "Atrocity crimes framing the responsibility to protect", In *Responsibility to protect: The global moral compact for the 21st century*, pp. 77-98. New York: Palgrave Macmillan US, 2009.

Schnabel, Albrecht. "the Responsibility to Rebuild". Knight, W. Andy and Frazer Egerton, (Eds.) *The Routledge handbook of the responsibility to protect.* London: Routledge, 2012.

Schneider, Catherine. "Les opérations extérieures de l'Union européenne en Afrique", *1er Symposium international sur la sécurité en Afrique" La sécurité en Afrique: Défis et perspectives"*.(2010).

Schmalenbach, Kirsten. "International responsibility for humanitarian law violations by armed groups", *Inducing Compliance with International Humanitarian Law. Lessons from the African Great Lakes Region*, Heike Krieger (ed),Cambridge University Press, (2015): 470-503.

Sheri, Rosenbergand, Ekkehard ,Strauss. "A Common Approach to the Application of the Responsibility to Protect". *Operationalizing the Responsibility to Protect A Contribution to the Third Pillar Approach*, Daniel Fiott Robert Zuber Joachim Koops (eds). The Madariaga, Brussels (2012):55-72.

Smith, Karen. "A reflection on the responsibility to protect in 2020", *Global Centre for the Responsibility to Protect* (2020).https://reliefweb.int/report/world/reflection-responsibility-protect-2020, accessed on 09th April 2023.

Soma, Valérie. "Le Droit d'intervention de l'Union Africaine", *Sciences Juridiques et Politiques* 1, no. 1 (2017).

Smit, Nico. "The Evolution of the Responsibility to Protect", E-International Relations (2008): 615-639.

Sprik, Lenneke. "Command responsibility in peacekeeping missions: Normative obligations of protection in a criminal law environment", *Journal of Conflict and Security Law* 22, no. 3 (2017): 497-522.

Sriram, Chandra Lekha. *Globalizing justice for mass atrocities: a revolution in accountability.* Routledge, 2013.

Stahn, Carsten. "Responsibility to protect: political rhetoric or emerging legal norm?", *Globalization and Common Responsibilities of States.* Routledge, (2017): 147-168.

Stamnes, Eli. "The Responsibility to Protect and» Root Cause "Prevention", *Norwegian Institute of International Affairs* (2010): 1-21.

Stearns, Jason K. "Helping Congo Help Itself: What It Will Take to End Africa's Worst War", *Foreign Aff.* 92 (2013).

Steenberghe, Raphael van. "The Notions of the Responsibility to Protect and the Protection of Civilians in Armed Conflict: Detecting Their Association and Its Impact Upon International Law", *Goettingen J. Int'l L.* 6 (2014): 81-144

Swedberg, Richard. "Exploratory research", *The production of knowledge: Enhancing progress in social science* (2020): 17-41.

Szasz, Paul C. "UN Forces and international humanitarian law", *International Law Studies* 75, no. 1 (2000).

Szurek, Sandra. "La responsabilité de protéger: du principe à son application. Quelques remarques sur les enjeux du law making process en cours", *dial.uclouvain.be* (2014).

Tardy, Thierry. "The dangerous liaisons of the Responsibility to Protect and the protection of civilians in peacekeeping operations", *Global Responsibility to Protect* 4, no. 4 (2012): 424-448.

Thakur, Ramesh. "The responsibility to protect at 15", *International Affairs* 92, no. 2 (2016): 415-434.

Thakur, Ramesh and Thomas, Weiss G. "R2P: from idea to norm—and action?", *Global Responsibility to Protect* 1, no. 1 (2009): 22-53

Thakur, Ramesh. "Peacebuilding and the Responsibility to Rebuild", *Asian International Studies Review* 19, no. 2 (2018): 1-12.

Roger, Thamba. "Financement des groupes armés et gouvernance démocratique en République démocratique du Congo", *Africa Development/Afrique et Développement* 44, no. 2 (2019): 77-97.

Tunkin, Grigory. "Is General International Law Customary Law Only?", *Eur. J. Int'l L.* 4 (1993)

UN Office of Legal Affairs (OLA) representative Mona Ali Khalil, panel discussion, "Humanitarian Law, Peacekeeping/Intervention Forces and Troop-Contributing Countries: Issues and Challenges," *Asian-African Legal Consultative Organization (AALCO)*, United Nations, New York, August 21, (2013)

Umutesi, Marie Béatrice. "Is reconciliation between Hutus and Tutsis possible?", *Journal of International Affairs* (2006): 157-171.

Upadhyay, Niteesh Kumar. "Law of Armed Conflict: Applications and Practice", *20-21 ISIL Y.B. Int'l Human. & Refugee L. 394* (2020-2021).

Van Steenberghe, Raphael. "The Law against War or Jus contra Bellum: A New Terminology for a Conservative View on the Use of Force?", *Leiden Journal of International Law* 24, no. 3 (2011): 747-788.

Vermeer-Künzli, Annemarieke. "A matter of interest: Diplomatic protection and state responsibility Erga Omnes", *International & Comparative Law Quarterly* 56, no. 3 (2007): 553-581.

Wakabi, Wairagala. "Ntaganda Convicted at ICC for Rape, Sexual Violence and Murder", *International Justice Monitor*, (2019) Last modified July 8, 2019 at https://www.ijmonitor.org, accessed on 11th January 2022.

Waszink, Camilla. "Protection of civilians under international humanitarian law: trends and challenges", *NOREF report* (2011).

Weiss, Herbert F. and Georges Nzongola-Ntalaja. "Decentralization and the DRC–an overview", *New York: Social Science Research Council* (2013).

Welsh, Jennifer M. "The responsibility to prevent: Assessing the gap between rhetoric and reality", *Cooperation and Conflict* 51, no. 2 (2016): 216-232.

. "The Security Council's Role in Fulfilling the Responsibility to Protect", *Ethics & International Affairs* 35, no. 2 (2021): 227-243.

Williams, Christopher. Explaining the Great War in Africa: How Conflict in the Congo Became a Continental Crisis in *The Fletcher Forum of World Affairs*, Vol. 37, No. 2 (Summer 2013): 81-100.

Williams, Paul D. "The R2P, Protection of Civilians and UN Peacekeeping Operations", *The Oxford Handbook of the Responsibility to Protect* (2016): 524-544.

Wharton, Sara. "The Evolution of International Criminal Law: Prosecuting'New'Crimes before the Special Court for Sierra Leone", *International Criminal Law Review* 11, no. 2 (2011): 217-239.

Whittle, Devon. "Peacekeeping in conflict: The Intervention Brigade, MONUSCO and the application of international humanitarian law to United Nations forces", *Geo. J. Int'l L.* 46 (2014).

Reports

African Union, Communiqué of the 381st meeting of the Peace and Security Council (5-7)20 June 2013 at https://www.peaceau.org/ on 9 November 2022.

Aldo Ajello, the EU Special representative for Africa's Great Lakes Region, Brussels, 17 September 2003, available at http://www.irinnews.org/Report/46206/DRC-EU-calls-Artemis-operation-a-bigsuccess on 31 October 2022.

Amnesty international at https://www.amnesty.org/en/location/africa/east-africa-the-horn-and- great-lakes/democratic-republic-of-the-congo/ , accessed on 11th January 2022.

Annual Activity Report of the African Commission on Human and Peoples' Rights, 1993-94, ACHPR/RPT17th at Annex XI.

Austrian Fund for Reconciliation, Peace and Cooperation at http://www.zukunftsfonds-austria.at/download/book_reconciliationfund_ForcedLaborInAustria.pdf, accessed on 11th January 2022.

Background Doc. DPH 2004, p. 30; Report DPH 2004, pp. 15-17; Report DPH 2005, p. 13

Ban Ki-moon. (2012a). Responsibility to Protect: Timely and Decisive Response. Report of the Secretary-General, UN Doc. A/66/874–S/2012/578, July 25.

Ban Ki-moon ,Responsibility to Protect: State Responsibility and Prevention. Report of the Secretary-General, UN Doc S/2013/399, July 9. (2013a).

Baromètre Sécuritaire du Kivu, La cartographie des groupes armés dans l'Est du Congo, opportunités manquées, insécurité prolongée et prophéties auto-réalisatrices, Février 2021. (Mapping armed groups in eastern Congo, missed opportunities, prolonged insecurity and self-fulfilling prophecies) Translated, at https://kivusecurity.nyc3.digitaloceanspaces.com/reports/39/2021%20KST%20rapport%20FR.pdf, accessed on 11th January 2022.

Canada, Debates of Parliament, 38th Parliament, 1st Session, Revised Han sard, No. 61 (February 21, 2005).

Carnegie Commission on Preventing Deadly Conflict, *Preventing Deadly Conflict: Final Report* (WashingtonDC: CarnegieCommissiononPreventingDeadlyConflict,1997).

Council of the EU, Democratic Republic of the Congo: EU adopts sanctions against a further 9

people, Press release, 29 may 2017 at https://www.consilium.europa.eu/en/press/press-releases/2017/05/29/rdc-sanctions/, accessed on 11th January 2022.

Colonel Felicia Maganwe, chief of staff of the force intervention brigade (fib) of monusco callsfor professionalism to achieve the expected results , beni: monusco's Malawian contingent trained in the jungle combat techniques, 07.04.2022 at https://monusco.unmissions.org/en, accessed on 1st August 2023.

Decision on the peace process in the Democratic Republic of the Congo doc. ex/cl/42 (iii) e, Executive council third ordinary session, 4 - 8 July 2003, Maputo (Mozambique) ex/cl/dec. 20 - 74 (iii).

Democratic Republic of the Congo, Human Rights Report 2022, 23.03.2023 at https://www.state.gov/wp-content/uploads/2023/03/415610, accessed on 1st August 2022.

Democratic Republic of the Congo, Populations at risk, 28.02.2023 at https://www.globalr2p.org/countries/democratic-republic-of-the-congo/, accessed on 1st August 2022.

"Draft of Arrangement on the Treatment of Persons Handed Over by the United Nations Organization Stabilization Mission in the Democratic Republic of the Congo (MONUSCO) to the DRC authorities"at https://digitallibrary.un.org/record/3978485?ln=en, accessed on 1st August 2022.

DR Congo: A comprehensive strategy to disarm the FDLR, 09.07.2009 at https://reliefweb.int/report/democratic-republic-congo/dr-congo-comprehensive-strategy-disarm-fdlr, accessed on 1st april 2022.

DRC: M23 armed group must stop killing civilians and respect international law on December 2, 2022 at https://www.amnesty.org/ see also Atrocity Alert No. 328:

DR Congo, International Justice and Genocide Victims Day by Global Centre for R2P, on December 7, 2022 at https://www.globalr2p.org/publications, accessed on 1st August 2022.

DR Congo: EU, US Sanction Top Officials, UN, AU Should Expand Action Against Rights Abusers, Press for Credible Elections, 1st June 2017 available at https://www.hrw.org/news/2017/06/01/dr-congo-eu-us-sanction-top-officials, accessed on 1st August 2022.

DR Congo: M23 Rebels Committing War Crimes, HUM. RTS. WATCH (Sept. 11, 2012), available at https://perma.cc/X2YU-49H8.

DR Congo: The atrocities of the Rwandan-backed M23 rebellion, 06.02.2023 available at https://www.hrw.org/fr, accessed on 1st August 2022.

DRC: Mapping Human Rights Violations, supra note 170, at 31, 463–64. The U.N.

DR Congo: Guterres 'outraged' over peacekeepers' aggression, calls for accountability on 31 July 2022 available at https://news.un.org/en/story/2022/07/1123692 accessed on 1st August 2022.

European Union, A Secure Europe in a Better World - European Security Strategy. Brussels, 2003.

European Commission, "EU Relations with Democratic Republic of Congo", 2010a.

FARDC and MONUSCO launch joint operations against ADF,16.11.2018 available at https://monusco.unmissions.org/en, accessed on 14th december 2023.

FIDH, Slaughter in Kasai: Crimes against humanity perpetrated to create chaos, Report 20/12/2007 at https://www.fidh.org on 31 October 2022.

Focus group with the population of Mbau , held at Mbau by Mugombozi, A. Félicité, on 12th June 2023.

General Thierry Lion in beni: " we are amidst sovereign and unilateral operations, prepared by the fardc " (interview), 18.11.2019 at https://monusco.unmissions.org/en, accessed on 17th december 2023.

Global Centre for The R2P, Democratic Republic of Congo, 1 September 2021 available at https://www.globalr2p.org/countries/democratic-republic-of-the-congo/ on 6th September 2022

Global Centre for the Responsibility to Protect ,Un Security Council And The Responsibility To Protect, 2 June 2022 https://www.globalr2p.org/calling-for-a-unsc-code-of-conduct/ accessed on 20th december 2023.

Global Centre for the Responsibility to Protect, Democratic Republic of the Congo, 31 May 2021 available at https://www.globalr2p.org/countries/democratic-republic-of-the-congo/ accessed on 20th december 2023.

High Level Panel on Threats, Challenges and Change,Report of the High-Level Panel on Threats Challenges and Change: A More Secure World: Our Shared Responsibility (A/59/565) (2nd December 2004).

Human Right Watch, DR Congo: Resurgent M23 Rebels Target Civilians 25 July 2022 at https://www.hrw.org/ on 12 September 2022.

International Crisis Group. (2011). A ceasefire and negotiations the right way to resolve the Libyan crisis. Retrieved from https://www.crisisgroup.org/middle-east-north-,africa/north-africa/libya/ceasefire-and-negotiations-right-way-resolve-libya-crisis accessed on 20th december 2023.

Implementing the responsibility to protect", Report of the Secretary-General UN Doc. A/63/677, 12 January 2009.

Interview with LTG Marcos Affonso da Costa, Force Commander & Head of the Military Component of MONUSCO in Goma held by Mugombozi, A. Félicité on 24th January in Goma at the MONUSCO headquarter.

Interview with a member of civil society of Rutshuru, interview held in Goma by Mugombozi, A. Félicité, 12.07.2023.

International Commission on Intervention and State Sovereignty, 'The Responsibility to Protect' (Ottawa: International Development Research Centre, 2001).

Interview with Joseph Kitausa, president of the Beni civil society, available at https://www.rfi.fr/fr/afrique/20220731-rdc-des-soldats-de-la-monusco-tuent-au-moins-personnes-dans-le-territoire-de-beni, accessed on 20th december 2023.

Interview with an "anonymous' FIB member held in Beni by Mugombozi, A. Félicité, Mavivi 20th June 2023.

La RDC s'oppose à la reconfiguration d'une brigade spéciale de la force onusienne, 'DRC opposes the reconfiguration of a special UN force brigade ' at https://www.lemonde.fr/afrique/article/2020/08/06/, accessed on 06 August 2020.

Letter dated 4 March 2013 from the Secretary General to the President of the Security Council S/2013/131.

Le déploiement de la brigade d'intervention est imminent, (21/04/2013) available at https://www.radiookapi.net/nations-unies/magazine-un, accessed on 20th december 2023.

L'état de siège a-t-il amélioré la sécurité dans l'est de la RDC ? on June 10th 2021, available at https://blog.kivusecurity.org/fr/tag/brigade-dintervention 13th January 2023, accessed on 20th december 2023.

"Letter to the Acting Chair of Special Committee on Peacekeeping Operations, United Nations, regarding immunities of civilian police and military personnel" in United Nations Juridical Yearbook 2004, New York, UN, 2007 at 323 (UN Doc ST/LEG/SER.C/42).

L'Union Européenne et la République démocratique du Congo available at https://www.eeas.europa.eu/republique-democratique-congo/lunion-europeenne-et-la-republique-democratique-du-congo_fr?s=94 on 1st November 2022.

Memorandum by Hersch Lauterpacht to the Committee on Crimes Against International Public Order entitled "Punishment of War Crimes" 6 (1942),at http://diginole.lib.fsu.edu/islandora/ object/fsu%3A547450.

MONUSCO rehabilitates major road in Beni to facilitate troops' and local populations' mobility, 25.02.2020 at https://peacekeeping.un.org/en accessed on 20th december 2023.

MONUSCO to track down FDLR after M23, 11.12.2013 available at https://monusco.unmissions.org/en/monusco-track-down-fdlr-after-m23 accessed on 2th october 2023.

MONUSCO recognizes a serious incident at the border between the DRC and Uganda, in Kasindi available at https://monusco.unmissions.org/en/monusco-recognizes-serious-incident-border-bet, accessed on 2th october 2023.

ONU. Transcription de la conférence de presse ONE UN en RDC, le 19 mai 2021 à Kinshasa.

Opérations contre les ADF : "L'appui de la MONUSCO aux FARDC est conséquent", 18 August 2021 at https://peacekeeping.un.org/, accessed on 2th october 2023.

Peace, Security and Cooperation Framework for the Democratic Republic of Congo and the Region, available at http://www.peaceau.org/uploads/scanned-on-24022013-125543.pdf, accessed on 2th october 2023.

Pete Jones, U.N. troops start military action against Congo's Rwandan rebels, available at https://www.reuters.com/article/congo-democratic-un-idINDEE9B90CI20131210, accessed on 2th october 2023.

RDC : Deux otages retrouvés après bombardement de plusieurs campements des rebelles ADF à Beni, December 1, 2018 at https://actualite.cd/2018/12/01/rdc.

Radio-Canada, Risque de nettoyage ethnique en République démocratique du Congo, selon l'ONU on 4 August 2017 at https://ici.radio-canada.ca/ 14 Septembre 2022.

Rapport du BCNUDH sur les violations des droits de l'homme à Goma, Sake et Minova. 15 Nov - 2 Dec 2012, OHCHR, published on 8 May 2013 accessed on 7th July 2022.

Reports by Human rights watch at https://www.hrw.org/africa/democratic-republic-c ongoRecent population displacements following military operations in bunyampuli, 12.078.2014 at https://monusco.unmissions.org/en, accessed on 1th jun 2023.

Recent population displacements following military operations in bunyampuli, 12.078.2014 at https://monusco.unmissions.org/en, accessed on 1th jun 2023.

Report on abuses and violations of human rights and international humanitarian law by ADF combatants and members of the defence and security forces in the territories of Beni in North Kivu and Irumu and Mambasa in Ituri, between 1 January 2019 and 31 January 2020(translated) para. 21 and 25 at https://www.ohchr.org/sites/default/fil es/Documents/Countries/CD/ADF_FR.pdf, accessed on 1th jun 2023.

Report of the Secretary-General, Model status-of-forces agreement for peace-keeping operations, 9October 1990, A/45/594, ("Model SOFA").

Report of the Secretary-General, 'Summary Study of the Experience derived from the establishment and operation of the force' (9 October 1958) UN Doc. A/3943, para. 127

Report of the Secretary-General on special measures for protection from sexual exploitation and sexual abuse, UN GA Off, 70th Session, UN Doc A/70/729 (2016).

Report of the UN Secretary-General, 'Implementing the responsibility to protect',' (A/63/677), 12 Jan. 2009.

Report of the Secretary-General, 'The role of regional and sub-regional arrangements in implementing the responsibility to protect', (A/65/877–S/2011/393), June 2011.

Report of the Secretary-General. In Larger Freedon: Towards Development, Security and Human Rights for All. U.N. Doc A/59/2005 (2005), accessed may 12, 2022, http://www.un.org/largerfreedom/contents.htm, accessed on 18th jun 2021.

Report of the Secretary General. Implementing the Responsibility to Protect. U.N. Doc. A/63/677 (12 may 2021).

Responsibility to protect: timely and decisive response', Report of the UN Secretary-General, 25 July 2012 (A/66/874-S/2012/578).

Romain Gras, DRC allows Uganda's army to enter Congolese territory to fight the ADF, 02.12.2021 at https://www.theafricareport.com/151989/drc-allows-ugandas-army-to-e nter-congolese-territory-to-fight-the-adf/, accessed on 15th jun 2023.

S/2022/967, Mid-term report of the Group of Experts pursuant to paragraph 6 of resolution 2641 (2022),16 December 2022 on https://documents-dds-ny.un.org/doc/ UNDOC/GEN/N22/757/87/PDF/N2275787.pdf, accessed on 1th jun 2023.

SADC, Communiqué of the Virtual Organ Troika Summit Plus Force Intervention Brigade - Troop Contributing Countries (FIB - TCC) and the Democratic Republic of Congo (DRC), August 5, 2020, Para 7 at https://www.sadc.int/latest-news on November 12, 2022.

SADC takes dispute over DRC force reconfiguration to UNGA at https://www.sardc.net/en/southern-african-news-features/sadc-takes-dispute-over-drc-force-reconfiguration-to-unga/, accessed on 1th jun 2023.

Special report of the Secretary-General on the Democratic Republic of the Congo and the Great Lakes Region, UN Doc S/2013/119, para 60-64.

Special Report of the Secretary-General on the Democratic Republic of the Congo and the Great Lakes Region, UN Doc S/2013/119, para 60-64 167.

Standard Operating Procedure the handling of detention in united nations peacekeeping operations and special political missions 2021 at https://peacekeeping.un.org/en/standard-operating-procedure-handling-of-detention-united-nations-peacekeeping-operations-and, accessed on 14th jun 2022.

Statement by Mr. Miguel de Serpa Soares Under-Secretary-General for Legal Affair on the 40th Annual Seminar for Diplomats on International Humanitarian Law jointly organized by the International Committee of the Red Cross and New York University School of Lawat https://www.un.org/ola/sites/www.un.org.ola/files/documents/2023/03/15032023-mss-ihl-icrc-nyu-seminar-speech.pdf, accessed on 1th jun 2023.

Statement of Ms Samia , South Africa-Tanzania Relations | President Ramaphosa hosts Tanzanian president Samia Suluhu Hassan, 16.03.2023 at #SABCNews and https://dailynews.co.tz/president-samia-attends-sadc-extra-ordinary-meeting/, accessed on 1th jun 2023.

"sokola2" to disarm the fdlr rwandan rebels, 30.01.2015 at https://monusco.unmissions.org/en, accessed on 1th jun 2023.

Tackling Sexual Violence Must Include Prevention, Ending Impunity—U.N. Official, U.N. News Centre (Apr. 27, 2010), https://perma.cc/2G4V-CARW, accessed on 1th jun 2023.

Tadziwana Kapeni, the brazilian jungle warfare mobile training team (jwmtt) wrapped up, on april 1, a training in the jungle warfare mobile techniques for the malawian contingent (malbatt) troops deployed within monusco force intervention brigade at https://monusco.unmissions.org/en, accessed on 17th February 2024.

Testimony of one of the survivors of the ADF kidnappings, interviewed in Oicha by Mugombozi, A. Félicité, June 2023.

The Responsibility to Protect. (2001). Report of the International Commission on the Intervention and State Sovereignty, retrieved from: http://responsibilitytoprotect.org/ICISS%20Report.pdf, accessed on 17th February 2024.

The UN Joint Human Rights Office (UNJHRO) in the DRC documented at least 2,024 civilians killed during 2021 by armed groups in North Kivu, South Kivu, Tanganyika and Ituri provinces

The report of the Secretary General Ban Ki-moon to the General Assembly, 2009.

The Copenhagen Process on the Handling of Detainees in International Military Operations: Principles and Guidelines, 2012 at http://um.dk/en/~/media/UM/English-site/Documents/Politics-d, accessed on 17th February 2024.

The Report of the Investigative Team of the SecretaryGeneral (S/1998/581), appendix, para. 96.

"The rule of law and transitional justice in conflict and post-conflict societies", UN Security Council, S/2004/616, 3 August 2004, p. 4.

The killings may, however, be violations of national law of the DRC. See "Martin Kobler, Head of MONUSCO, Strongly Condemns the Killing of UN Peacekeeper by M23," *MONUSCO Press Release,* August 28, 2013.

The Responsibility to Protect: Report of the International Commission on Intervention and State Sovereignty (2001)(hereinafter ICISS REPORT], 2.24, 6.17.

The Christmas Massacres: LRA attacks on Civilians in Northern Congo, Hum. Rts. Watch (Feb. 16, 2009), https://perma.cc/W3ZM-24DT accessed on 7th July 2022.

"the M23 is a militia of the Rwandan army" (MONUSCO)9081E SÉANCE, MATIN CS/14952 29 JUIN 2022, https://press.un.org/fr/2022/cs14952.doc.htm accessed on 1st July 2022.

Travel restriction concerned individuals and entities listed in annex II and extended the assets freeze provision of the 1970 resolution, at http://www.nato.int/nato_staticassets/pdf/pdf_2011_03/20110927_1103,ll-UNSCR, accessed on 19th jun 2023.

TV5 Monde, RDC : l'Union Européenne maintient ses sanctions contre le camp Kabila, sans surprise, 24.12.2021 at https://information.tv5monde.com/afrique.

U.N. High Comm'r for Hum. Rts. (OHCHR), Democratic Republic of the Congo, 1993– 2003: Report of the Mapping Exercise Documenting the Most Serious Violations of Human Rights and International Humanitarian Law Committed within the territory of the Democratic Republic of the Congo between March 1993 and June 2003, 259 (Aug. 2010) https://perma.cc/6SEG-LB2C [hereinafter DRC: Mapping Human Rights Violations], accessed on 17th February 2024.

UN , A New Partnership Agenda: Charting a New Horizon for UN Peacekeeping. New York: DPKO/DFS, (2009). paragraphs 40, 55, 68.

UNA-UK, The Responsibility to Protect In detail, Feb 25, 2022 https://una.org.uk/r2p-detail accessed on 18th June 2022.

UN, Murder of UN experts in DRC, 16 August 2017 at https://news.un.org/ on 14 September 2022.

UN Security Council, Press Statement on Democratic Republic of Congo, UN Doc. SC/11108, August 29, 2013.

UN Secretary-General, 'Implementing the Responsibility to Protect: Report of the Secretary-General', UN GAOR, 63rd Sess., Agenda Items 44 and 107, UN Doc. A/63/677, 12 January 2009.

United Nations , DRC: Victims' harrowing accounts indicate Government complicity in ethnic-based massacres in Kasai – UN report 4 August 2017 at https://www.ohchr.org/en/press-releases, accessed on 17th February 2024.

United Nations. Security Council, Special report on the events in the Ituri, January 2002– December 2003, New York, 16thJuly 2004, p. 32. S/2004/573.

United Nations, Report of the Special Committee on Peacekeeping Operations and its Working Group on the 2007 Resumed Session, UN Doc. A/61/19 (Part III), June 12, 2007.

United Nations Mission in Democratic Republic of Congo Must Transform into 'Robust, Flexible, Highly Mobile' Entity, Security Council Told, 14.03.2014 at https://press.un.org/en/2014/sc11316.doc.htm, accessed on 17th February 2024.

United Nations Secretary-General, Report of the Secretary General, We the Peoples: The Role of the United Nations in the Twenty-First Century, (A/54/2000) (27th March 2000), paragraph 217.

United Nations Secretary-General, Report of the Secretary-General, Implementing the Responsibility to Protect, (A/64/677) (12th January 2009).

Thesis

Aggar, Samia. "La responsabilité de protéger : un nouveau concept ?" PhD diss., Bordeaux, 2016.

Casiez-Piolot, Lenaïg. "La responsabilité de prévenir", PhD diss., Aix-Marseille, 2017.

Joly, Françoise. "The Responsibility to Protect: from doctrine to practice 'R2P'and protection of civilians: case study: DRC", PhD diss., Dublin City University, 2015.

Kirenge, Getrudah Sidi. "An Assessment of African Union's Application of the Responsibility to Protect Doctrine", PhD diss., United States International University-Africa, 2017.

Mugombozi, Akonkwa Félicité. "Examination of the impact of the United Nations Security Council Resolution 2098 on the protection of civilians in North-Kivu, Democratic Republic of the Congo", Master diss., Kampala International University, 2018.

Ntamwira, Cheshe Thomas. "The responsibility of the International Organization for damages caused to the civilians; Case of UN during peacekeeping operations in North- Kivu", Master diss., Kigali Independent University (ULK), 2018.

Vries de, Michelle. "The Resposibility to Protect in the DRC conflict", Master diss. Radboud University, 2017.

Williams, Sarah. "Hybrid and Internationalized Criminal Tribunals: Jurisdictional Issues", PhD diss., Durham University, 2009.

Wynn-Pope, Phoebe A. "The Responsibility to Protect Against Crimes Against Humanity and Genocide: Effective Operationalisation of the Principle", PhD diss., University of Melbourne, Melbourne Law School, 2008.